Cooking
Allergy-Free

COOKING
allergy-free

SIMPLE INSPIRED MEALS **FOR EVERYONE**

JENNA SHORT

The Taunton Press

Dedication To my husband, my better half—food would mean nothing if I couldn't share it with you—and to my sweet baby Eytan—let the journey begin.

 The Taunton Press
Inspiration for hands-on living®

The Taunton Press, Inc., 63 South Main Street, PO Box 5506, Newtown, CT 06470-5506
email: tp@taunton.com

Editor: Carolyn Mandarano
Dietitian Nutritionist: Colleen Fogarty Draper, MS, RD
Food and Nutrition Consultant: Rachel Begun, MS, RDN, Boulder, CO
Copy Editor: Li Agen
Indexer: Heidi Blough
Cover, Interior, Layout design: Rita Sowins/Sowins Design
Illustrator: Jenna Short
Photographer: Helen Norman
Food Stylist: Bill Scepansky
Prop Stylist: Nan Whitney

The following names/manufacturers appearing in *Cooking Allergy Free* are trademarks: Anolon®, Bob's Red Mill®, Bragg®, Calphalon®, Cuisinart®, Earth Balance®, Ener-G Egg Replacer®, Frantoia®, Global®, Guinness®, Heartland®, KitchenAid®, Lea & Perrins®, Le Creuset®, Magimix®, Microplane®, Morton®, Nutella®, Prince®, Robot Coupe®, Sriracha®, Terra Stix®, Victorinox®, Vitamix®, Wüstof®.

Library of Congress Cataloging-in-Publication Data in progress
ISBN # 978-1-62710-396-1

Printed in the United States of America
10 9 8 7 6 5 4 3 2 1

Safety Note
When purchasing packaged ingredients to make the recipes in this cookbook, it is essential to read the ingredients and allergen statements on all labels to ensure avoiding the ingredients that are of concern to you and the people you are cooking for. We have noted "read ingredients statement" where recipes call for packaged ingredients. Should you make substitutions with packaged ingredients, it's important to read the labels for ingredients and allergen statements.

In the headnotes, cooking tips, variations, and serving suggestions of many of the recipes in this cookbook, there are suggestions for substituting ingredients or pairing the recipe with certain foods or other recipes in this cookbook. These suggestions may contain allergens not contained in the recipe itself, so please always be sure to read ingredients statements and be aware of allergens for these suggestions.

Acknowledgments

Being pregnant and writing a cookbook was no piece of cake . . . ooohhh cake! And so it goes . . . For the past nine months, every recipe I wrote I would "have" to test and eat (luckily I had no food aversions!). It hasn't been easy giving birth to these two "babies" at the same time, but both were worth it and I am excited to see what they become. This has been an unbelievable journey, one that would not have been possible without the love and support of those around me. I would like to recognize a few people for their continuous dedication to me and my life's work.

My parents, for always supporting my crazy life decisions and always believing that it would lead me to do something with food and design that they could be proud of. And, of course, for allowing me to make a mess of their kitchen! Thank you for raising me to believe that anything is possible.

My husband, for making it all possible. Thank you for believing in me and always pushing me to be better. I know it hasn't been easy! You inspire me and I am so proud of you. I am the lucky one.

My brother, my forever partner in crime. Here's to being a kid forever.

Liat Justin, for thinking that my food is good enough to write a book.

Grandma Joyce, for teaching me the joys of sharing food with others.

Jonathan Lindenauer, Michael Castellano, Samuel Griffin, and the '08 team at *Bon Appétit* magazine—you taught me everything I need to know about being a chef and designer and working in a "real" kitchen. From supremes to dicing an onion and so much in between, my food and design wouldn't be nearly as exciting without the journey we shared. You taught me the rules—and exactly how to break them! I am forever grateful for your time, patience, and knowledge.

To everyone who worked at or contributed to ShortBreadNYC in those first years in New York City. Thank you for believing in me and carrying things up and down my four-story walkup. Great things start small but can only be taken as far as the support you are given. I owe all my success to you. Thanks Joe Tuckman, for buying the first batch of cookies; you really got the ball rolling.

To the friends I have made during my time in Israel, for "suffering" through all my taste tests and for all the new foods you taught me about. Thank you for your input in the making and tasting of this book.

Thank you Colleen Draper Fogarty for your nutritional brilliance. You truly live the allergen-free and thoughtful way of life, and we all have much to learn from you. I look forward to watching your girls grow up and learning from you for years to come. Thanks also to Rachel Begun for your technical expertise in ensuring the information in this book is accurate.

Carolyn Mandarano at Taunton Press and Regina Brooks from Serendipity Literary Agency, for your countless hours of work on this project; you have been an amazing resource and source of support. Thank you for your patience in helping me through this new and exciting process. I look forward to many more amazing projects together.

Photographer Helen Norman, for capturing the love in my food. Designer Rita Sowins, for breathing life into this creation. Being a designer and photographer myself, I appreciate the amount of work and energy that goes into something like this. Thank you to food stylist Bill Scepansky and copy editor Li Agen for your dedication to this project. Don't think for a second that any of your hard work went unnoticed, no matter how picky I was.

And last but certainly not least, to all the foodies, home cooks, and adventure seekers out there. Keep exploring and trying new things. Food is about creativity, love, and travel. Never stop searching for more; the world is full of endless tastes and exploration. Eat well and travel often!

If you have questions feel free to email me at jenna@shortbreadnyc.com; my mailbox is always open.

Contents

Introduction

While majoring in graphic design at the Art Institute of Boston, I spent a semester abroad eating my way through Italy—quite literally! Upon my return, I discovered that not only had I gained 60 pounds but also had become allergic to dairy in the process. Because of my new-found allergy and my vast love of food, I decided to add some of my creativity from graphics to cooking, all with the idea that I—and anyone with a dietary restriction—deserved delicious food regardless of an allergy. Thus began my journey as a foodie, chef, and baker.

Today, it's not unusual for at least one person sitting at your dinner table to have a food intolerance or allergy. If you're one of those people, you might feel left out of a great meal if the cook didn't account for your needs. The purpose of this book is to include everyone in the same meal. Food is emotional, nostalgic, and, most important, about togetherness, and to be able to include everyone sitting around your table in that experience is priceless.

I developed the recipes in this book to be first and foremost delicious and satisfying. But I've also used color-coded icons (see p. 29) with each recipe so you can easily discern which are suited for those with one or more of the most common food allergies—wheat, milk, nuts, eggs, shellfish, fish, soy, and corn. Recipes that are appropriate for vegetarians, vegans, and those who eat gluten-free are also indicated with an icon.

I want you to look at this book as a way to add versatility to your cooking repertoire, from menu planning to shopping to creating a meal. In addition to each recipe providing an icon to indicate its allergy appropriateness, I've also included variations for how to change that recipe so that it works for people with one or more of the other most common allergens. This means the recipes are adaptable, no matter who is joining your table. I hope this inspires you to be free to adjust these recipes, as well as your own favorites, for anyone sitting at your table, not just those with food allergies.

But this book goes beyond strictly providing simple, flavorful allergy-free recipes. You will also find information about cooking with fresh and healthful foods, tips for how to develop your cooking skills, and menu options for occasions when you entertain, as well as strategies for keeping a well-stocked pantry for all of your dietary needs, health and otherwise.

For the last 10 years, since my time in Italy, I have spent countless hours reworking some of my favorite recipes to make them suitable for everyone to enjoy. I hope you and your family find the recipes in this book unique, delicious, and inspiring.

Chapter 1

Kitchen Essentials for Allergy-Free Cooking

Kitchen Essentials

This book is a great start for you to take charge of your health and the health of your family and to make a difference in how you enjoy your food. Although there has been a rise in food allergies and sensitivities, the good news is there are many ingredients available to use for cooking that replace the commonly offending foods and can even make your diet more nutritious.

In many ways you need to be your own nutritionist, so you must learn about your own health and nutrition and experiment with what does and does not work with your body. (If you are concerned you have a real issue, you should seek the help of a health care professional to diagnose potential food allergies, sensitivities, and celiac disease.) You may find that you, your family members, and your friends struggle with food reactions, allergies, intolerances, and even particular preferences. It can get complex to honor these differences, so let's first review some concepts that might help you understand what you are dealing with at home and then work on setting up your pantry to assist in all of your dietary choices.

FOOD ALLERGIES VS. SENSITIVITIES

What Is a Food Allergy?

A food allergy is when the body mistakenly identifies a food as foreign or harmful and triggers an immune reaction to attack the allergen. Symptoms can be experienced within just a few minutes and up to several hours after coming into contact with the food. Local symptoms such as itching, swelling, and hives often occur. More serious symptoms such as trouble breathing, a drop in blood pressure, and even anaphylaxis, a potentially life-threatening reaction, can also occur. Any food can cause an allergic reaction, but eight foods are responsible for 90% of all reactions. They are milk, eggs, soy, peanuts, tree nuts, shellfish, fish, and wheat.

What Is the Difference between Celiac Disease and Gluten Sensitivity?

Celiac disease is an autoimmune disorder in which the body's immune system triggers an attack on the intestines every time gluten is eaten. Gluten is a collective term for a group of proteins found in the grains wheat, rye, and barley and any foods made from these grains. The villi, the fingerlike projections in the intestines, become damaged and are unable to absorb nutrients into the blood, which can lead to nutrient deficiencies and other long-term health consequences, including a greater likelihood for other autoimmune disorders, anemia, osteoporosis, infertility, neurological conditions, and even some types of cancer. Celiac disease can affect many systems of the body, not just the gastrointestinal (GI) system. While gastrointestinal symptoms such as bloating, gas, diarrhea, and constipation are common, people with celiac disease often experience other symptoms such as migraines, achy joints, tingling in the fingers and toes, and foggy brain. Some people show no outward symptoms at all.

While the symptoms of non-celiac gluten sensitivity (or simply gluten sensitivity) often overlap with celiac disease, they are two distinct conditions. Gluten sensitivity is not an autoimmune disorder. We know this because antibodies to gluten are not produced and there is no intestinal damage like we see with celiac disease. Currently, there is no test for gluten sensitivity. It is diagnosed by ruling out celiac disease and wheat allergy through proper testing and then conducting an elimination diet to see if symptoms go away when taking gluten out of the diet and then return again when gluten is reintroduced back into the diet. We also don't know yet if there are long-term consequences to eating small amounts of gluten.

What Is a Food Sensitivity?

A food sensitivity is a negative reaction to a food that doesn't involve the immune system. One example is lactose intolerance, in which lactose, the sugar in milk, is not digested well and leads to uncomfortable GI symptoms. People can be sensitive to a wide variety of foods and experience many different symptoms, including GI symptoms, migraines, skin rashes, joint pain, and asthma.

What Is an Elimination Diet?

When food allergies and celiac disease have been ruled out through proper testing but symptoms still persist, an elimination diet may be conducted under the supervision of a physician and/or dietitian to identify if a certain food or foods may be the cause. An elimination diet involves removing many of the foods known to cause symptoms for a period of time, and then adding them back one at a time to see if the symptoms return. An elimination diet can also be specific to just one food that is suspected for causing symptoms. It is recommended to conduct an elimination diet under the care of a knowledgeable health professional as he or she is trained to properly identify the trigger food(s) and can help tailor a meal plan that meets all nutrient needs while removing foods from the diet.

WHAT IS VEGETARIANISM VS. VEGANISM?

A **vegetarian** does not eat meat, chicken, fish, or shellfish, but may choose eggs and milk.

A **lacto-ovo vegetarian** avoids meat and chicken, but chooses eggs and milk.

A **pescatarian** avoids all animal protein sources except fish and shellfish. Due to the additional protein variety, a pescatarian will find it easier to meet his or her nutritional requirements.

A **vegan** does not consume animal foods of any kind and makes food choices in accordance with environmental sustainability. This includes eliminating meat, chicken, fish, eggs, milk, and honey. It is possible to eat a healthy, balanced diet as a vegan, but it requires organization and planning to ensure you are getting sufficient amounts of protein, calcium, vitamin B12, and vitamin D.

HOW CAN I BE A NUTRITIONIST, FOODATARIAN, AND GREAT COOK?

Whatever your diet and health interests are, it is important to keep it simple and fun! Start slow when making changes in your diet. When choosing your favorite recipes and modifications in this book, keep the following guidelines in mind:

» Check out the website of the Food Allergy Resource & Education organization (FARE), which is an excellent resource for information about living with food allergies (www.foodallergy.org).

» If you have celiac disease or gluten-related disorders, visit the website for the National Foundation for Celiac Awareness (NFCA) (www.celiaccentral.org).

» Choose whole, organic, seasonally fresh, locally grown foods and grass-fed meats whenever possible.

» Cook and eat lots of plant foods, including vegetables, fruits, and legumes.

» Watch for unnecessary food additives in the products you cook with.

» Emphasize a variety of oils. Choose avocados and various nuts and seeds to increase the variety of healthy fats in your cooking.

» Get your omega-3 fats from wild, cold-water fish, seafood, flax seeds, chia seeds, and walnuts.

» Use filtered water that is not stored in plastic for prolonged periods of time.

» Avoid artificial colors, sweeteners, and other unnecessary added ingredients.

» Evaluate your food and recipe choices for adequate inclusion of vitamins and minerals and your recipe choices to ensure maximum nutrient density and variety.

» Make sure you are maximizing calcium from leafy greens, cow's milk, or fortified alternative milks.

» Make sure you maximize vitamin D from the sun, fortified milks, fatty fish, and egg yolks.

» Most important, eat consciously. Take a few breaths. Celebrate your cooking, your kitchen, and your meals. Eat with love and kindness and in good company

» Re-invigorate the time you spend cooking and eating in your kitchen with this book!

CONSCIOUS COOKING

If you, a family member, or a guest have a serious or life-threatening allergy, you know how important it is to avoid cross-contact of allergens in the kitchen. Otherwise, there is a chance an epi-pen and a trip to the emergency room will be necessary. Celiac disease is another example of how even the slightest of crumbs can have detrimental effects. Care and vigilance is required when shopping and cooking with food allergens in mind.

At the Store

Always read ingredients statements and signage every time you shop. When shopping, keep problematic foods separate from other foods—place them in a different grocery cart and keep them separate at the checkout counter; store in separate bags. Avoid foods from bulk bins, salad bars, and the deli counter since there could be cross-contact at these sites.

At Home

When you get home, follow these guidelines to help limit cross-contact:

Set Up a Storage System. Use squeeze bottles for condiments and other liquids to eliminate double dipping. If possible, simply choose condiments free from the allergen; if this is not possible, clearly label the option that is allergen-free or gluten-free. Store allergen- and/or gluten-free foods on separate shelves in the refrigerator, freezer, and pantry.

Use clean equipment and dishes. Based on the food(s) that need to be avoided and when necessary and possible, use separate utensils (for food prep and eating) and small appliances. Prepare and cook allergen- and/or gluten-free dishes first and with clean equipment. Be sure the surface you're using is clean as well. Depending on your needs, consider a dedicated space for food prep.

Wash frequently. Wash and sterilize hands, silverware, dishes, equipment, and surfaces—anything that comes into contact with the allergen- or gluten-free food being prepared. Use hot, soapy water when washing.

STOCKING YOUR PANTRY

To set up a basic kitchen, you need to stock some essential ingredients. It goes without saying that fresh, unprocessed foods are better for you than highly processed foods with unwanted ingredients. When dealing with food allergies, sensitivities, and celiac disease, it's important to be aware of hidden ingredients in the foods you purchase that are related to the ingredients you need to avoid. I've listed here ingredients that are great to have on hand. Note that many of these recommended ingredients will have one of the common allergens or gluten, so they may be safe for some but not all. Be sure to check and read all labels for listed ingredients and hidden allergens. It is also important to compare labels between brands of a similar product, as one many contain an allergen while another may not.

Oils

Air, heat, light, and age affect the quality and shelf life of many types of oils. Be sure your oils are stored in airtight containers and in a place that is not exposed to heat or light. If you seldom use a particular oil in your pantry, smell or taste it before adding it to your food.

Olive oil. There are a number of distinctions between olive oils—extra-virgin, virgin, pure, regular, and refined. The difference is based on what number press of the olives it came from. For instance, extra-virgin olive oil (EVOO) comes from the first cold press of the olives. Refined olive oil indicates the taste and acidity were chemically modified. When buying, look for these clues to choose a good-quality olive oil: price (this is one item where more expensive means better quality) and storage container (the oil should be stored in a dark-colored glass—not clear—bottle or can). At home, store the olive oil in the refrigerator; it should harden. I store my good olive oils in the fridge; when I need them, I run the bottle under hot water for a minute or two so the oil will liquefy.

As a general rule I always use EVOO when it comes to cooking. It is a healthy, natural oil that has a complex and rich flavor that accentuates your food. Use the best quality EVOO you can afford—you'll taste the difference. My favorite is Frantoia®, imported from Spain.

Canola oil. This oil is the lowest in saturated fat, making it ideal for baking and frying. It's a good alternative to olive oil.

Nut oils. These types of oils—walnut, almond, and hazelnut, to name a few—are perfect in salad dressings and dips (they aren't good for cooking). People with tree nut allergies should avoid nut oils.

Vegetable oil. The most commonly used oil by home cooks, vegetable oil is also the least expensive of all oils. It is a blend of several types of oils, and the oils used vary from one brand to another and sometimes within the same brand. Be sure to read the ingredient statement to check for potential allergens.

Corn oil. Most commonly found in margarine, corn oil is surprisingly low in saturated fats and perfect for frying over medium heat. If you are allergic to corn, use vegetable or canola oil instead.

Peanut oil. Use peanut oil only when frying at high heat. This oil has a very high smoke point, meaning it won't burn your food when frying. However, it has the highest level of saturated fats. People allergic to peanuts should avoid peanut and tree nut oils.

Sesame oil. This oil is derived from sesame seeds, and it's high in antioxidants and polyunsaturated fats. Sesame oil adds great flavor, especially for Asian and Middle Eastern dishes. Because sesame seeds and tree nuts have proteins in common, don't use this oil if you're allergic to nuts.

Vinegars

Vinegar breaks down protein fibers, so adding it to marinades or braising liquids will help tenderize meat. Like oils, vinegars are susceptible to air, heat, and light. Once opened, store vinegar in a cool, dark place. You can even refrigerate them—and should if they are fruit- or herb-based. Vinegars are best stored in a glass container.

The acidic taste of vinegar often reduces the need for salt in many dishes. It also can cut the amount of fat in a recipe because it balances flavors without needing additional cream, butter, or oil.

I keep balsamic vinegar and apple cider vinegar in my pantry at all times because of their varied uses, but there are other types of vinegars used in several recipes in this book that are great to have on hand as well. There are a wide range of flavors available, so be sure to taste and experiment.

Balsamic vinegar. This popular Italian vinegar is known for its sweet flavor and mild acidity. It's terrific for deglazing pans, for dressing salads and vegetable dishes, and for seasoning everything from grilled meat to poached fruit.

Apple cider vinegar. Made from fermented apples, apple cider vinegar is inexpensive and tangy. While it may not be the best choice for vinaigrettes, it works great in chutneys, stews, and marinades as a tenderizer. It also has a wide range of medicinal uses, including soothing sunburned skin, aiding in weight loss, and minimizing heartburn.

Rice vinegar. Also called rice wine vinegar, this vinegar is made from rice. Rice vinegars are popular in Asian countries and are milder and less acidic than apple cider or balsamic vinegar.

Red-wine vinegar. This is used primarily in vinaigrettes and for making marinades, stews, and sauces. It is a staple in French cooking.

White vinegar. This is the cheapest of all the vinegars because it is used for all the mundane jobs, like making pickles, cleaning out limescale from pots, and washing windows. Distilled from alcohol, it's a bit too harsh for most recipes.

White vinegar can be made from a variety of starch sources, including gluten-containing grains. Distilled white vinegar technically should test to below 20 parts per million of gluten, the threshold considered gluten-free by the FDA. However, some people with celiac disease and gluten sensitivity report reacting to distilled vinegars derived from gluten-containing grains, so use with caution.

Herbs and Spices

Herbs, whether fresh or dried, are key to flavorful and unique cooking. You'll need to buy fresh herbs based on your recipe, but you should keep a well-stocked pantry of dried herbs and spices; don't forget to replace them every few months or so (they don't last forever!). Although the list is endless, here are some basic spices to have on hand. Spice and seasoning blends and powders made with more than one spice can contain allergens as binders. Be sure to read labels.

- » Allspice
- » Basil
- » Bay leaves
- » Cardamom
- » Chili powder
- » Cloves
- » Crushed red pepper flakes
- » Ground cumin
- » Curry powder
- » Garlic powder
- » Ground cinnamon
- » Ground ginger
- » Ground mustard
- » Nutmeg
- » Oregano
- » Parsley
- » Poppyseeds
- » Salt and pepper
- » Sesame seeds
- » Thyme
- » Turmeric

Condiments

Soy sauce, honey, harissa, anchovy paste, fish sauce, and tahini paste (I like Prince® brand) are a few of my go-to staples to enhance the flavor of a dish. They can often contain allergens, so be diligent in reading labels based on your allergy to be sure they're safe for you. Some brands make allergy-free versions, such as gluten-free soy sauce (I like Bragg® Liquid Aminos as a gluten-free soy sauce substitute) and ketchup. Various mustards, hoisin sauce, Sriracha®, and chili sauce are other staples I use regularly in my cooking. For most of these condiments, 1 teaspoon can make all the difference in a dish, bringing out new and exciting flavors when combined with just the right amount of other ingredients.

The list below contains condiments I always keep stocked in the fridge or pantry. Most last for a long time, too. Be sure to read the product's ingredient statement for hidden allergens or gluten.

- » Chili sauce
- » Dijon mustard
- » Ketchup
- » Mayonnaise
- » Nam pla (Thai fish sauce)
- » Soy sauce (contains wheat/gluten, unless labeled gluten-free)
- » Spicy brown mustard
- » Sriracha
- » Tahini paste (contains sesame seeds)
- » Teriyaki sauce (contains soy sauce often made with wheat/gluten)
- » Tomato paste
- » Worcestershire sauce (may contain wheat/gluten); I like Lea & Perrins®

Flours

With a host of flours on store shelves you might wonder if you need to stock them all in your pantry. While the answer is no, some flours are better for some types of cooking because they behave differently. When you're cooking or baking for someone with food allergies, it's important to know the base of the flour—wheat, corn, rice, and the like—so you can choose what's appropriate. Be mindful of cross-contact with flours. For example, if you have celiac disease or a gluten sensitivity, use a gluten-free flour blend for your dish as well as for rolling out dough.

All-purpose flour. Unbleached, all-purpose flour is just what the name says—good for almost any use. This is what many people use in some types of baking, to flour a work surface when rolling out dough, or to add to soups and sauces as a thickener. All-purpose flour is milled from wheat, which is a gluten-containing grain.

Bread flour. Also milled from wheat, a gluten-containing grain, this type of flour has more protein than all-purpose, so it helps with gluten development. Bread flour typically results in a heavier and denser loaf and is used when a chewy or elastic crumb is desired.

Pastry flour. Because it has a lower protein content than all-purpose and bread flours, pastry flour is typically used for delicate cakes and pastries. It is also milled from wheat, a gluten-containing grain, and is unbleached.

Cake flour. Typically sold in a box, cake flour has the lowest protein of the flours because it is bleached; the bleaching process is what weakens the protein. Cake flour is normally used for angel food cakes and chiffon. It is milled from wheat, a gluten-containing grain.

Whole wheat flour. Whole wheat flour is ground from the wheat kernel (also called wheat berry) and contains all of the bran and germ. Whole wheat flour gives baked goods a dense texture and doesn't rise as much as white flour. Whole white wheat flour is becoming more widely available. This type of flour is lighter in color and milder in flavor than whole wheat, so generally requires less sweetener in a recipe where it's used. Wheat is a gluten-containing grain.

Because whole wheat flour creates a dense product, don't simply substitute the same amount of whole wheat flour for a "regular" type of flour. The rule to follow is three-quarters whole wheat to one-quarter "regular" flour.

Rye flour. Various types of rye flours are available—some with different grinds of the rye berries and different percentages of bran and germ. Dark, medium, light, and pumpernickel rye are a few. Rye contains gluten.

Corn flour/cornmeal. Corn flour is a finely ground ingredient used for baking. Cornmeal, also ground from corn, has a heartier texture. In some places, polenta is also called cornmeal. Cornmeal is available in white, yellow, and blue, depending on the color of the corn. Corn contains something called "corn gluten," which isn't the same gluten that affects people with celiac disease or gluten sensitivity. If you have celiac disease, make sure the corn flour you choose is 100% corn.

Semolina flour. Semolina flour is manufactured by coarsely grinding the endosperm of a type of wheat called durum. Semolina has a consistency similar to sugar and is typically used to bake specialty breads. It is also used to produce couscous and other pastas. Semolina flour contains gluten.

Gluten-Free Flours

It's easy to make your own gluten-free flour blend (see the recipe below). If you'd rather buy one off the shelf, try Bob's Red Mill® Gluten-Free. Of the manufactured brands, I find its consistency is most like that of regular flour. For people with celiac disease, I recommend buying certified gluten-free flour blends, so as to avoid cross-contact with gluten.

GLUTEN-FREE FLOUR RECIPE

MAKES ABOUT 4 CUPS

1⅓ cups rice flour
1⅓ cups tapioca flour
1⅓ cups cornstarch
1 tablespoon potato flour

Sift all ingredients together and store for up to 3 months in an airtight container. Use it as a 1-to-1 substitution for all-purpose flour.

Sorghum flour. Sorghum flour has a light color and bland flavor that make it a versatile option in gluten-free baking. Since it is milled from the whole grain, it's also higher in fiber and protein.

White rice flour. The bland taste of this flour doesn't alter the flavor of dishes. It comes in a range of textures (from regular to fine) that affect consistency; coarser grinds can make for grainy baked goods.

Brown rice flour. This flour is milled from brown rice, which still contains the bran, giving it a heavier texture, but also making it more nutritious than white rice flour.

Teff. Teff is a very tiny cereal grain native to Africa that's rich in protein, calcium, iron, and potassium. It has a sweet, nutty flavor and can be served alone as a hot cereal or mixed into a variety of baked goods.

Tapioca flour. This flour is made from the root starch of the cassava plant. It adds chewiness and stretch to gluten-free baked goods.

Gar-Fava flour. This flour is a protein and fiber-rich blend of garbanzo beans (chickpeas) and fava beans, which lend an earthy flavor to baked goods. It provides a great texture for a variety of gluten-free baked goods.

Garbanzo bean flour. This flour is made by grinding garbanzo beans (also called chickpeas) into a fine protein-rich flour. It has a fuller and richer in flavor than rice flour.

Coconut flour. This high-fiber, protein-rich flour is an excellent gluten-free flour. It gives baked goods a mild sweetness and rich texture. It requires more liquid than other flours, so use it in recipes specifically designed for it. Coconut is considered a tree nut, so coconut flour should be avoided by those with tree nut allergies.

Almond flour. Also called almond meal, almond flour is made by grinding raw blanched almonds into a fine powder. Combine it with other gluten-free flours to add a hint of nuttiness plus healthy fats, fiber, and protein. Almonds are a tree nut.

Other Ingredients for Gluten-Free Baking

Cornstarch. Cornstarch is ground from corn kernels. This flavorless powder is used as a binder or thickening agent, and it's added in baked goods to make them lighter in texture.

Arrowroot. Arrowroot is a fine, white powder that resembles cornstarch and is used as a thickener.

Xanthan gum. Xanthan gum is another binding agent that enables rising, reduces crumbling, and gives your baked goods an elastic texture similar to that which gluten provides. However, I find that it adds an odd aftertaste, so I leave it out of my recipes.

Sugars

Sugar takes many forms (and colors), but those I use most often—and recommend you have on hand—are the solid types. Each adds something different to a dish.

Granulated sugar. By far the most popular, granulated sugar, also called white sugar, is the type most frequently called for in recipes. It adds sweetness and moisture to baked goods.

Confectioners' sugar. Also known as powdered sugar, this type is 10 times finer than granulated sugar, which is why it's also known as 10X. It's used mainly in icings and frostings and to dust the tops of cakes and cookies. Confectioners' sugar contains cornstarch so when serving it to someone with a corn allergy, use the corn-free recipe below.

CORN-FREE CONFECTIONERS' SUGAR

MAKES 5 CUPS

²/₃ cup granulated sugar
1 teaspoon potato starch

Grind the sugar and potato starch together in a food processor or blender until powdery. Use as needed in your recipe. This is also a great substitute for regular confectioners' sugar at Passover.

Dark brown sugar. Dark brown sugar is granulated sugar with a small amount of molasses added to it to give it a richer color and flavor.

Light brown sugar. Also granulated sugar with a bit of molasses, but light brown sugar has less molasses than dark brown. Its flavor is not as intense as dark brown.

Demerrara sugar. A light, almost blonde sugar, demerrara comes in coarse crystals. Its color and flavor—caramel like—is a natural byproduct of the crystallization during processing cane juice into sugar crystals. Demerrara is also called turbinado sugar.

Chemical Leaveners

Baking powder is a chemical leavening shortcut. It's made up of a base, an acid salt, and the addition of either baking soda, cream of tartar, or cornstarch. The mixture releases carbon dioxide into batter or dough, forming bubbles, which will cause the batter or dough to rise. Recipes that contain butter-

milk or other acidic ingredients usually call for just baking soda instead of or in addition to baking powder to avoid too much acid in your recipe. Each of the chemical leaveners contain different levels of acid, which is why we use different ones and different amounts depending on the recipe and how much acid it needs to create the proper rise.

Baking powder has an indefinite shelf life while sealed. Once opened, it can last between 6 and 18 months. Ideally, it should be stored in a cool, dry place. Avoid keeping it in the fridge, because any moisture that may result from condensation can ruin it. To check if your baking powder is still good, test it by adding a teaspoon to a bit of water. If it fizzes, you're good to go.

Salt and Pepper

Salt and pepper are a cook's best friend. When used in the right proportion, salt enhances the flavor of food and pepper adds a bit of zing.

Salt. The three most common types of salt are kosher, coarse (like sea salt or fleur de sel), and table salt. Kosher salt is best used for cooking because it is non-iodized and dissolves faster. My go-to brand is Morton®. Sea salt or fleur de sel is a finishing salt, so you sprinkle it on food just before serving. Finely ground table salt is what the name implies—good for use at the table.

Black pepper. This is one of the most common spices home cooks use to add a little kick and seasoning to food. Freshly ground black pepper (from a mill) is common in recipes to add the most spicy flavor, but ground black pepper you buy from the market can always be substituted. White pepper is less pungent than black pepper, and red pepper is more spicy.

What does "add salt and pepper to taste" mean? Most recipes will tell you to "season to taste" or "adjust the seasoning." This is because some ingredients in a recipe could make your dish too salty or seasoned to your liking—or not seasoned enough. It is very important to always taste your food as you're cooking it and again before serving and adjust the salt and pepper.

Breadcrumbs

We all know what breadcrumbs are but based on their size and degree of dryness, they are used for different things. Store-bought dry breadcrumbs might come with various flavor enhancers (Italian style, for instance, which has Italian seasonings thrown in) and are used for breading food. Fresh breadcrumbs are used more as a stuffing ingredient. Panko breadcrumbs are made from crustless bread, so they're lighter than regular dry breadcrumbs and don't absorb as much oil when fried, so stay somewhat crisp. Store-bought breadcrumbs will almost always contain wheat and gluten if they are not gluten-free. They may also contain other allergens. Always check labels.

Making your own breadcrumbs from leftover bread is super-easy. If you can't eat wheat or gluten, make some from gluten-free bread so you're never without. To make your own breadcrumbs, cube some stale bread and add it and seasonings if you like (a little salt, pepper, and dried herbs) to a food processor. Process until coarse crumbs form. You can also toast the crumbs if you like.

Stock

When any of the recipes say to use stock you have the option here to use several ingredients—beef stock, chicken stock, vegetable stock, or water. Recipes often suggest certain types of stock that will best suit or complement the other ingredients, but feel free to experiment with different stocks, including using whatever you have on hand. In a lot of cases, I choose vegetable stock so that I can serve whatever dish I am making to vegetarians (assuming that the rest of the dish is vegetarian friendly).

One note on water: While water will suffice as a substitute for stock, especially when you're trying to make a recipe allergy-friendly, it won't contain the same flavors as stock, so won't give your recipe the same impact. Be sure to adjust the seasonings in your recipe if you use water.

I often buy low-sodium stock at the grocery store, but when I have leftover bones or vegetable trimmings, I like to make a pot of stock and freeze it in quart containers to use later. Follow the recipe below to make your own stock. If you choose to purchase packaged broths or stocks, be sure to read the ingredients statements, as they can contain gluten or allergens.

STOCK

MAKES ABOUT 2 QUARTS

Leftover bones from cooked or raw chicken or meat
Celery
Onions (peeled)
Carrots
Fresh parsley
2 teaspoons kosher salt
1 teaspoon black pepper

Put the bones in a large stockpot and cover with cold water. Add the vegetables, herbs, and salt and pepper. (If you like, roast the bones before boiling them for a bit more flavor. Arrange the bones in a heavy roasting pan and drizzle them with a bit of vegetable oil (check the ingredient statement). Roast at 400°F for about 30 minutes and then continue with the recipe.)

Bring to a boil and immediately reduce the heat to barely a simmer. Simmer, uncovered, for at least 4 hours, skimming the foam from the surface occasionally. Remove the bones and strain the stock. Store in quart containers for up to 5 days in the refrigerator and up to 3 months in the freezer.

Chocolate

There are many brands of chocolate to choose from, but more important than the brand is what type of chocolate you need for a recipe. Once you figure out the type, there are few ways to help make a decision on brand—taste, price, and form, meaning squares, bars, big blocks, or chips.

Chocolate will keep for a year at room temperature, if stored below 70°F. Wrap it in a few layers of plastic to keep it as airtight as possible and put it in a dark cupboard, away from strong-smelling foods.

You can store chocolate in the refrigerator or freezer, but a moist environment isn't ideal. If you do chill your chocolate, bring it to room temperature while still wrapped to prevent condensation from forming, as any water on the chocolate can interfere with its ability to melt smoothly.

Note that you will see "chocolate liquor" written in an ingredients list for most types of chocolate. Chocolate liquor is the basis of all types of chocolate, formed by grinding cacao beans into a smooth, liquid paste. Nothing is added, and it does not contain alcohol, despite its name. Chocolate is often made with lecithin, which most often comes from soy or eggs. In addition, because so many chocolate manufacturers make products with add-ins and seasonings, and because plain chocolate is often manufactured on the same equipment as chocolates with these add-ins, always be sure to read ingredient decks and voluntary statements about manufacturing practices.

Unsweetened. Containing no sugar, unsweetened chocolate is pure chocolate liquor. It is very bitter, so can't be used in place of semisweet or bittersweet chocolate. Unsweetened chocolate is also known as baking chocolate.

Bittersweet. Bittersweet chocolate is a dark chocolate that contains less than a third sugar, as well as cocoa butter, vanilla, and sometimes lecithin as a binder. Bittersweet and semisweet chocolates can generally be used interchangeably, though bittersweet will give a less sweet result.

Semisweet. Semisweet chocolate, also a dark chocolate, has at least 35 percent cocoa solids. It also contains sugar (though there are no regulations about the amount, generally it's about half as much as the cocoa) but no milk products.

Milk chocolate. A solid chocolate, milk chocolate is made with milk in the form of milk powder, liquid milk, or condensed milk added. Milk chocolate is generally eaten out of hand and isn't widely used in baking.

White chocolate. A combination of sugar, milk, and cocoa butter makes white "chocolate"—not a chocolate at all since it doesn't contain any cocoa solids.

Cocoa powder. Cocoa powder is used for baking and for drinking with added milk and sugar. Cocoa is available as natural or Dutch-processed. Natural cocoa creates a leavening action that allows the batter to rise during baking; it has a more acidic chocolate flavor. Dutch-processed cocoa is slightly milder in taste, with a deeper and warmer color than natural cocoa.

Chunks vs. chips. Although some of the decision of using chocolate chunks vs. chips in baking comes down to what you have on hand, you do need to know that chocolate chips behave differently than bar or block chocolate. This is because the chips have been formulated to retain their shape when baked.

Carob chips. Another option to chocolate when making chocolate chip cookies is to substitute chocolate chips with carob chips. Carob chips are made with carob powder, which comes from the pod of the Mediterranean carob tree. Carob's flavor is a not as intense as chocolate, but carob is similar enough to be an excellent vegan substitute.

Milk Products

There's some confusion around lactose intolerance and milk allergy. A milk allergy is an immune response to the protein in milk. The symptoms experienced can range from mild to quite severe, and can even be fatal. Lactose intolerance does not involve the immune system or the milk protein. It occurs when lactose, the milk sugar, cannot be broken down by the digestive system. It causes uncomfortable symptoms, such as gas, bloating, cramping and diarrhea, but it is not life threatening.

In recent years, many products have been developed that don't contain milk but that simulate its characteristics in baking and cooking. You'll now find nut milk, tofu yogurt and sour cream, soy cheese, and dairy-free butter. One of my favorite butter substitutes is Earth Balance®. Earth Balance contains a wide array of products, some of which contain corn, soy, and other allergens. Always be sure to read labels before purchasing. In some recipes, you can replace butter with oil, and I've indicated that in my recipes where appropriate.

Nuts

I love the taste and texture of nuts in just about any recipe. When I've used nuts as a topping or garnish, though, feel free to leave them out—the dish will still be delicious. When I've used tahini, a paste made from ground sesame seeds, you can substitute it with other oils or butter, though oils and butter won't mimic tahini's taste or texture.

Eggs

There are a number of substitutes for eggs (see "Recommended Substitutions" on p. 30). Many times I will try a recipe without eggs (in my banana bread, for example) to see what happens (in this case, the banana bread turned out fantastic!). My point is, don't be afraid to experiment. But make sure to always keep the same liquid-to-dry-ingredient ratio. A great egg substitute is a product called Ener-G Egg Replacer™, which also happens to be vegan and gluten-free. Always read the ingredients statements of egg replacers to check for unwanted allergens or gluten.

Shellfish

Crustaceans (shrimp, crab, and lobster) and mollusks (clams, mussels, oysters, scallops, octopus, and squid) all make up shellfish. Some people with shellfish allergies are allergic to both groups, though some are allergic to just one. However, allergists usually advise to avoid both groups even if you are allergic to just one. Note that there are no shellfish recipes in this book.

Fish

While fish is a great source of lean protein and omega-3 fatty acids, these nutrients can often be found in vegetarian and vegan foods. Whether you are allergic to fish or are vegan, look for other options to get the proper nutrients in your diet. Be on the lookout, too, for fish used in store-bought condiments, like Worcestershire sauce, which contains anchovies.

Soy

When you have a soy allergy, you have to be careful with a lot of store-bought products. Some contain soy lecithin used as a binder; others, like soy sauce, tofu, and edamame—all made from soy beans—are more recognizable culprits. When cooking, use substitutes like almond and coconut milks instead of soy milk, or stick with cow's milk products.

Corn

Like soy, corn products and byproducts are everywhere and can sneak into packaged foods and ingredients where you would least expect it. As with any allergy, be diligent about reading labels and don't be afraid to try new safe ingredients. When a recipe calls for cornstarch, try potato starch instead.

Vegetarian and Vegan

Because so many of us are looking to eat a more plant-based diet, many of my recipes are appropriate for vegetarians and vegans. Grains, beans, fruits, vegetables, and, for vegetarians, milk and eggs, are all part of a healthful, balanced diet.

ALLERGEN AND DIET KEY

I created the fun icons you'll see throughout the book as a way for you to instantly recognize what dish is appropriate for you. In "Variation" sidebars you'll find substitutions for other allergies.

wheat-free (not gluten-free)   milk-free (not dairy-free)   nut-free   egg-free   shellfish-free   fish-free   soy-free   corn-free   vegetarian   vegan   gluten-free

ALLERGENS   DIETARY NOTIFICATIONS

If you have lactose intolerance, a milk or egg allergy, or eat a vegan diet, look to the substitutions below to adapt recipes to meet your needs. Just keep in mind that the substitute you choose may effect the flavor of the dish, so be sure to taste your food—you may need to add a bit more salt, sugar, or lemon juice.

INSTEAD OF 1 EGG
- 1 tablespoon ground flax meal plus 3 tablespoons water
- ¼ cup blended tofu (contains soy)
- ½ banana (though your recipe will have a bit of banana flavor)
- ¼ cup applesauce (this makes baked goods really moist, and it allows you to cut down on fat in the recipe)
- 3 tablespoons vegan mayonnaise plus ¼ teaspoon baking powder (read ingredients statement for other allergens or unwanted ingredients)
- ¼ cup soy or almond milk (contains nuts) plus 1 teaspoon apple cider vinegar until it starts to curdle

INSTEAD OF 1 CUP COW'S MILK
- 1 cup soy milk
- 1 cup almond milk (contains nuts)
- 1 cup rice milk
- other alternative milk of your choice

INSTEAD OF 1 CUP REGULAR YOGURT
- 1 cup silken tofu (contains soy) blended with 2 tablespoons lemon juice
- 1 cup soy yogurt
- 1 cup tofu sour cream (contains soy)

INSTEAD OF 1 CUP BUTTERMILK
- 1 cup soy milk plus 1 teaspoon apple cider vinegar

INSTEAD OF 1 STICK BUTTER
Vegan fats contain the same number of calories as animal fats, so don't overdo the use of fats of any kind. Always read labels for butter substitutes to make sure you are avoiding necessary allergens.
- 1 stick vegan margarine or any butter substitute (Earth Balance is the one I use most)
- 1 stick vegetable shortening

INSTEAD OF 1 TABLESPOON HONEY
- 1 tablespoon pure maple syrup
- 1 tablespoon Silan (date honey)
- 1 tablespoon agave nectar

KITCHEN EQUIPMENT

As you can imagine, the range of kitchen products on the market is vast. You may find yourself asking if you really need some of the things being sold as must-haves. I've compiled a list of the basic every-day items I use in my home kitchen. As a general rule, buy good-quality stainless steel and heat-resistant equipment. It might be more expensive up front, but it will last you a lifetime.

- » **Stand mixer.** I swear by my KitchenAid® and prefer the smaller artisan model because of the tilting head, which I find easier to work around.

- » **Food processor.** I like the Magimix® and Robot Coupe®.

- » **Blender.** Although this is not a must, a blender is a nice addition to my kitchen and really aids in making soups, smoothies, sauces, and soups. The Vitamix® brand is terrific.

- » **Cookware.** Calphalon®, Anolon®, Le Creuset®, and Cuisinart® are my top choices.

- » **Knives.** Make sure you have a good chef's knife, paring knife, and large serrated knife for cutting breads. I like Global®, Wüsthof®, and Victorinox® brands.

- » **Stainless tongs.** Necessary for frying and flipping meats.

- » **Measuring cups and spoons.** I prefer stainless steel to plastic; you can find cups online that have a full set of odd sizes, including $\frac{2}{3}$ and $\frac{3}{4}$, which I find very helpful in baking.

- » **Ice cream scoops.** Buy several sizes for varied uses, including making uniform cookies and muffins.

- » **Microplane®.** Necessary for zesting citrus and grating spices.

- » **Offset spatula.** Must-have for baking and prepping.

- » **Fish spatula.** Perfect when working with delicate ingredients.

- » **Heat-safe silicone spatulas.** A must-have for everything else!

Prep Work

The French call it *mise en place,* which literally means "putting in place" and is used in professional kitchens to refer to organizing and arranging everything. Before attempting a new recipe, make sure you have all the ingredients and utensils out that you may need. That way you don't have to go searching for things with dirty hands. I also measure out what I will need before I start, which keeps me and the kitchen organized and leaves very little room for mistakes. As you finish with ingredients, put them away. This will make for easier cleanup later.

Measuring Ingredients

When measuring out ingredients using cup or spoon measures, make sure that the cup is completely full and use the back of a knife to level off the cup. Don't dip a measuring cup into a large container of dry ingredients, like flour or sugar. Instead, spoon it into the measuring cup. If you scoop, you compact the ingredient, so the amount is likely to be more than what's called for in your recipe. Measurements in recipes, especially in baking, are not suggestions, so follow the directions.

Knife Skills

Knowing how to work with a knife will make the process of cooking easier and more fun. Here are a few tips. Regardless of what kind of cutting you're doing, for stability, wrap your fingers around the knife handle but use your thumb and index finger to steady the blade.

Slicing. Rest the tip of the blade on a cutting board; raise the heel of the knife, then slice downward while pushing the blade forward.

Chopping. Position the knife as for slicing and make quick downward strokes. It's important to protect the fingers of your nonworking hand by tucking them into a "claw" when slicing and chopping.

Mincing. Holding the knife parallel to you, rock it up and down without raising the heel more than an inch or so. Stabilize the knife with your other hand.

Smashing garlic. On a cutting board, place an unpeeled clove under the flat side of a chef's knife and press down with your fist or hand to crush the clove. Remove and discard skin.

What is "cutting on the bias"? Cutting on the bias is making a 45-degree cut. I like to use do this when I want to create a more sophisticated look for things like crostini.

TIPS FROM A PROFESSIONAL KITCHEN

I've learned a lot over my years of cooking professionally. Some of these are common sense but worth repeating.

- » Always taste your food before serving.

- » Read through the recipe before starting to cook.

- » Know the difference between chemical leaveners (see p. 22 for more information). They have different purposes for the outcome of your baked goods and can't be substituted for one another.

- » Make sure to clean as you go or you will end up with a pile of dirty dishes.

- » Experiment with flavors and keep track of your changes to a recipe as you make them.

- » Keep two side towels on hand at all times—one to dry off your hands and one to take things out of the oven. Trying to take a pan out of the oven with a wet towel from hand drying will result in some nasty burns.

- » When cleaning a blender or food processor, add hot water and soap then turn on the machine for a few seconds to start the cleaning process before removing the unit from the base.

- » When baking, check for doneness by poking the top of the baked item with your finger. If it bounces back and is golden brown and firm to the touch, the baked item is done. While others will advise to test for doneness by piercing the cake with a skewer or knife, I am firmly opposed to this method because piercing will let out all of the steam, making for a very dry result.

- » When boiling soups and water for pasta, rest a heatproof spatula across the pot to prevent the contents from boiling over.

Chapter 2

Starters

MAKES 12 TO 14 CUPS;
SERVES 4 TO 6
Nutrition information per cucumber
cup: Calories: 28.9, Total Fat: 1.8g,
Cholesterol: 2.4mg, Sodium: 39.3mg,
Total Carbohydrates: 2.7g, Dietary
Fiber: 0.7g, Sugars: 0.1g, Protein: 0.9g

Greek Salad Cucumber Cups

2 large cucumbers (not
English), unpeeled

½ small red onion, finely
chopped

½ red bell pepper, finely
chopped

1 large tomato, seeded
and finely chopped

¼ cup finely chopped
Kalamata or other black
olives

½ teaspoon crushed red
pepper flakes

¼ cup fresh feta,
crumbled; more for
garnish (optional)

¼ cup chopped fresh flat-
leaf parsley; more for
garnish (optional)

1 lemon, zested and
juiced

1 tablespoon red-wine
vinegar

1 tablespoon extra-virgin
olive oil

½ tablespoon dried
oregano

Kosher salt and freshly
ground black pepper

This very simple appetizer is light and tasty. After scooping out the cucumber flesh, use the tip of a paring knife to remove any remaining cucumber seeds.

1. Peel the cucumbers, leaving thin strips of skin down the entire length for color. Trim the ends, then cut into 1-inch slices (you should end up with 12 to 14 slices total). Use a melon baller or small spoon to scoop out the center of each cucumber slice, leaving a dip in the center for the filling. Be sure you don't scoop through the bottom of the slice.

2. In a large bowl, mix the onions, bell peppers, tomatoes, olives, red pepper flakes, feta, parsley, lemon zest and juice, vinegar, olive oil, and oregano. Season with salt and pepper to taste. Fill the cucumber cups with the salad mixture, garnish with additional parsley and/or feta if desired, and serve.

VARIATION

 Leave out the feta or replace it with crumbled tofu and an additional ½ teaspoon salt (or to taste).

MAKES 1¹⁄₄ CUPS MARMALADE; SERVES 8 TO 10
Marmalade nutrition information per ¹⁄₂ teaspoon:
Calories: 156.2, Total Fat: 11g, Cholesterol: 0mg, Sodium:
156.4mg, Total Carbohydrates: 14.4g, Dietary Fiber: 1g,
Sugars: 11.7g, Protein: 0.6g

Mustard Raisin Marmalade on Toasted Crostini

1 cup golden raisins

¹⁄₄ cup balsamic vinegar

1 tablespoon whole-grain mustard (check ingredient statement)

1¹⁄₂ tablespoons capers plus 1 teaspoon caper juice

1 shallot, minced

1 tablespoon fresh lemon juice, plus more as needed

¹⁄₂ teaspoon ground cumin

¹⁄₂ cup olive oil, plus more for the baguette

Kosher salt and freshly ground black pepper

1 baguette (store-bought—check ingredient statement—or home-made; recipe on p. 216)

The marmalade is easy to make and will keep for about 2 weeks when refrigerated. Spread on crostini, it makes a delicious appetizer. Or dollop a spoonful on the Sweet Potato Soup on p. 72 (omit the pecan garnish) for a unique flavor combination.

1. Position a rack in the center of the oven and heat the oven to 350°F.

2. In a small saucepan, bring the raisins, vinegar, and 2 tablespoons water to a boil. Remove from the heat, cover, and let the raisins steep until the mixture is cool, about 30 minutes. Transfer the cooled raisin mixture to a food processor and add the mustard, capers and juice, shallots, lemon juice, and cumin. Process, adding the oil in a thin stream, until the mixture is smooth. Check the consistency. If the mixture seems too thick, add warm water 1 teaspoon at a time until you reach the desired spreadable consistency. Season with salt, pepper, and additional lemon juice to taste. Set aside.

3. Just before serving, cut the baguette into thin (about ¼-inch) slices on the diagonal, brush with olive oil on one side, and sprinkle with salt and pepper. Toast until golden brown, 5 to 10 minutes. Serve the crostini with the marmalade.

COOK'S TIP

Use ½ cup dried figs, apricots, or cherries in place of the raisins as a crostini topping or a dipping sauce for grilled or roast chicken or turkey (you might need to thin the mixture with a bit of olive oil or water to use as a dipping sauce).

VARIATION

To make this recipe wheat-free and gluten-free, serve the marmalade on crostini made from gluten-free bread or on gluten-free crackers. Or eliminate the crostini altogether and use the marmalade as a dipping sauce for chicken or tofu.

WINE PAIRING

The high acidity and flowery nature of German Riesling will pair perfectly with this crostini.

Herb Pesto–Stuffed Mushrooms

¼ cup olive oil

25 large white mushrooms, stems and caps separated and washed

2 tablespoons unsalted butter

1 cup finely chopped onions

¼ cup finely chopped celery

2 cloves garlic, finely chopped

½ teaspoon dried oregano, crumbled

1½ teaspoons kosher salt

1 teaspoon freshly ground black pepper

½ cup dried breadcrumbs (check ingredient statement)

½ cup finely grated Parmesan cheese

¼ cup chopped fresh flat-leaf parsley

Instead of the Herb Pesto, stuff the mushrooms with Pistachio Pesto (p. 238) or Arugula–Almond Pesto (p. 239) for variety. Just be aware that those fillings are not nut-free.

1. Position a rack in the center of the oven and heat the oven to 400°F.

2. Pour the oil into a large, shallow baking pan. Put the mushroom caps, stemmed sides down, in the pan and bake until the mushrooms exude liquid, about 10 minutes. Remove from the oven and let cool slightly; leave the oven on.

3. While the mushroom caps are baking, finely chop the mushroom stems. Melt the butter in a 12-inch heavy skillet over moderately high heat until the foam subsides, then sauté the chopped mushroom stems, onions, celery, garlic, oregano, salt, and pepper until the vegetables are golden brown, 5 to 6 minutes. Transfer the mixture to a large bowl and let cool slightly, then add the breadcrumbs, Parmesan, and parsley. Stir to combine.

4. Turn the mushroom caps over and mound the filling into the caps, pressing gently so that you don't break the caps. Bake in the original baking pan on the center rack in the oven until the stuffing is golden brown, 15 to 20 minutes. Serve hot.

VARIATIONS

 Replace the Parmesan with ¼ cup tofu cream cheese, which has the same salty flavor as the Parmesan and will bind the rest of the ingredients together. Replace the 2 tablespoons butter with 2 tablespoons olive oil.

 To make this dish vegan, follow the substitutions for making the dish milk-free and use vegan breadcrumbs (or you can make your own breadcrumbs by toasting and grinding vegan bread).

 Instead of the breadcrumbs, toast a few slices of gluten-free bread and crush them in a food processor to make gluten-free breadcrumbs. You can also crush gluten-free crackers.

SERVES 6 TO 8
Nutrition information per serving (based on 8 servings): Calories: 179.5, Total Fat: 12.3g, Cholesterol: 42.4mg, Sodium: 580.6mg, Total Carbohydrates: 6.1g, Dietary Fiber: 1.1g, Sugars: 1.6g, Protein: 15.3g

Thai Chicken Lettuce Cups

2 tablespoons olive oil

1 pound ground chicken

1 clove garlic, minced

1 teaspoon ground ginger

1/2 cup thinly sliced scallions (white and light green parts)

One 8-ounce can water chestnuts, drained and coarsely chopped

3 tablespoons hoisin sauce (check ingredient statement)

2 tablespoons gluten-free soy sauce

1 tablespoon rice vinegar

1 tablespoon fish sauce (nam pla; check ingredient statement)

2 teaspoons Sriracha or other hot chili sauce (check ingredient statement)

1 teaspoon kosher salt

FOR SERVING

1/3 cup peanuts, chopped

1/4 cup roughly chopped fresh cilantro

1/4 cup roughly chopped fresh mint

1/4 cup roughly chopped fresh basil, preferably Thai

12 Bibb lettuce leaves

These lettuce cups make a fun appetizer, though you could have them as a full meal, too. Serve the ingredients tapas-style and let guests create their own combination. Try one of the dips on pp. 243 and 244 or double the sauce here and reserve half of it for dipping.

1. Heat the olive oil in a large nonstick skillet over medium-high heat. Add the chicken, garlic, and ginger to the pan and cook for about 6 minutes, or until the meat is no longer pink and cooked through.

2. While the chicken is cooking, make the sauce: Combine the scallions, water chestnuts, hoisin sauce, soy sauce, rice vinegar, fish sauce, Sriracha, and salt in a large bowl.

3. Remove the chicken from the heat and transfer to the bowl with the sauce (draining off any fat that has accumulated in the pan). Toss to combine thoroughly.

4. Place the chopped nuts and herbs in four small bowls for serving. Serve tapas style, with the chicken mixture in a bowl, lettuce on a plate, and nuts and herbs in their bowls on the side. To eat, spoon about 1 large tablespoon of chicken on top of a lettuce leaf. Top with the chopped peanuts and herbs.

This dish pairs well with a light pilsner beer. If you can get your hands on Thai beer like Chang or Singha, it would make for an even more authentic accompaniment. Note that beer contains wheat and gluten.

VARIATIONS

 Leave out the peanuts when serving. You can also use crunchy Asian noodles, but these contain wheat and/or gluten.

 Replace the chicken with 1 to 2 blocks of extra-firm tofu. Cut the tofu into 1-inch cubes, place them on several layers of paper towels, cover with more paper towels, and top with a cutting board or plate to drain excess liquid. Let stand for several minutes, pressing down occasionally. Once the tofu is prepped, follow the recipe as written.

COOK'S TIP

Nam pla is an Asian fish sauce that's an essential ingredient in Thai cooking. You can find it in the Asian section of large grocery stores or in specialty markets. If you can't find it, use Worcestershire sauce instead (check ingredient statement).

SERVES 6

Nutrition information per serving: Calories: 139.4, Total Fat: 6.6g, Cholesterol: 30.1mg, Sodium: 59.3mg, Total Carbohydrates: 2.3g, Dietary Fiber: 0.6g, Sugars: 0.8g, Protein: 17.2g

Asparagus Beef Rolls with Horseradish Cream

FOR THE HORSERADISH CREAM

½ cup prepared horseradish (check ingredient statement)

½ cup heavy cream

1 cup sour cream

1 lemon, juiced, plus more lemon juice as needed

1 teaspoon kosher salt, plus more as needed

½ teaspoon cayenne

½ teaspoon freshly ground black pepper, plus more as needed

2 tablespoons chopped fresh flat-leaf parsley

FOR THE ROLLS

½ pound hanger steak

Kosher salt and freshly ground black pepper

1 pound fresh asparagus, bottoms trimmed

COOK'S TIP

If you don't see hanger steak at your market, you can use flat-iron steak, strip steak, or even flank steak instead.

Although beef and horseradish is a traditional combination, you can also use boneless chicken breasts instead of the beef. For another delicious option (though it won't be fish-free), use smoked salmon instead of the beef and thinly sliced cucumbers in place of the asparagus. Be sure to pound the beef until it's about ⅛ inch thick before rolling. If you like, make extra cream to serve as a dipping sauce with the rolls.

MAKE THE HORSERADISH CREAM

Combine the cream ingredients in a medium bowl. Season to taste with additional salt, black pepper, and lemon juice. Set aside.

MAKE THE FILLING AND ASSEMBLE THE ROLLS

1. Heat a gas or charcoal grill on high. Season the steak on both sides with salt and black pepper and grill over medium heat for 4 to 5 minutes on each side (or until the beef registers about 125°F on an instant-read thermometer). Transfer the steak to a cutting board and tent with foil. Let rest for 10 minutes, then thinly slice on a diagonal.

2. While the beef is resting, blanch the asparagus. Fill a large skillet with about 2 inches of salted water and add the asparagus. Cook the asparagus until it's bright green, 1 to 2 minutes, then transfer to a bowl of ice water to stop the cooking. Cut the asparagus spears into 2½-inch lengths.

3. Spread 1 teaspoon of the cream on each slice of beef, then place 2 lengths of asparagus (only one with a tip) on top of the cream at one end. Roll up the slices tightly and secure with a toothpick if needed to keep the meat from unrolling. Arrange the rolls, seam side down, in a baking dish or on a parchment-lined baking sheet, cover with plastic wrap, and refrigerate for 1 to 2 hours. Remove the toothpicks before serving.

VARIATION

 Replace the heavy cream with soy milk and replace the sour cream with silken tofu or tofu sour cream.

MAKES 16 MINI BURGERS
Burger only nutrition information (per 1 burger):
Calories: 123.2, Total Fat: 3.6g, Cholesterol: 0mg,
Sodium: 42.5mg, Total Carbohydrates: 16.2g,
Dietary Fiber: 3.9g, Sugars: 2.6g, Protein: 7.3g

Edamame Sliders with Sweet Red Pepper Jam

FOR THE BURGERS

2 cups frozen shelled edamame

One 15-ounce can black beans, undrained

1 cup sliced button mushrooms

½ cup cashews

4 cloves garlic

½ teaspoon ground cumin

1 teaspoon gluten-free soy sauce (read ingredient statement)

2 teaspoons kosher salt

1 teaspoon freshly ground black pepper

3 cups chickpea flour (read ingredient statement), plus more as needed

Vegetable oil, for frying (read ingredient statement)

FOR SERVING

Brioche Buns (p. 228) or store-bought slider rolls (check ingredient statement)

Sweet Red Pepper Jam (p. 240)

½ cup arugula

This recipe is very flexible, so experiment with different types of beans and vegetables; just be sure to keep the same proportions of ingredients. Make the gluten-free variation of brioche buns for this recipe or serve the burgers as "meatballs" for your gluten-free crowd instead.

1. Put the frozen edamame and black beans, including the liquid, in a large saucepan and warm through on low heat to thaw the edamame, about 20 minutes. Combine the edamame–black bean mixture, mushrooms, cashews, garlic, cumin, soy sauce, salt, and pepper in a food processor and process to a smooth paste. Transfer to a large bowl.

2. Slowly add the chickpea flour to the edamame mixture just until it becomes thick (you may need more or less than the 3 cups). Put the bowl in the refrigerator for 20 minutes so the mixture stiffens and becomes easier to shape.

3. Scoop out a small handful of cold edamame mixture and use your hands to shape 16 mini burger patties. Heat enough oil in a large sauté pan to cover the bottom, add the patties (don't crowd them), and fry them over medium heat for 4 to 5 minutes total, or until golden brown on both sides. Remove and drain on a paper towel–lined plate. Cook the patties in two batches if necessary, adding more oil as needed.

4. To serve, set one patty on each bun and top with Sweet Red Pepper Jam and 2 arugula leaves. If you'd like, secure with a long fancy toothpick for presentation and to prevent the ingredients from falling out while serving.

VARIATIONS

  To make this recipe wheat-free and gluten-free, use the gluten-free Mini Goat Cheese Brioche Buns (p. 233) or other gluten-free slider rolls. Check ingredient statement for other allergens.

 Replace the soy sauce with 1 teaspoon lemon juice or balsamic vinegar.

Eggplant Caponata

1 small eggplant, unpeeled and diced

½ cup small-diced fennel

½ cup small-diced red bell peppers

1 cup small-diced red onions

3 cloves garlic, thinly sliced

3 tablespoons extra-virgin olive oil

Kosher salt and freshly ground black pepper

1 tablespoon tomato paste (check ingredient statement)

2 tablespoons dry red wine

1 tablespoon Worcestershire sauce (check ingredient statement)

¼ cup quartered pitted black olives

1 tablespoon capers, drained

2 tablespoons minced fresh flat-leaf parsley

1 tablespoon minced fresh mint

Crostini or crackers, for serving (optional)

This dip is a great appetizer or party snack; serve with crackers (gluten-free or regular) or crostini. You can also use it as a fresh topping on baked flaky white fish, such as cod or halibut. Check the label of your Worcestershire sauce to see if it contains malt vinegar. If it does, leave it out to make this recipe gluten-free.

1. Position a rack in the center of the oven and heat the oven to 450°F.

2. In a medium bowl, mix the vegetables with the olive oil and salt and pepper to taste. Spread the vegetables on a foil-lined baking sheet and roast in the oven for 15 to 25 minutes, until browned and tender.

3. Meanwhile, in a medium bowl, stir together the tomato paste, wine, Worcestershire sauce, olives, capers, parsley, and mint. When the vegetables are done, add them to the mixture and toss to coat.

VARIATIONS

 For a wheat-free and gluten-fee option, use gluten-free Worcestershire and choose gluten-free crostini or crackers. Check ingredient statement for other allergens.

 Worcestershire sauce contains anchovies, so if you have a fish or seafood allergy, eliminate it from the recipe.

COOK'S TIP

Trim the fennel fronds from the bulb when you get home from the market. Slice the stalks off close to the bulb. When you're ready to prep the fennel, peel the outer layer from the bulb with a paring knife or peeler (this layer has stringy fibers), then cut the bulb into wedges and dice it for the recipe.

WINE PAIRING

A classic Italian red wine from the Chianti region will bring out the flavors of the eggplant and tomatoes.

MAKES FOUR 6-INCH TARTS
Nutrition information per tartlet: Calories: 193.8,
Total Fat: 11.3g, Cholesterol: 0mg, Sodium: 34.4mg,
Total Carbohydrates: 20.4g, Dietary Fiber: 4.3g,
Sugars: 1.6g, Protein: 6g

Tahini Tartlets with Spinach and Mushrooms

FOR THE TARTLET SHELLS

½ cup unbleached all-purpose flour (read ingredient statement)

¼ cup almond flour (read ingredient statement)

2 tablespoons cornstarch

1 teaspoon kosher salt

Freshly ground black pepper

1 tablespoon chopped fresh rosemary

1 tablespoon chopped fresh thyme

3 tablespoons tahini paste, plus more as needed

3 tablespoons ice water

Olive oil, for the tartlet pans

FOR THE FILLING

2 tablespoons olive oil, for frying

1 small red onion, finely chopped

½ teaspoon ground cloves

4 cups fresh spinach

1 leek, thinly sliced and thoroughly cleaned (including green leaves)

12 to 15 baby portabella mushrooms, thinly sliced

1 teaspoon kosher salt

Freshly ground black pepper

1 lemon, juiced

Tahini paste, which is made from sesame seeds and olive oil, adds great flavor to dishes. In these tarts, the fresh herbs and tahini paste in the shell complement the earthy flavor of spinach and mushrooms. Serve this at your next get-together—your guests will be impressed!

MAKE THE TARTLET SHELLS

1. Position a rack in the center of the oven and heat the oven to 375°F.

2. Combine the flours and cornstarch in a medium bowl; season with the salt and a few grinds of pepper. Add the herbs, tahini paste, and ice water; using your hands, work the dry ingredients into the wet ingredients until a dough forms. Add more tahini, ½ teaspoon at a time, if the dough is too crumbly.

3. Grease four 6-inch tartlet pans or ramekins with olive oil. Portion the dough evenly into 4 parts. Form each portion into a ball and press 1 dough ball evenly into the bottom and up the sides of each tartlet pan or ramekin. Use a knife to trim the dough flush with the edge of the pans. Prick the bottoms with a fork, making air holes to prevent the dough from bubbling as it bakes. Place the tartlet pans on a baking sheet and bake until golden, about 15 minutes.

4. The tartlet shells will puff slightly during cooking, so after removing them from the oven, use the back of a tablespoon to push them gently down into place. Let the shells cool slightly, then invert each pan and turn out the shells onto a wire rack; let cool completely. Alternatively, you can serve them in the pans or ramekins.

MAKE THE FILLING AND SERVE

1. Heat the oil in a large skillet over medium heat. Add the onions and cloves and cook until the onions are lightly browned, 5 to 6 minutes. Add the spinach, leeks, and mushrooms and cook until the spinach is just wilted, about 3 minutes. (Use tongs to toss the spinach in the mixture as it cooks down.) Season with the salt, a few grinds of pepper, and lemon juice and cook for about 2 minutes longer.

2. Evenly portion the filling among the tartlet shells, sprinkle with a bit more salt (if desired), and serve hot.

VARIATIONS

 To make the tartlet shells gluten-free, replace the all-purpose flour with a gluten-free flour blend of your choice. Although it can be difficult to get gluten-free dough to rise, the tartlet crust doesn't need to rise, so it is okay to use.

 Because some people who have a nut allergy are also allergic to sesame, you might need to replace the tahini in this recipe. Use sunflower seed butter or olive oil.

 Replace the 2 tablespoons cornstarch in the crust dough with 2 tablespoons of potato starch. The change won't affect the flavor because it is just used for binding the dough.

MAKES APPROXIMATELY TEN 2-INCH SQUARES

Nutrition information per 1 square: Calories: 138.6, Total Fat: 5.8g, Cholesterol: 0mg, Sodium: 24.3mg, Total Carbohydrates: 17.9g, Dietary Fiber: 1.3g, Sugars: 0.4g, Protein: 4.2g

Mushroom and Onion Flatbread

½ recipe Pizza Dough (p. 218)

8 ounces baby portabella mushrooms, thinly sliced

1 medium red onion, thinly sliced

¼ cup olive oil, plus more for the pan

1 tablespoon sea salt

Freshly ground black pepper

1 tablespoon finely chopped fresh thyme

WINE PAIRING

The grapefruit-like acidity of a Sauvignon Blanc will complement the richness of the mushrooms and thyme in this dish.

This starter can be served warm or at room temperature, so it's great when entertaining. The pizza dough will need a couple of hours to rise, so plan that into your schedule (or make the dough ahead and refrigerate for up to 24 hours before making the flatbread). As an alternative to a starter, serve the flatbread with a green salad or soup. It pairs especially well with the Split Pea and French Lentil Soup on p. 66.

1. Make the pizza dough according to Step 1 in the directions on p. 218; once the dough has risen, cut it in half and tightly wrap one half in plastic wrap and refrigerate for another use.

2. Combine the mushrooms and onions in a medium bowl, drizzle with the oil, salt, pepper, and thyme, and set aside.

3. Position a rack in the center of the oven and heat the oven to 450°F.

4. Drizzle olive oil generously on a rimmed baking sheet. With your hands, gently pull the dough as you spread it on the baking sheet; you want the dough to be thin—between ⅛ and ¼ inch thick. Spread the mushroom mixture across the dough evenly, then bake for 15 to 20 minutes, or until golden brown. Allow the flatbread to cool for 5 minutes before cutting into 2-inch squares and serving.

MAKES 15 TO 20 MEATBALLS; SERVES 4 TO 6
Nutrition information per serving (based on 6 servings): Calories: 290.4, Total Fat: 23.4g, Cholesterol: 87.5mg, Sodium: 834.3mg, Total Carbohydrates: 4g, Dietary Fiber: 1.4g, Sugars: 0.3g, Protein: 16.1g

Israeli Meatballs with Tahini Glaze

1 pound ground beef
  (85% lean)

1/2 cup finely chopped
  onions

3/4 cup finely chopped
  fresh flat-leaf parsley

1/4 cup sesame seeds

2 teaspoons kosher salt

1 teaspoon freshly ground
  black pepper

1 teaspoon ground cumin

1/2 teaspoon turmeric

1/3 cup toasted pine nuts

1 egg yolk

Vegetable oil, for the
  pan (read ingredient
  statement)

Simple Tahini Dip
  (p. 244), for serving

Don't be shy about using your hands in cooking—they're a great tool. When making meatballs, as in this recipe, mixing the ingredients together with your hands will ensure everything is thoroughly combined.

People with a tree nut allergy might experience similar symptoms when eating sesame seeds. Simply eliminate them from this recipe to be safe.

1. Combine the ground beef, onions, 1/2 cup of the parsley, the sesame seeds, salt, pepper, cumin, turmeric, pine nuts, and egg yolk together in a bowl. Mix until well combined.

2. Scoop out a bit of the mixture (with your fingers or a spoon) and shape into tablespoon-sized meatballs.

3. Heat a large skillet with a thin layer of vegetable oil over medium-high heat. Arrange as many meatballs as possible in the pan and cook until they're golden brown on all sides, 5 to 7 minutes. Repeat this process until all the meatballs have been cooked, adding more oil as needed. Let the meatballs cool slightly, drizzle with the Simple Tahini Dip, and sprinkle with the remaining 1/4 cup chopped parsley.

COCKTAIL PAIRING

Serve with a classic Mediterranean ouzu/arak shot or cocktail with a hint of lemon.

VARIATION

 Simply leave out the pine nuts if you have an allergy. It will affect the flavor only slightly but will not affect the consistency or texture of the meatballs.

COOK'S TIP

If you like your meat well done, lower the heat to medium low and cook each batch of meatballs for an extra 5 minutes.

SERVES 4 TO 6
Nutrition information per serving (based on 6 servings): Calories: 82.7, Total Fat: 2g, Cholesterol: 62mg, Sodium: 31.2mg, Total Carbohydrates: 13.4g, Dietary Fiber: 3.8g, Sugars: 1.4g, Protein: 7g

Deconstructed Sabich

1 recipe Simple Tahini Dip (p. 244)

1 medium eggplant, unpeeled, cut into 1-inch pieces and fried until golden brown

1 russet potato, unpeeled, cut into 1-inch pieces, and fried until golden brown

1/2 cup cherry tomatoes, quartered

2 large eggs, hard boiled and halved

1/4 cup thinly sliced red onions

1/4 cup finely chopped fresh flat-leaf parsley

1/4 cup finely chopped fresh mint

Sea salt and freshly ground black pepper

Olive oil

If you have never had a Sabich, you must try this recipe. Sabich is a traditional Iraqi/Israeli sandwich eaten on Shabbat (Saturday) mornings. This is a different take on the traditional serving method, with the ingredients spread out separately. If you'd rather, stuff the ingredients in a pita and eat as a sandwich.

Portion about ¾ cup of the Simple Tahini Dip among four small bowls, reserving the rest for garnish. Top with the eggplant, potatoes, tomatoes, eggs, and onions (in that order) in even portions. I like to keep each ingredient in separate areas of the bowl for color and presentation. Drizzle with the reserved ¼ cup of the Simple Tahini Dip and top with the freshly chopped herbs. Sprinkle with the sea salt and black pepper, drizzle with olive oil, and then serve.

SERVES 8 TO 10
Nutrition information per 1 skewer with 1 tablespoon dipping sauce: Calories: 147, Total Fat: 8.6g, Cholesterol: 26mg, Sodium: 129.6mg, Total Carbohydrates: 5.5g, Dietary Fiber: 0.8g, Sugars: 3.7g, Protein: 13.3g

Thai Peanut and Lime Chicken Skewers

FOR THE CHICKEN

1 pound boneless, skinless chicken breast halves, thinly sliced into long strips (you should have 12 to 15 strips, depending on the size of the breasts)

1 teaspoon Asian sesame oil

1 garlic clove, minced

1/2 teaspoon crushed red pepper flakes

1 teaspoon kosher salt

1 teaspoon freshly ground black pepper

Fifteen 8-inch wooden skewers, soaked in warm water for at least 30 minutes

FOR THE DIPPING SAUCE

1/2 cup creamy peanut butter

2 tablespoons lime juice, plus more as needed

2 tablespoons rice vinegar

1 tablespoon sugar, plus more as needed

1 teaspoon Sriracha or other hot chili sauce (check ingredient statement)

Kosher salt and freshly ground black pepper

Vegetable oil, for the pan (read ingredient statement)

Black sesame seeds, for garnish

These skewers come alive with the flavorful dipping sauce, but you can eliminate the sauce and serve the skewers on their own if you have a nut allergy. If you like, turn this dish into a light meal by serving 4 or 5 skewers over a bed of rice noodles (vermicelli) with the sauce drizzled over the top and sprinkled with a mix of chopped mint, cilantro, and peanuts.

MARINATE THE CHICKEN

In a large bowl, toss the chicken strips with the sesame oil, garlic, red pepper flakes, salt, and pepper. Marinate in the refrigerator for at least 1 hour and up to 3, then thread a strip of chicken onto each skewer.

MAKE THE DIPPING SAUCE

In a small bowl, whisk together the peanut butter, lime juice, vinegar, sugar, Sriracha, and 1/2 cup water until well combined. Season to taste with salt, pepper, and more lime juice and sugar, if desired. Set aside.

COOK THE SKEWERS AND SERVE

1. Heat a gas or charcoal grill or grill pan over high heat. If using a grill pan, brush it with oil. Working in batches, sear the chicken until cooked through, 1 to 2 minutes per side.

2. Sprinkle the skewers with the sesame seeds and serve with the dipping sauce on the side.

VARIATION

Replace the chicken with 1 to 2 blocks of extra-firm tofu cut into 1-inch cubes. Lay them on several layers of paper towels, cover with more paper towels, and top with a cutting board or plate to drain excess liquid. Let stand for several minutes, pressing down occasionally. Once the tofu is prepped, follow the recipe as written, threading 3 or 4 cubes onto a skewer. By replacing the tofu for chicken, this recipe is no longer soy-free.

MAKES 24 STUFFED TOMATOES; SERVES 12
Nutrition information per serving (based on 2 tomatoes): Calories: 63.3, Total Fat: 4.1g, Cholesterol: 14.5mg, Sodium: 25.7mg, Total Carbohydrates: 3.6g, Dietary Fiber: 0.5g, Sugars: 1.6g, Protein: 3.7g

Moroccan Stuffed Tomatoes

24 large roma tomatoes

1 tablespoon kosher salt, plus more for the tomatoes

Vegetable oil, for the pan (read ingredient statement)

1½ pounds ground beef (90% lean)

1 large onion, finely chopped

¾ cup dried breadcrumbs (check ingredient statement)

½ cup finely chopped fresh flat-leaf parsley

¼ cup finely chopped fresh mint

¼ cup pine nuts, chopped or left whole

2 tablespoons sesame seeds

1 large egg

1 teaspoon ground turmeric

1 teaspoon ground cumin

1 teaspoon freshly ground black pepper

Unlike stuffed cherry tomatoes, this appetizer requires a fork and knife. Choose the largest roma tomatoes at your market, and be sure to buy a low-fat ground beef to help minimize the amount of liquid as it cooks. Save the tops of the tomatoes and use in one of the delicious tomato salad recipes (see pp. 74 and 77).

1. Cut off the top one-quarter from each tomato using a small serrated knife (save the tops for another use). Using a spoon (a grapefruit spoon is great if you have one), scoop out the seeds and pulp and discard. Sprinkle the insides of the tomatoes with salt, then place them, cut side down, on paper towels and allow them to drain for about 20 minutes.

2. Position a rack in the center of the oven and heat the oven to 350°F. Lightly oil a 13x9x2-inch baking dish.

3. In a large bowl, mix the ground beef with the remaining ingredients, including the remaining 1 tablespoon salt. Fill the tomatoes to the top with the meat stuffing. Arrange them in the prepared dish, standing them straight up close to one another (touching is fine).

4. Bake the tomatoes until the meat is cooked through, about 1 hour. Let cool for at least 10 minutes, then transfer from the baking dish to a serving dish that has sides. Serve warm.

VARIATION

Instead of the regular breadcrumbs, toast a few slices of gluten-free bread and crush them in a food processor to make gluten-free breadcrumbs. You can also crush gluten-free crackers to make breadcrumbs.

MAKES 24 BLINIS
Nutrition information per 1 blini: Calories: 40.8, Total Fat: 2.6g, Sodium: 111.3mg, Total Carbohydrates: 2.5g, Dietary Fiber: 0.3g, Sugars: 0.4g, Protein: 1.9g

Blinis Topped with Lemon Whip and Smoked Salmon

1/3 cup buckwheat flour (read ingredient statement)

1/4 cup unbleached all-purpose flour (read ingredient statement)

1 teaspoon kosher salt

1 teaspoon baking powder

1 large egg, lightly beaten

2/3 cup buttermilk

2 tablespoons unsalted butter, melted

Vegetable oil (read ingredient statement)

1/3 cup mascarpone

1 lemon, zested and juiced

1 tablespoon finely chopped fresh chives, plus 1/4 cup cut into 1-inch lengths

4 ounces smoked salmon, thinly sliced

Sea salt

Blinis are like little pancakes, and they can be garnished with savory or sweet toppings. If you're entertaining, make the blinis up to 4 hours ahead of serving; layer them between sheets of parchment and store, covered, at room temperature until ready to use.

1. Sift the flours, salt, and baking powder into a medium bowl. Gradually whisk in the egg and buttermilk until fully incorporated and smooth, then stir in the melted butter.

2. Coat a large frying pan with oil and heat over medium-high heat. Drop the batter into the frying pan, 2 teaspoons per blini, and cook for about 2 minutes, or until the first side is golden brown (lift one edge of the blini with a spatula to check). Flip the blini and cook for another 2 minutes on the other side until browned. You can cook more than 1 blini at a time, but make sure they don't touch as they're cooking. Transfer the cooked blinis to a wire rack to cool. Repeat until you have used up all the batter, adding more oil as necessary.

3. Make the lemon whip by combining the mascarpone, lemon zest and juice, and the 1 tablespoon chopped chives in a medium bowl.

4. To serve, arrange the blinis on a platter. Spread each with 1 teaspoon lemon whip. Top with a slice of salmon, garnish with 1 or 2 lengths of chives, sprinkle with sea salt, and serve.

WINE PAIRING

Any light crisp white wine will pair nicely with this dish, but Champagne is ideal. If you are feeling really adventurous, break out a bottle of vodka for an authentic experience.

VARIATION

 Substitute 2/3 cup soy milk plus 1 teaspoon apple cider vinegar for the buttermilk. Replace the butter with 2 tablespoons Earth Balance or another butter substitute, and use 1/3 cup tofu cream cheese instead of the mascarpone. Earth Balance butter spreads contain corn and sometimes soy. If you have a corn or soy allergy, choose butter substitutes that do not contain them.

MAKES ABOUT 14 SLIDERS
Nutrition information per 1 slider: Calories: 226.8, Total Fat: 11.2g, Cholesterol: 93.7mg, Sodium: 214.8mg, Total Carbohydrates: 5.4g, Dietary Fiber: 0.5g, Sugars: 0.7g, Protein: 26.1g

Turkey Sliders with Cilantro–Lime Aïoli

FOR THE BURGERS

6 cloves garlic, minced

1/3 cup mayonnaise (check ingredient statement)

1 cup finely diced onions

2 tablespoons finely chopped fresh chives

1 tablespoon ground cumin

1 tablespoon kosher salt, plus more as needed

4 pounds ground turkey

1/2 cup dried breadcrumbs (check ingredient statement)

Freshly ground black pepper

FOR SERVING

Brioche Buns (p. 228) or store-bought slider rolls (check ingredient statement)

Cilantro–Lime Aïoli (p. 242)

1/2 cup arugula

If you don't want to serve these as sliders, make the patties and serve over a bed of arugula (lightly dressed with olive oil and a pinch of kosher salt) for a light dinner for four (3 to 4 burgers per serving). Or shape the mixture into meatballs and serve with pasta.

1. Heat a gas or charcoal grill on high.

2. Combine the garlic, mayonnaise, onions, chives, cumin, and 1 tablespoon salt in a large bowl; add the ground turkey and breadcrumbs and mix well. Scoop out a bit of the mixture and roll into a golf ball–sized ball, then flatten into a patty and place on a platter. Repeat with the remaining mixture. (You should have about 14 patties.) Sprinkle the patties with salt and black pepper. Grill the burgers over medium heat for 3 to 4 minutes on each side, until cooked through.

3. To serve, cover the bottom of each bun with a burger, spread with 1 tablespoon Cilantro–Lime Aïoli, and then top with a few arugula leaves and the bun tops.

VARIATION

Instead of the regular breadcrumbs, toast a few slices of gluten-free bread and crush them in a food processor to make gluten-free breadcrumbs. Serve the turkey burgers on gluten-free slider rolls.

Chapter 3

Soups & Salads

SERVES 6
Nutrition information per serving: Calories: 326.2, Total Fat: 11.9g, Cholesterol: 92.4mg, Sodium: 726mg, Total Carbohydrates: 28.9g, Dietary Fiber: 2.8g, Sugars: 5.6g, Protein: 26.3g

Turkey, Spinach, and White Bean Soup

FOR THE SOUP

2 medium onions, finely chopped

1 tablespoon fresh rosemary, chopped, or 1½ teaspoons dried rosemary

2 tablespoons olive oil

One 9-ounce bag spinach, chopped

7 cups vegetable stock (check ingredient statement)

One 15-ounce can white beans, rinsed and drained

½ cup orzo or other small-shaped pasta (check ingredient statement)

1 large clove garlic, minced

2 teaspoons lemon juice

Kosher salt and freshly ground black pepper

FOR THE MEATBALLS

1 pound ground turkey

½ cup finely ground fresh breadcrumbs (check ingredient statement)

1 large egg yolk

1 scallion, minced (white and light green parts)

2 teaspoons kosher salt

1 teaspoon freshly ground black pepper

3 tablespoons olive oil

Freshly shaved Parmesan cheese (optional)

This is my family's favorite soup, and I make it for them whenever I am home for a visit. They call it "Turkey Ball Stoop," or TBS for short. What is "stoop"? When the soup sits for a few hours or overnight, the consistency ends up somewhere between soup and stew—hence stoop! This is an easy weeknight meal—and also makes plenty of leftovers for later in the week.

MAKE THE SOUP

In a large saucepan, cook the onions and rosemary in the oil over medium heat, stirring, until the onions are softened, about 5 minutes. Add the spinach, toss to coat with oil, and cook for 1 minute. Add the stock, white beans, and orzo and bring to a simmer. Continue simmering, stirring occasionally so the orzo doesn't stick to the bottom of the pot, for 15 minutes. While the soup simmers, prepare the meatballs.

MAKE THE MEATBALLS

1. Combine all the meatball ingredients except the oil in a large bowl. Shape the mixture into meatballs about 1 inch in diameter.

2. Heat the oil in a 9-inch skillet over medium-high heat until hot. Cook the meatballs, in batches if needed, until browned, about 3 minutes; note that the meatballs will not be cooked all the way through. Transfer the meatballs to the soup once browned.

FINISH THE SOUP AND SERVE

Once all of the meatballs are added, simmer the soup for 10 to 15 minutes, until the meatballs are cooked though. Stir in the minced garlic and lemon juice, then season with salt and pepper to taste. Serve garnished with shaved Parmesan, if using.

COOK'S TIP

Be sure to taste your food and season it with salt and pepper (or other seasoning used in your recipe) before serving. Salt will accentuate the flavors of a dish, and pepper adds a touch of pungent flavor itself. Too little of these well-loved spices and your dish will be bland. Too much and the food's flavors will be overpowered. Start with small amounts when seasoning and retaste as you go to find just the right balance.

VARIATIONS

  Substitute gluten-free pasta for the orzo in the soup, and make homemade breadcrumbs from gluten-free bread for use in the meatball mixture. Check the ingredient statement for other allergens. If you would prefer not to use breadcrumbs at all, just leave out the egg yolk as well to give the meat a firmer consistency for frying.

   To make the soup egg-free, vegetarian, and vegan, use precooked lentils in place of the ground turkey and leave out the egg. Start with ¼ cup breadcrumbs (read ingredient statement) and add more if needed so the mixture holds together. Serve without the shaved Parmesan.

SERVES 4 TO 6
Nutrition information per serving (based on 6 servings): Calories: 229.6, Total Fat: 3.3g, Polyunsaturated Fat: 0.7g, Monounsaturated Fat: 1.7g, Cholesterol: 2.4mg, Sodium: 978.6mg, Total Carbohydrates: 39.7g, Dietary Fiber: 8.9g, Sugars: 10g, Protein: 7.6g

Sunchoke Soup

4 to 6 small leeks (white and light green parts), trimmed, cut on the diagonal, and rinsed well

1 pound sunchokes, peeled and quartered

1 small head cauliflower, trimmed and cut into quarters

3 large cloves garlic

3 medium carrots, peeled and quartered

3 medium parsnips, peeled and cut into 1-inch-thick rounds

2 tablespoons olive oil

1 teaspoon kosher salt, plus more as needed

¼ teaspoon freshly ground black pepper, plus more as needed

2 fresh oregano sprigs

2 cups chicken stock (check ingredient statement)

COOK'S TIP

It's imperative you let your vegetables cool before processing in a food processor or blender. The blade of these devices generates a lot of heat when processing and when added to already hot vegetables, the combined heat can cause the mixture to shoot out of the blender or food processor, resulting in a huge mess and sometimes burns.

Fall is one of my favorite times of year because the markets are lined with every type and color of vegetable imaginable, from colorful tomatoes and potatoes to flavorful greens and herbs. But for me, the most exciting veggie of the fall season is the sunchoke, or Jerusalem artichoke. Its consistency is very much like a fingerling potato, but its shape is more akin to fresh ginger and its flavor is more complex, like a parsnip. I love to purée sunchokes into a soup, chop and roast them to serve with a roast chicken, or even finely slice and fry into chips. Whichever preparation you choose, you will be pleasantly surprised with the exciting new flavor you have found.

1. Position a rack in the top and bottom third of the oven and heat the oven to 375°F.

2. Spread the leeks and sunchokes on a large rimmed baking sheet. Spread the cauliflower, garlic, carrots, and parsnips on another large rimmed baking sheet and drizzle all of the vegetables with the olive oil and sprinkle with the salt and pepper. Sprinkle the oregano on top of the cauliflower–carrot mixture. Roast both sheets of vegetables for 20 to 25 minutes, until golden brown, swapping the position of the sheets halfway through cooking. Remove the oregano and let the vegetables cool slightly.

3. Put all of the vegetables in the bowl of a food processor. Turn the food processor on and add enough chicken stock (start with 1 cup and go up to 2 cups) to the vegetables until you have reached a creamy consistency. Pour the purée back into the saucepan and keep hot for serving. Taste and season with more salt and pepper if necessary.

VARIATION

Replace the chicken stock with either vegetable stock (read ingredient statement) or water.

SERVES 4 TO 6
Nutrition information per serving (based on 6 servings): Calories: 137.3, Total Fat: 10.3g, Cholesterol: 0mg, Sodium: 500.1mg, Total Carbohydrates: 10.1g, Dietary Fiber: 3.8g, Sugars: 1.6g, Protein: 3.8g

Caramelized Cauliflower Soup

1 medium head cauliflower, cut into florets and florets thinly sliced

1 tablespoon olive oil, plus more as needed

1/2 teaspoon ground nutmeg

Kosher salt and freshly ground black pepper

1 large shallot, chopped

1 large clove garlic, chopped

3 cups vegetable stock (check ingredient statement)

1 teaspoon finely chopped fresh thyme, plus fresh thyme leaves

1 tablespoon white balsamic vinegar

1/2 cup hazelnuts, toasted and chopped, for serving

Caramelizing cauliflower brings out its naturally nutty flavor. This soup is delicious on its own, and it also makes the perfect starter to the Perfect Roast Chicken on p. 99. For a heartier meal, serve the soup over a bed of Creamy Polenta (p. 179).

1. Position a rack in the center of the oven and heat the oven to 450°F.

2. Spread the cauliflower florets on a rimmed baking sheet. Drizzle with the olive oil and sprinkle with the nutmeg, 1 teaspoon salt, and 1/2 teaspoon pepper; toss to coat. Bake for 35 to 45 minutes, tossing halfway through, until the cauliflower is fully roasted and the edges are golden brown. Transfer to another baking sheet or large platter and let cool completely.

3. While the cauliflower is roasting, make the broth. Heat 1 tablespoon oil in a large saucepan and sauté the shallots and garlic for about 5 minutes, until softened. Add the vegetable stock, chopped thyme, and vinegar and bring to a simmer. When the cauliflower is cool to the touch, add it along with the stock to the bowl of a food processor or blender and process until smooth. Pour the purée back into the saucepan and keep hot for serving. Season to taste with salt and pepper.

4. To serve, portion the soup among serving bowls and top with the fresh thyme leaves and chopped hazelnuts.

VARIATION

Omit the nuts when garnishing. If you'd like, use crushed artisanal potato chips or breadcrumbs to replace the texture and look of the toasted nuts. Check ingredient statement for other allergens, such as wheat.

SERVES 6 TO 8

Soup nutrition information per serving (based on 8 servings): Calories: 264.1, Total Fat: 7g, Cholesterol: 21.4mg, Sodium: 731.7mg, Total Carbohydrates: 33.7g, Dietary Fiber: 3.1g, Sugars: 9.8g, Protein: 16.1g

Matzo ball nutrition information per serving (based on 1 matzo ball): Calories: 36.3, Total Fat: 1.4g, Cholesterol: 27.9mg, Sodium: 22.3mg, Total Carbohydrates: 4.3g, Dietary Fiber: 0.2g, Sugars: 0.2g, Protein: 1.4g

Mom's Chicken Soup with Matzo Balls

FOR THE SOUP

2 tablespoons olive oil

3 large onions, diced

3 to 5 large cloves garlic

1 tablespoon black peppercorns

Kosher salt and freshly ground black pepper

2 bone-in skinless chicken breasts

4 medium carrots, halved lengthwise and thinly sliced

1 celery stalk, thinly sliced

1 medium potato, diced

1 medium sweet potato, diced

1 leek, halved lengthwise and thinly sliced

3 to 4 quarts (12 to 16 cups) chicken stock (read ingredient statement)

1 lemon, juiced

FOR THE MATZO BALLS

1/2 cup matzo meal (read ingredient statement)

2 large eggs, lightly beaten

2 tablespoons vegetable oil (read ingredient statement)

1 teaspoon kosher salt

1/4 teaspoon freshly ground black pepper

1 teaspoon dried parsley (or a combination of your favorite dried herbs)

2 tablespoons plain seltzer

Whenever I feel homesick, I make this soup—not because it tastes really good (even though it does!) or is true comfort in a bowl—but because it takes me back to the days of my youth and my mom cooking this soup. Your mom's chicken soup is probably the best, too, but the added advantage of this recipe is that it's super easy to make.

Be sure to use bone-in chicken for this recipe. The bones not only add flavor but also help to keep the chicken moist. (Bone-in breasts are typically cheaper than boneless, too.) If you buy breasts with skin on, simply remove it before browning to keep the fat content in the soup low and the end result less greasy.

MAKE THE SOUP

1. Heat 1 tablespoon of the olive oil in a large (12-quart) stockpot over medium-high heat. Stir in the onions, garlic, peppercorns, 1/2 teaspoon salt, and 1/2 teaspoon black pepper and cook, stirring occasionally, until the onions are glistening and golden brown, about 5 minutes. Add the chicken and brown for 3 minutes on each side to seal in the flavor. Transfer the chicken to a plate.

2. Add the remaining 1 tablespoon olive oil, the carrots, celery, potatoes, sweet potatoes, and leeks to the pot. Stir and then let cook until the vegetables are brown, 5 to 8 minutes. Return the chicken to the pot and pour in the stock until the pot is about three-quarters full. Bring to a boil, then reduce to a simmer and cook, covered, for 1 to 3 hours. Remove the chicken breasts, shred the chicken, and return it to the soup (discard the bones). An hour before serving, make the matzo balls.

MAKE THE MATZO BALLS

1. Mix all of the matzo ball ingredients together in a large bowl. Cover and chill for 30 minutes.

2. Run your hands under water so they are thoroughly wet. Shape the chilled matzo mixture into 1-inch-diameter balls; drop the matzo balls into the simmering soup as they're rolled. Cover the pot and cook the soup with the matzo balls for 30 to 40 minutes.

COOK'S TIP

Leeks are very dirty, so they must be cleaned thoroughly before using. Slice the leeks as directed, then put them in a medium bowl and fill with water. Use your hands to swish the leeks through the water, then remove the leeks with a spider or spoon, leaving the dirty water behind. Soak again, swishing to remove lingering dirt, and remove one more time. Continue another time if needed until the leeks are clean. Let dry before using them in the recipe.

FINISH THE SOUP

Season to taste with the lemon juice and more salt and pepper. Serve hot.

VARIATIONS

 Use cornmeal in place of the matzo meal. It will have a different consistency but will be equally as delicious. Note: These corn-meal balls won't be appropriate for someone with a corn allergy.

 Replace the chicken stock with vegetable stock or water and leave out the chicken for a faux chicken soup. Read ingredient statement for other allergens.

SERVES 6
Nutrition information per serving:
Calories: 119.4, Total Fat: 8g, Cholesterol: 0mg, Sodium: 447.5mg, Total Carbohydrates: 12.1g, Dietary Fiber: 3.5g, Sugars: 0.9g, Protein: 3g

Tomato and Almond Gazpacho

FOR THE SOUP

4 large tomatoes, halved (use the most in-season you can find; on-the-vine tomatoes will work when out of season)

1 shallot, chopped

1 large clove garlic, chopped

½ cup chopped celery

½ cup chopped unpeeled cucumbers

½ cup chopped red bell peppers

1 jalapeño (cut open and seeds removed for less heat, if desired)

2 teaspoons red-wine vinegar

1 tablespoon kosher salt

½ teaspoon sugar

FOR SERVING

10 to 12 whole almonds

8 to 12 heirloom cherry tomatoes, halved (mixed colors if possible)

1 avocado, cut into ¼-inch cubes

6 raspberries, halved

6 fresh basil leaves

8 to 12 very thin slices of jalapeño (seeds removed for less heat)

2 tablespoons olive oil

Fleur de sel or other coarse sea salt and freshly ground black pepper

Gazpacho, the classic chilled tomato-based soup, has many variations. Many years ago, while on assignment in Baja Mexico, I tasted the most flavorful gazpacho, with garden-fresh heirloom tomatoes, a bit of heat from jalapeños, and the perfect balance of puréed vegetables as the base and chopped vegetables for the garnish.

Use the most in-season tomatoes you can find; their sweetness will balance the tartness of the raspberries. Roasting the tomatoes will caramelize them and bring out their flavor—plus add a beautiful color.

1. Position a rack in the center of the oven and heat the oven to 350°F.

2. Arrange the tomatoes, cut side up, on a rimmed baking sheet and roast for 10 minutes.

3. Transfer the tomatoes and their juices to a blender, along with the shallots, garlic, celery, cucumbers, bell peppers, and jalapeño. Blend on low until smooth, 1 to 2 minutes, then strain through a fine-mesh sieve into a large bowl (press down on any solids left in the sieve to get all of the juices from the vegetables). Season the soup with the vinegar, salt, and sugar. Refrigerate until cold. (The soup can be made to this point and refrigerated for up to a week before serving.)

4. While the soup is chilling, toast the almonds in a small, dry skillet over medium heat until they are fragrant and beginning to color, 5 to 8 minutes. Watch carefully to ensure they don't burn. Set aside until you're ready to serve the soup.

5. To serve, evenly portion the halved cherry tomatoes, avocado, raspberries, basil, jalapeño slices, and almonds among soup bowls. Pour the soup into the bowls over the vegetables, portioning it evenly, drizzle with olive oil, and season with fleur de sel and black pepper. Serve immediately. (Alternatively, portion the soup into bowls first, then top with the garnishes.)

VARIATION

 Make this soup nut free by eliminating the almonds from the garnish.

SERVES 6 TO 8
Nutrition information per serving (based on 8 servings): Calories: 118.8, Total Fat: 2.6g, Cholesterol: 0mg, Sodium: 27.7mg, Total Carbohydrates: 20.2g, Dietary Fiber: 6.2g, Sugars: 2.2g, Protein: 5.7g

Split Pea and French Lentil Soup

2 tablespoons olive oil

1 medium onion, cut into ½-inch dice

2 medium carrots, cut into ½-inch dice

2 stalks celery, cut into ½-inch dice

1 clove garlic, minced

1 teaspoon dried thyme

1 cup dried green split peas

1 cup dried French lentils

8 cups vegetable stock (read ingredient statement)

2 bay leaves

Kosher salt and freshly ground black pepper

COOK'S TIP

You'll likely find several brands of vegetable stock at your local grocery store. You can use a low-salt version—or even water in place of the stock—but be sure to taste and adjust the seasoning before serving.

If you can't find French lentils, double the amount of split peas and make this a split pea soup.

1. Heat the olive oil in a large stockpot over medium heat. Add the onions, carrots, celery, garlic, and thyme and cook for 4 to 6 minutes, until the onions are translucent and slightly golden brown.

2. Add the peas, lentils, stock, and bay leaves and bring to a boil. Reduce the heat and simmer, covered, for 1 to 2 hours, until the peas have dissolved and the soup has thickened. Remove and discard the bay leaves and season to taste with salt and pepper. Keep warm over low heat and stir occasionally until ready to serve.

SERVES 8 TO 10
Nutrition information per serving (based on 10 servings): Calories 352.5, Total Fat: 5.4g, Cholesterol: 0mg, Sodium: 359.3mg, Total Carbohydrates: 55.6g, Dietary Fiber: 13.3g, Sugars: 2.5g, Protein: 17.2g

One-Pot Veggie Soup

1 tablespoon olive oil

1 medium onion, diced

3 medium carrots, diced

2 celery stalks, sliced

4 large cloves garlic, crushed

8 cups water or vegetable stock (read ingredient statement)

Two 19-ounce cans beans (such as chickpea, white, or black), rinsed and drained

1 cup uncooked gluten-free grain (such as rinsed quinoa or buckwheat)

One 14½-ounce can diced tomatoes, with their juices

About 9 ounces leafy greens (such as kale, spinach, or collard greens)

1 tablespoon kosher salt, plus more as needed

1 teaspoon freshly ground black pepper, plus more as needed

The beauty of this soup is its versatility. You can switch a few of the ingredients and still be guaranteed a delicious meal. It's a great soup for using up what you have on hand or when you discover beautiful leafy greens at the market. I've made this soup with spinach, rice, and white beans and again with quinoa, black beans, and kale. Feel free to play around with the ingredients but maintain the same technique and process of making the soup. Be aware that many grains contain gluten, so if you're on a gluten-free diet, use one that is gluten-free.

1. Heat the olive oil in large stockpot over medium heat. Add the onions, carrots, celery, and garlic; cook for 4 to 6 minutes, until the onions are golden brown.

2. Add the water or stock, then stir in the beans, grain, and tomatoes with their juices. Bring to a boil, reduce the heat to low, and simmer, covered, for 20 minutes. Stir in the greens, salt, and pepper. Simmer for another 10 to 15 minutes, until the grain is tender. Taste and adjust the seasoning if needed, then serve.

COOK'S TIP

The longer you cook soup, the more time the flavors have to develop. But be sure to cook soup at a gentle simmer, not a strong boil, which kills the nutrients in the vegetables.

SERVES 6 TO 8

Nutrition information per serving (based on 8 servings): Calories: 168.8, Total Fat: 4.2g, Cholesterol: 0mg, Sodium: 976.8mg, Total Carbohydrates: 30.4g, Dietary Fiber: 6.5g, Sugars: 4g, Protein: 7.1g

Kale and Barley Soup

8 cups vegetable stock (check ingredient statement)

1 cup pearl barley

2 teaspoons kosher salt

2 tablespoons olive oil, plus more for drizzling

3 cups chopped onions

Sea salt and freshly ground black pepper

8 cups coarsely chopped stemmed kale leaves

3/4 cup sliced scallions (white and light green parts)

3 tablespoons chopped fresh mint

2 tablespoons fresh lemon juice

You can't always find kale in your grocery store, so you can easily substitute any other leafy green that's in season, like spinach or collard greens. Even the leaves from a celery stalk make a great addition to the healthfulness and flavor of this soup.

1. Bring 2 cups of the stock, 4 cups water, the barley, and kosher salt to a boil in large stockpot. Reduce the heat to medium low, cover, and simmer until the barley is tender, about 40 minutes.

2. Meanwhile, heat 2 tablespoons oil in a heavy medium skillet over medium-high heat. Add the onions, sprinkle with sea salt, and sauté until golden brown, stirring often, about 15 minutes. Add the sautéed onions and the remaining 6 cups stock to the pot with the barley. Add the kale and simmer until the greens are tender, about 15 minutes. Add the scallions and mint; simmer for another 5 minutes. Add the lemon juice, taste, and season the soup with sea salt and pepper if needed.

3. To serve, portion the soup among serving bowls and drizzle each with olive oil.

COOK'S TIP

Top with crumbled feta for an interesting variation. Keep in mind this means the dish will no longer be milk-free.

VARIATION

 Replace the pearl barley with 1 cup rinsed quinoa and follow the recipe directions.

SERVES 4 TO 6

Nutrition information per serving (based on 6 servings): Calories: 153.9, Total Fat: 2g, Cholesterol: 0mg, Sodium: 97.7mg, Total Carbohydrates: 29.9g, Dietary Fiber: 11.3g, Sugars: 0.6g, Protein: 10.9g

Broccoli–Cauliflower Soup

2 medium heads broccoli, cut into florets

1 medium head cauliflower, cut into florets

1 serrano chile

2 large shallots

4 large cloves garlic

6 to 8 cups vegetable stock (read ingredient statement) or water

1 cup quick-cooking oats

2 lemons, juiced

Kosher salt and freshly ground black pepper

Every head of broccoli and cauliflower is a different size, so you might need to adjust the amount of stock or water to get a consistency you like. Start with the least amount of stock called for in the recipe and increase it until you're satisfied with the consistency.

The serrano chile (hotter than a jalapeño but not as hot as a habanero) will add a bit of heat to this soup. To reduce that amount of heat, slice open the chile and remove the seeds before adding it to the soup.

1. Combine the broccoli florets, cauliflower florets, serrano, shallots, and garlic in a food processor; process until chopped, then pour into a large soup pot. Pour enough of the vegetable stock or water to just cover the vegetables and bring to a boil over high heat.

2. Cover the pot and simmer the soup for about 20 minutes, until the vegetables are very tender. In batches, pour the soup into the food processor or a blender and purée (hold a folded dishtowel over the lid to prevent splashes), or leave the soup in the pot and use an immersion blender to purée until smooth. Pour the puréed soup back into the pot (if necessary), bring to a boil, then reduce the heat. When the soup is just simmering, slowly stir in the oats. Allow the oats to cook for about 5 minutes, stirring as the soup thickens. Add the lemon juice and season to taste with salt and pepper.

VARIATION

To make this wheat-free and gluten-free, replace the 1 cup oats with 1 cup certified gluten-free oats or rinsed quinoa and cook the soup for another 15 to 20 minutes, until the oats or quinoa are tender.

SERVES 6 TO 8

Nutrition information per serving (based on 8 servings): Calories: 389.4, Total Fat: 13g, Cholesterol: 42.5mg, Sodium: 156.8mg, Total Carbohydrates: 49g, Dietary Fiber: 4.7g, Sugars: 2.8g, Protein: 19.1g

Kubbe in Sweet and Sour Swiss Chard Soup

FOR THE SOUP

4 scallions (white and light green parts), trimmed

6 large cloves garlic

2 stalks celery, trimmed

1 bunch Swiss chard, stemmed

10 to 12 cups chicken stock (read ingredient statement) or water

2 medium zucchini, cut into ¼-inch dice

2 medium turnips, cut into ¼-inch dice

¾ cup fresh lemon juice

FOR THE DUMPLINGS

1 cup uncooked fine bulgur wheat

2 cups semolina, plus more as needed

2½ teaspoons kosher salt

1 pound ground beef (85% lean)

1 medium onion, finely chopped

¼ cup finely chopped fresh flat-leaf parsley

1 teaspoon freshly ground black pepper

1 tablespoon sesame seeds

Vegetable oil, for the pan (read ingredient statement)

This dish was one of the first things my mother-in-law, Georgette, taught me how to make. She was born in Morocco, doesn't speak a word of English, and is an amazing cook; most important, she decided that if I were going to steal her son away then I at least would need to know how to make him his favorite foods. It was only a few months into dating when she spent an afternoon teaching me how to prepare some Moroccan delights. This soup is one of my favorites. Making the kubbe—meat-stuffed dumplings—is a bit of a labor of love but well worth it. Make a double batch and freeze some for later.

MAKE THE SOUP

1. Put the scallions, garlic, celery, and half of the chard in a blender. Add 1 cup water and blend until the vegetables are pulverized. Roughly chop the remaining chard.

2. Pour the chicken stock or water (start with 10 cups and add more if desired) into a large soup pot and bring to a boil. Add the diced zucchini, diced turnips, and chopped Swiss chard to the stock and cook for 5 to 7 minutes, until the vegetables are fork-tender. Add the puréed vegetables to the soup and cook for another 10 minutes. Add the lemon juice, starting with ½ cup and adding more until you reach the desired taste. The soup should be quite sour.

MAKE THE DUMPLINGS

1. Soak the bulgur wheat in about 1 cup water for 30 minutes, until the wheat has absorbed the water and has expanded; it shouldn't be soupy. Transfer to a large bowl and add the semolina and ½ teaspoon of the salt; work the ingredients together into a dough and knead until the dough is elastic. Add more water if necessary to create a pliable dough. If the dough is too wet, let it stand for 30 minutes or add a small amount of semolina.

2. While the bulgur wheat is soaking, make the meat filling. Combine the ground beef with the onions, parsley, the remaining 2 teaspoons salt, the pepper, and the sesame seeds.

COOK'S TIP

Uncooked stuffed dumplings can be frozen. Freeze them on a baking sheet; once frozen, seal them in a zip-top bag and return them to the freezer. They'll last for 3 to 4 months.

3. When the dough is elastic, take a piece and shape it into a ball about the size of a golf ball (about 2 inches). You'll need to keep your hands wet to prevent the dough from sticking to them. Arrange the dough balls on a lightly oiled baking sheet. Use one thumb to make an indentation in the dough ball, forming a shell. The sides of the shell should be thin, so you will need to reposition your thumb to create the hollow shell. Your dough should make about 15 to 20 shells.

4. Using a small teaspoon or your fingers, stuff the shells with the meat filling, then stretch the dough to enclose the filling.

FINISH THE SOUP

Bring the soup to a boil and then gently add the dumplings one at a time. Use a long wooden spoon to stir the soup and make sure the dumplings are not stuck to the bottom of the pot. Continue to boil the soup and let the dumplings cook for about 20 minutes; the dumplings will rise to the surface when they're done (don't let them overcook or they will disintegrate). Serve the hot soup as soon as the dumplings have cooked through.

VARIATIONS

 If you have an allergy to nuts, omit the sesame seeds, which can cause a similar reaction.

  To make this appropriate for vegetarians and vegans, use cooked mashed peas or lentils in place of the ground beef following the same recipe directions. Use vegetable broth or water instead of chicken broth for the soup base. If substituting with vegetable broth, read the ingredient statement for other allergens.

SERVES 8 TO 10
Nutrition information per serving (based on 10 servings): Calories: 186.1, Total Fat: 12.6g, Cholesterol: 18mg, Sodium: 502.5mg, Total Carbohydrates: 17.2g, Dietary Fiber: 3.2g, Sugars: 2.2g, Protein: 2.7g

Sweet Potato Soup Topped with Buttered Pecans

FOR THE SOUP

2 tablespoons unsalted butter

1 cup finely chopped onions

1 cup finely chopped leeks (white and light green parts), washed well and drained

3 large cloves garlic, minced

3 large carrots, thinly sliced (about 1½ cups)

1 bay leaf

3 medium sweet potatoes or yams, peeled, halved lengthwise, and thinly sliced

One ½-pound russet potato, peeled, halved lengthwise, and thinly sliced

6 cups chicken stock, plus more as needed (read ingredient statement)

¾ cup dry white wine

Kosher salt and freshly ground black pepper

FOR THE BUTTERED PECANS

1 cup chopped pecans

2 tablespoons unsalted butter

1 teaspoon kosher salt

Olive oil, for serving

This velvety, flavorful soup makes a great first course to a roast chicken or beef dinner, but is also delicious on its own when served with a salad (I like baby arugula with sliced pears) or pancetta-wrapped homemade croutons. Make the soup ahead—it keeps for up to 2 days in the fridge—and reheat gently on the stove when ready to serve.

MAKE THE SOUP

1. Heat the butter in a large soup pot over medium heat and cook the onions, leeks, garlic, carrots, and bay leaf until the onions are softened and slightly golden, about 5 minutes. Add the sweet potatoes, russet potato, stock, wine, and 1½ cups water and bring to a simmer. Cover and cook for 15 to 20 minutes, until the potatoes are very tender. Remove and discard the bay leaf.

2. Transfer the potato mixture to a blender (in batches if necessary) and purée until smooth. (Hold a dry kitchen towel on top of the blender before turning it on to prevent the contents from splashing out and burning you.) Return the purée to the soup pot, add more broth to adjust the consistency, then season to taste with salt and pepper.

MAKE THE BUTTERED PECANS

In a medium skillet, cook the pecans in the butter with the salt over medium heat, stirring occasionally, for 10 minutes, or until golden brown. Transfer the cooked pecans to a paper towel–lined plate to drain excess oil. If you're not serving the soup right away, store the pecans in an airtight container for up to 2 days.

TO SERVE

Portion the soup among serving bowls and top each serving with a few pecans and a drizzle of olive oil.

VARIATIONS

 Replace the butter in the soup with olive oil or a butter substitute. Omit the buttered pecans. If using a butter substitute, check the ingredient statement for other allergens.

 Instead of the pecans, garnish the soup with an artisanal potato chip like Terra Stix® to maintain the crunch provided by the nuts (check the ingredient statement for other allergens). You can also garnish with a few sliced scallions or a dollop of Mustard Raisin Marmalade (recipe on p. 38).

 VG Replace the chicken stock with vegetable stock (check the ingredient statement for other allergens).

 V Replace the chicken stock with vegetable stock, and use olive oil instead of butter (check the ingredient statement for other allergens).

Tomato and Watermelon Salad

1 large seedless watermelon, cut into 1-inch cubes

6 cups tomatoes, halved or quartered (I like a mix of Campari and cherry, multicolored if possible)

1 teaspoon fleur de sel

2 tablespoons olive oil

1½ tablespoons red-wine vinegar

1 tablespoon chopped fresh basil

1 tablespoon chopped fresh flat-leaf parsley

1 tablespoon chopped fresh mint

Kosher salt and freshly ground black pepper

½ cup sliced almonds, lightly toasted (optional)

1 cup feta (optional)

Tomatoes and watermelon seem like an unlikely combination, but they're delicious together. This recipe treats them simply so that their flavors sparkle. This salad is best made in summer, when the star ingredients are at their freshest.

Combine the watermelon and tomatoes in a large bowl. Sprinkle with fleur de sel and toss to coat. Let stand for 15 minutes. Whisk together the olive oil, vinegar, and herbs and add to the melon mixture. Season to taste with salt and pepper. To serve, portion among salad bowls and top with the toasted almonds and feta, if you like.

VARIATIONS

 Omit the feta to make this recipe milk-free.

 Eliminate the almonds to make this dish nut-free.

COOK'S TIP

Salt brings out the flavor of ingredients, and the flaky texture of fleur de sel will enhance the flavor of the tomatoes without overwhelming it. Fleur de sel, like other sea salts, is harvested by hand, so it is pricey, but the flavor can't be beat. If you don't have fleur de sel, though, you can use another coarse salt.

SERVES 6 TO 8
Nutrition information per serving (based on 8 servings): Calories: 53.6, Total Fat: 3.6g, Cholesterol: 0mg, Sodium: 29.7mg, Total Carbohydrates: 5.5g, Dietary Fiber: 1.4g, Sugars: 2.6g, Protein: 0.6g

Moroccan Carrot Slaw

1 pound carrots, peeled

1 clove garlic, minced

1 teaspoon sweet paprika, preferably Moroccan

1 teaspoon ground cumin

1 teaspoon ground cinnamon

1/2 teaspoon cayenne

1 tablespoon sugar

2 tablespoons lemon juice

Kosher salt and freshly ground black pepper

2 tablespoons extra-virgin olive oil

1 tablespoon chopped fresh flat-leaf parsley

This simple slaw features staple spices of Moroccan food—paprika, cumin, cayenne, and cinnamon—and is perfect served with a Moroccan-themed meal, including the tagine on p. 100. This recipe is also a great addition to a tapas party.

Many Moroccan dishes feature dried fruits and nuts, so consider topping this salad with dried cranberries and chopped pecans to make it a bit heartier.

Shred the carrots into long sticks using a box grater. Transfer to a large serving bowl and add the garlic, paprika, cumin, cinnamon, cayenne, sugar, and lemon juice. Toss to combine and season to taste with salt and pepper. Chill for at least an hour. Before serving, season again with salt and pepper, drizzle with olive oil, and sprinkle on the chopped parsley.

SERVES 4 TO 6
Nutrition information per serving (based on 6 servings): Calories: 93.2, Total Fat: 7.1g, Cholesterol: 0mg, Sodium: 48.3mg, Total Carbohydrates: 6.3g, Dietary Fiber: 1.3g, Sugars: 2.4g, Protein: 1g

Bloody Mary Salad

3/4 cup finely chopped red onions

3 tablespoons sherry vinegar, divided

3 pints cherry tomatoes, halved

1 cup finely chopped celery hearts

2 tablespoons prepared horseradish (read ingredient statement)

1 tablespoon gluten-free Worcestershire sauce (read ingredient statement)

1/2 teaspoon celery seeds

1/4 cup olive oil

Kosher salt and freshly ground black pepper

This salad has all the tangy flavors of a bloody Mary. When entertaining, I like to serve it on a long, narrow plate accompanied by a shot of vodka for a palate cleanser. Use different-colored cherry tomatoes for the best presentation.

Not all brands of Worcestershire sauce are gluten-free, so be sure to check the label.

1. Put the onions in a large bowl and pour 1 tablespoon of the sherry vinegar on top; let the onions sit for about 10 minutes, then add the tomatoes and celery.

2. Whisk the remaining 2 tablespoons sherry vinegar, the horseradish, Worcestershire sauce, and celery seeds in a medium bowl. Slowly drizzle in the olive oil and whisk until emulsified. Pour the dressing on top of the tomato salad and toss to coat. Season to taste with salt and pepper. Set aside to marinate (the longer it sits, the more intense the flavor will be). Serve cold or at room temperature.

SERVES 6 TO 8

Nutrition information per serving (based on 8 servings): Calories: 132.3, Total Fat: 5.7g, Cholesterol: 0mg, Sodium: 10.9mg, Total Carbohydrates: 20.7g, Dietary Fiber: 6.4g, Sugars: 0.2g, Protein: 6.4g

Spiced Butternut Squash and Lentil Salad

1 cup dried lentils

5 cups butternut squash, peeled, seeded, and cut into 1-inch cubes

3 tablespoons olive oil

1 teaspoon ground cumin

1 teaspoon sea salt, plus more as needed

4 cups baby arugula

¼ cup thinly sliced fresh mint leaves

2 tablespoons red-wine vinegar

Freshly ground black pepper

Goat cheese crumbles, for serving (optional)

Dried cranberries, for serving (optional)

Not only are lentils naturally gluten-free, but they are a good source of fiber, protein, and a bunch of minerals and vitamins, too.

1. Put the lentils in small bowl, cover with cold water, and soak for about 10 minutes; drain.

2. Cook the lentils in boiling salted water until tender, about 30 minutes. Drain the lentils, rinse under cold water, and drain again.

3. Position a rack in the center of the oven and heat the oven to 425°F.

4. Put the butternut squash in a large bowl and toss to coat with 2 tablespoons of the olive oil, the cumin, and sea salt. Arrange in a single layer on a rimmed baking sheet and roast for 20 to 30 minutes, until golden brown. Let cool completely.

5. In a large bowl, toss the cooked lentils, roasted squash, arugula, mint, vinegar, and the remaining 1 tablespoon oil. Season to taste with salt and pepper. Portion the salad among serving plates and sprinkle with goat cheese and dried cranberries, if using.

VARIATION

Eliminate the goat cheese from the salad to make it milk-free.

COOK'S TIP

Buy precooked lentils to cut down on the prep time for this dish.

SERVES 8 TO 10
Nutrition information per serving (based on 10 servings): Calories: 259.4, Total Fat: 10.1g, Cholesterol: 0mg, Sodium: 104.6mg, Total Carbohydrates: 37.5g, Dietary Fiber: 2.4g, Sugars: 2g, Protein: 6.6g

Pine Nut and Olive Orzo Salad

One 16-ounce package orzo

¼ cup pine nuts, lightly toasted (see tip below)

1 small red onion, finely chopped

½ cup finely chopped fresh flat-leaf parsley

¼ cup Kalamata olives, halved

1 pint cherry tomatoes, quartered

1 cucumber, unpeeled and diced

1 lemon, zested and juiced

¼ cup olive oil

Kosher salt and freshly ground black pepper

Orzo looks like a long grain of rice, so people often confuse it with rice even though it's a short cut pasta. If you don't have celiac disease or a gluten sensitivity, use orzo in more than just this salad. It works well in soups, casseroles, and more. This salad is delicious with Greek Chicken Skewers on p. 104

1. Bring a pot of water to a boil and cook the orzo according to the package directions, then drain and rinse.

2. While the pasta is boiling, combine the pine nuts, onions, parsley, olives, tomatoes, cucumbers, lemon zest and juice, and olive oil in a large bowl. Stir to combine.

3. Pour the cooked, drained pasta into the tomato-nut mixture and stir to combine. Season to taste with salt and pepper, stir again, then serve.

VARIATION

 Make this recipe wheat-free and gluten-free by replacing the orzo with a small gluten-free pasta (read the ingredient statement for other allergens).You can also substitute quinoa (cook according to the package directions) for the orzo.

COOK'S TIP

Toasting nuts is easy. Spread the nuts on a rimmed baking sheet and toast in a 450°F oven for about 5 minutes. If you'd rather work on the stovetop, spread the nuts in a large frying pan and toast over medium-high heat for about 5 minutes. Whichever method you choose, keep an eye on the nuts—they go from toasted to burnt very quickly!

SERVES 6 TO 8

Nutrition information per serving (based on 8 servings): Calories: 114.7, Total Fat: 1.3g, Cholesterol: 0mg, Sodium: 5.6mg, Total Carbohydrates: 24.8g, Dietary Fiber: 4.2g, Sugars: 8.4g, Protein: 2.1g

Barley, Fig, and Mixed Greens Salad

1 cup pearl barley

3 teaspoons kosher salt

2 teaspoons freshly ground black pepper

4 scallions (white and light green parts), thinly sliced on an angle

¼ cup balsamic vinegar

2 tablespoons olive oil

1 pound fresh figs, stemmed and quartered

2 cups mixed greens

1 teaspoon chopped fresh thyme

³/4 cup chopped pecans, toasted

Barley, mixed greens, and nuts make a great salad foundation, so don't be afraid to try different fresh or dried fruits or vegetables in place of the figs and pecans here. I like fresh pears with walnuts in the fall and a beet and orange combination in summer. If you like, add crumbled feta or goat cheese to the combination here for a richer flavor. If you add cheese, this salad is no longer milk-free.

1. Bring 3½ cups water to a boil then add the barley, 1 teaspoon salt, and 1 teaspoon pepper. Return to a boil, then reduce to a simmer and cook until the liquid is absorbed and the barley is tender, 30 to 40 minutes.

2. Transfer the cooked barley to a large bowl and let cool, then add the scallions, balsamic vinegar, olive oil, remaining 2 teaspoons salt, and remaining 1 teaspoon pepper and toss to combine. Gently toss in the figs and greens. Top with the chopped thyme and pecans to serve.

WINE PAIRING

Pair this salad with a crisp Pinot Grigio to bring out the flavors of the figs.

COOK'S TIP

Barley is wheat-free but not gluten-free. However, there is the potential for barley to be contaminated with wheat. Those with a wheat allergy might want to try the variation.

VARIATION

Quinoa is wheat-free and gluten-free and is a good substitute for the pearl barley in this recipe. Cook quinoa according to the package directions, then continue with the recipe as directed.

SERVES 8

Baguette nutrition information per serving: Calories: 187.5, Total Fat: 0.9g, Cholesterol: 0mg, Sodium: 292.6mg, Total Carbohydrates: 37.8g, Dietary Fiber: 1.2g, Sugars: 0.5g, Protein: 6.2g

Salad nutrition information per serving: Calories: 78.8, Total Fat: 7.8g, Cholesterol: 1.5mg, Sodium: 38.5mg, Total Carbohydrates: 1.9g, Dietary Fiber: 0.4g, Sugars: 0.9g, Protein: 1.1g

Garlic Arugula Crostini Salad

FOR THE CROSTINI

1 baguette, store-bought (check ingredient statement) or homemade (see p. 216), halved lengthwise and cut into thirds

2 large cloves garlic, peeled

2 tablespoons olive oil

1 tablespoon sea salt

FOR THE SALAD

3 tablespoons olive oil

3 tablespoons fresh lemon juice

1 tablespoon mayonnaise (check ingredient statement)

8 cups arugula

Kosher salt and freshly ground black pepper

Block Parmesan cheese, shaved into large strips with a vegetable peeler

COOK'S TIP

Make the crostini up to 4 hours ahead and let stand at room temperature until you're ready to use.

This very simple salad can also be served as a starter if you cut the baguette into smaller slices. It's also delicious (as a salad or starter) garnished with thinly sliced grilled chicken breast.

1. Position a rack in the center of the oven and heat the oven to 400°F.

2. Arrange the bread in a single layer on a baking sheet. Rub the inside of the bread with the garlic cloves, drizzle with the 2 tablespoons olive oil, and sprinkle with the sea salt. Bake until golden brown, about 10 minutes.

3. To make the salad, whisk together the olive oil, lemon juice, and mayonnaise. Put the arugula in a large bowl and drizzle with the olive oil mixture. Sprinkle generously with salt and pepper and toss to coat.

4. To serve, portion the arugula evenly among the toasted crostini and top with shaved Parmesan. Sprinkle with freshly ground black pepper.

VARIATION

Feel free to leave out the Parmesan if you eat milk-free. If you don't have a nut allergy, use some toasted pine nuts instead of the cheese for the extra texture in each bite. Be sure to check the baguette ingredient statement to ensure there is no milk or butter.

SERVES 4 TO 6
Nutrition information per serving (based on 6 servings): Calories: 222.9, Total Fat: 11.2g, Cholesterol: 0mg, Sodium: 50mg, Total Carbohydrates: 28g, Dietary Fiber: 5g, Sugars: 1.3g, Protein: 9.3g

Quinoa and Herbed Fennel Salad

4 tablespoons olive oil

2 fennel bulbs, trimmed and thinly sliced

2 teaspoons kosher salt, plus more as needed

1 teaspoon freshly ground black pepper, plus more as needed

2 lemons, juiced

2 teaspoons ground cumin

2 teaspoons sugar

1 cup quinoa, rinsed

1 chile, seeded and chopped (use a serrano, jalapeño, or Thai, based on how spicy you like your food)

1 cup chopped fresh cilantro

1 cup chopped fresh mint

COOK'S TIP

Quinoa has a natural coating called saponin, which can make it taste bitter. Boxed quinoa is often pre-rinsed, but give it a quick rinse anyway. While the water is running, rub the seeds with your fingers to help remove the coating, then let drain before using in your recipe.

If you haven't yet discovered quinoa, you're missing out on a healthy pantry staple—it's a great source of protein, fiber, iron, and magnesium. Many people think quinoa is a grain, but it's technically a seed that can be used like other whole grains. It has a nutty flavor that shines in salads like this one.

1. Heat 3 tablespoons of the olive oil in a large skillet over medium heat. Add the fennel and season with 1 teaspoon each salt and pepper. Cook, stirring occasionally, until the fennel is just tender and lightly golden, 10 to 12 minutes. Stir in half of the lemon juice, the cumin, and sugar and cook for 1 minute until fragrant. Season to taste with salt and pepper and set aside.

2. Meanwhile, in a medium saucepan, combine the quinoa, the remaining 1 teaspoon salt, and 1¼ cups water and bring to a boil over high heat. Reduce the heat to medium low, cover, and simmer until the quinoa is tender, 15 to 20 minutes. Remove from the heat and let stand, covered, for 5 minutes. Fluff with a fork and transfer the quinoa to a large bowl.

3. Add the remaining lemon juice and remaining 1 tablespoon olive oil to the quinoa and stir to combine with a fork. Add the fennel mixture, chile, and herbs; toss gently and season with salt and pepper to taste. Transfer the salad to a serving bowl or individual bowls.

SERVING SUGGESTION
Pair this salad with Lamb Shawarma with Pomegranate–Mint Salsa on p. 130.

SERVES 2 TO 4
Nutrition information per serving (based on 4 servings): Calories: 444.2, Total Fat: 19.2g, Cholesterol: 51mg, Sodium: 259.1mg, Total Carbohydrates: 42g, Dietary Fiber: 2.2g, Sugars: 18.8g, Protein: 34.6

Thai Noodle Salad with Grilled Skirt Steak

FOR THE DRESSING

2 Thai chiles, thinly sliced

1/2 cup lemon juice

1/2 cup gluten-free Worcestershire sauce (read ingredient statement)

1/3 cup sugar

2 teaspoons peeled and minced fresh ginger

1 clove garlic, chopped

2 teaspoons kosher salt

FOR THE SALAD

1/2 package (6 ounces) rice noodles (read ingredient statement)

2 cups fresh cilantro, coarsely chopped

1 cup fresh mint leaves, coarsely chopped

1 cup fresh basil leaves, coarsely chopped

4 to 8 large butter lettuce leaves

1 pound skirt steak, cooked medium rare and thinly sliced on an angle

1/2 cup peanuts, chopped

This Thailand-inspired main dish salad tastes really fresh thanks to the herbs and high acidity of the dressing. Grilled fish or chicken pairs nicely with this salad if you don't eat beef.

1. In a large bowl, whisk together the dressing ingredients. Set aside.

2. Put the rice noodles in a large heatproof bowl and cover with boiling water. Allow the noodles to sit for 3 to 5 minutes until al dente. Drain, then pour back into the large bowl.

3. Add the chopped herbs and the dressing to the noodles and toss to coat.

4. To serve, line individual bowls or one large serving platter with lettuce leaves and place the noodle mixture on top. Top with a few slices of steak and chopped peanuts.

VARIATIONS

 To make this salad nut-free, eliminate the peanuts.

  Instead of grilled steak, top with seared sesame tofu. Cut 1 to 2 blocks of extra-firm tofu into strips about 1 by 3 inches, place them on several layers of paper towels, cover with more paper towels, and top with a cutting board or plate to drain excess liquid. Let stand for several minutes, pressing down occasionally. Heat 1 tablespoon Asian sesame oil in a nonstick pan over medium-high heat, add the tofu, and cook for about 5 minutes, turning the tofu strips to brown both sides.

This variation is not soy-free. Sesame oil should be avoided by those with a sesame allergy. Some people with nut allergies may choose to avoid the sesame oil as well.

SERVES 4 TO 6

Nutrition information per serving (based on 6 servings): Calories: 170.9, Total Fat: 9.5g, Cholesterol: 0mg, Sodium: 8.9mg, Total Carbohydrates: 20.9g, Dietary Fiber: 5.2g, Sugars: 0.4g, Protein: 9.4g

Bulgur Wheat Tabbouleh Salad

1 cup bulgur wheat

1 teaspoon kosher salt, plus more as needed

1 lemon, juiced

1 clove garlic, minced

¼ cup extra-virgin olive oil

1 large cucumber, unpeeled and diced

1 pint cherry tomatoes, quartered

½ cup fresh flat-leaf parsley, finely chopped

½ cup fresh mint, finely chopped

Freshly ground black pepper

Many major supermarkets carry bulgur wheat, but if yours doesn't have it, check your local health food store or Middle Eastern market.

1. Put the bulgur wheat and salt in a large bowl and cover with 1½ cups water. Let soak for 30 to 40 minutes, until all the water is fully absorbed. Fluff with a fork.

2. While the bulgur is soaking, whisk the lemon juice and garlic in a medium bowl, then slowly whisk in the olive oil. Add the cucumbers, tomatoes, and herbs and season to taste. Pour over the fluffed and cooled bulgur and toss to coat. Season to taste with salt and pepper and serve.

VARIATION

 Replace the cooked bulgur with cooked quinoa. Bring 1 cup rinsed quinoa, 1 teaspoon salt, and 1¼ cups water to a boil in a medium saucepan over high heat. Reduce the heat to medium low, cover, and simmer until the quinoa is tender, 15 to 20 minutes. Remove from the heat and let stand, covered, for 5 minutes. Fluff with a fork and transfer to a large bowl.

SERVES 4 TO 6
Nutrition information per serving (based on 6 servings): Calories: 241.5, Total Fat: 14g, Cholesterol: 0mg, Sodium: 30.2mg, Total Carbohydrates: 25.8g, Dietary Fiber: 3.4g, Sugars: 4g, Protein: 5.1g

Quinoa and Baby Spinach Salad with Cranberries and Pecans

1 cup quinoa, rinsed

1 teaspoon kosher salt

¼ cup olive oil

1 lemon, zested and juiced

3 tablespoons prepared mustard (read ingredient statement)

Kosher salt and freshly ground black pepper

One 6-ounce bag baby spinach, rinsed and roughly chopped

¼ cup dried cranberries

¼ cup pecan halves

If you have a mustard allergy, use prepared horseradish in place of the mustard in the dressing (though be sure to read the ingredient statement to confirm allergens). Feel free to sprinkle on some fresh herbs right before serving—try mint, flat-leaf parsley, cilantro, thyme, or dill.

To make this a main dish salad, add grilled chicken, fish, or shrimp. You can also sprinkle feta or goat cheese on top, too. (Note that this dish will no longer be milk-free, fish-free, or seafood-free with any of these additions.)

1. In a medium saucepan, combine the quinoa, salt, and 1¼ cups water and bring to a boil over high heat. Reduce the heat to medium low, cover, and simmer until the quinoa is tender, 15 to 20 minutes. Remove from the heat and let stand, covered, for 5 minutes. Fluff with a fork and transfer the quinoa to a large bowl.

2. While the quinoa cools, whisk together the olive oil, lemon zest and juice, and mustard in a small bowl. Season the dressing with salt and pepper to taste.

3. Toss the baby spinach into the quinoa and drizzle with the dressing to coat. Top with the cranberries and pecans and serve.

VARIATION

 To make this dish nut-free, leave out the pecans.

SERVES 6 TO 8
Nutrition information per serving (based on 8 servings): Calories: 245.3, Total Fat: 7.8g, Cholesterol: 0mg, Sodium: 539.1mg, Total Carbohydrates: 37.1g, Dietary Fiber: 5.5g, Sugars: 13.7g, Protein: 9.8g

Barley, Asparagus, and Mushroom Salad Topped with Gingered Tofu

FOR THE TOFU

1 package extra-firm tofu, cut into 1-inch cubes (read ingredient statement)

1 tablespoon brown sugar

2 tablespoons gluten-free soy sauce (read ingredient statement)

1 teaspoon finely grated fresh peeled ginger

1 teaspoon Asian sesame oil

1 clove garlic, grated

FOR THE SALAD

1 tablespoon Asian sesame oil

1 cup pearl barley

2 teaspoons kosher salt

1 pound asparagus, bottoms trimmed, and spears cut into 2-inch pieces

10 ounces large shiitake mushrooms, stems removed

2 teaspoons olive oil

4 to 5 scallions, thinly sliced (white and light green parts; about 1½ cups)

(continued)

This recipe breaks down into three distinct processes. While none are overly time-consuming, you can make everything ahead and assemble the salad when ready to eat.

If you don't have agave nectar, you can use honey instead, but keep in mind that this salad will no longer be vegan.

MARINATE AND ROAST THE TOFU

1. Position a rack on the center of the oven, and heat the oven to 375°F.

2. Put the tofu cubes on several layers of paper towels; cover with more paper towels and top with a cutting board to drain excess liquid. Let stand for several minutes, pressing down occasionally.

3. Arrange the tofu in a single layer in a rimmed baking dish. Combine the brown sugar, soy sauce, ginger, sesame oil, and garlic in a small bowl. Pour the mixture over the tofu and toss to coat. Let stand for 25 minutes. Remove the tofu from the marinade and arrange in a single layer on a baking sheet. Bake for 35 minutes, rotating halfway through cooking. Let cool completely.

MAKE THE SALAD

1. Heat the sesame oil in a large heavy saucepan over medium-high heat. Add the barley and cook for 3 minutes, until lightly toasted. Add 5 cups water and 1 teaspoon of the salt. Bring to a boil, then reduce to a simmer and cook for 45 minutes, until the barley is tender. Drain and let cool completely. Pour the barley into a large bowl.

2. Cook the asparagus in boiling water for 2 to 4 minutes (depending on the size of the spears), until crisp. Drain and plunge into ice water to stop the cooking. Pat dry and add to the barley.

3. Heat a grill pan over medium-high heat. Brush the tops of the mushrooms with the olive oil. Add the mushrooms to the pan, oiled side down. Cook for 5 minutes, until browned. Sprinkle evenly with the remaining 1 teaspoon salt. Let cool slightly, then slice the mushrooms thinly and add to the barley mixture, along with the scallions.

(continued)

Barley, Asparagus, and Mushroom Salad *(continued)*

FOR THE DRESSING

1 tablespoon Asian
    sesame oil

¼ cup rice-wine vinegar

2 tablespoons gluten-
    free soy sauce (check
    ingredient statement)

2 tablespoons agave nectar

2 teaspoons finely grated
    peeled fresh ginger

1 garlic clove, minced

Toasted black sesame
    seeds, for garnish
    (optional)

WINE PAIRING

Serve with chilled junmai
sake. Junmai sake is a pure
sake, meaning no additional
sugars or starches have been
added. It is a medium-sweet,
high-acid sake. Like other
sakes, junmai sake is a rice
wine and can be found at
most liquor stores.

MAKE THE DRESSING

Whisk together all of the dressing ingredients in a small bowl.

ASSEMBLE THE SALAD

Drizzle the dressing over the barley mixture and toss to coat. Evenly portion among serving plates, and top each serving with the gingered tofu and sesame seeds, if using. Serve at room temperature or chilled.

VARIATIONS

  Substitute cooked quinoa for cooked pearl barley. Bring 1 cup quinoa, 1 teaspoon salt, and 1¼ cups water to a boil in a medium saucepan over high heat. Reduce the heat to medium low, cover, and simmer until the quinoa is tender, 15 to 20 minutes. Remove from the heat and let stand, covered, for 5 minutes. Fluff with a fork and transfer to a large bowl.

 Tree nuts and sesame seeds have proteins in common, so someone with a nut allergy might experience similar symptoms when eating sesame seeds. Although this recipe is nut-free, it does contain large amounts of sesame, so you might want to use regular olive oil instead of sesame oil and leave out the sesame seed garnish.

Wheat Berry, Apple, and Smoked Salmon Salad with Feta

1 cup wheat berries

1½ cups diced Gala apples

½ cup thinly sliced red onions

½ cup chopped walnuts, toasted

3 celery stalks, thinly sliced

6 ounces smoked salmon, cut into 1-inch pieces

2 tablespoons olive oil

1 lemon, zested and juiced

2 tablespoons whole grain mustard (read ingredient statement)

1 teaspoon capers, drained and finely chopped

1 teaspoon kosher salt

1 teaspoon freshly ground black pepper

1 cup feta, crumbled, for serving (optional)

COOK'S TIP
Some health food stores sell presoaked or pre-cooked wheat berries, which will allow you to make this recipe when you are short on time.

Use wheat berries as you would rice—in a stir-fry, soup, or even chili. Wheat berries are tough, so they do take a little time to cook.

1. Place the wheat berries in a medium saucepan, cover with water, and bring to a boil over high heat. Reduce the heat, cover, and simmer gently for 1 hour, stirring occasionally. Drain and rinse.

2. In a large bowl, combine the wheat berries, apples, onions, walnuts, celery, and smoked salmon pieces.

3. In a small bowl, whisk together the olive oil, lemon zest and juice, mustard, capers, salt, and pepper. Drizzle over the wheat berry–apple mixture and toss to coat. Serve, garnished with crumbled feta, if using.

VARIATIONS

 Omit the feta to make the salad milk-free.

  Replace the cooked wheat berries with cooked quinoa. Bring 1 cup quinoa, 1 teaspoon salt, and 1¼ cups water to a boil in a medium saucepan over high heat. Reduce the heat to medium low, cover, and simmer until the quinoa is tender, 15 to 20 minutes. Remove from the heat and let stand, covered, for 5 minutes. Fluff with a fork and transfer to a large bowl.

  Omit the feta and the smoked salmon—the salad is still delicious without them.

Chapter 4

Mains

SERVES 4 TO 6
Nutrition information per serving (based on 6 servings): Calories: 236.4, Total Fat: 16.1g, Cholesterol: 43.3mg, Sodium: 93.6g, Total Carbohydrates: 4.6g, Dietary Fiber: 1.3g, Sugars: 0.9g, Protein: 19.1g

Grilled Chicken with Pistachio Pesto

Pistachio Pesto
(recipe on p. 238)

1 pound boneless, skinless chicken breasts, cut into 1-inch-thick strips

Vegetable oil, for the grill (read ingredient statement)

Kosher salt and freshly ground black pepper

The pistachio pesto is quite versatile—try it on tofu or grilled fish.

1. Make the pesto and transfer 3 tablespoons to a shallow pan; add the chicken strips and toss to coat.

2. Heat a grill or grill pan on medium high and oil the grill or pan. Sprinkle the chicken with salt and pepper, lay the strips on the grates, and cook for about 3 minutes. Flip the chicken strips and cook until they're cooked through, another 2 to 3 minutes.

3. To serve, top with the remaining pesto and serve.

WINE PAIRING

You might naturally lean toward a red wine because this is a meat dish. But because the flavors are light and summery, instead pair it with something refreshing. Try a Sancerre or Sauvignon Blanc.

SERVING SUGGESTION

Serve on a bed of Creamy Polenta (recipe on p. 179).

VARIATION

  Substitute 1 to 2 blocks of extra-firm tofu for the chicken. To prepare the tofu, cut it into 1-inch strips, then place on several layers of paper towels; cover with more paper towels and top with a cutting board to drain excess liquid. Let stand for several minutes, pressing down occasionally. Tofu contains soy, so this variation will not be soy-free.

SERVES 6 TO 8

Chicken mole nutrition information per serving (based on 8 servings), without accompaniments: Calories: 348.2, Total Fat: 10.6g, Cholesterol: 130.6mg, Sodium: 645.1mg, Total Carbohydrates: 9.9g, Dietary Fiber: 3.4g, Sugars: 0g, Protein: 52.4g

Spicy Pulled Chicken Mole Tacos

4 pounds boneless, skinless chicken thighs

2 teaspoons kosher salt, plus more as needed

½ teaspoon freshly ground black pepper, plus more as needed

2 tablespoons vegetable oil (read ingredient statement)

4 cups Homemade Salsa (recipe on p. 245 or use store-bought—read ingredient statement)

2 serrano chiles, finely chopped

3 bay leaves

1 cup brewed black coffee, regular or decaf (read ingredient statement)

1 teaspoon chili oil

¼ cup cocoa powder (read ingredient statement)

3 large cloves garlic, crushed

TO SERVE

Soft flour tortillas (read ingredient statement)

Shredded lettuce

Sour cream

Guacamole (recipe on p. 155)

Cooked rice (read ingredient statement)

This is a great dish to make with kids or to serve at a large party. Make serving fun by spreading out the mole and accompaniments as a taco bar. This dish is made in a slow cooker, so you can make it ahead and keep it warm until ready to serve. Leave out the serranos if you want to keep the mole mild.

1. Season the chicken with salt and pepper. Warm the vegetable oil in a medium stockpot or Dutch oven over medium-high heat, then add the chicken and brown. Once it's golden brown, transfer to a slow cooker (the chicken will not be cooked through).

2. While the chicken is browning, combine the remaining ingredients, then add to the chicken in the slow cooker. Cover and cook on low for 8 to 10 hours.

3. Remove the chicken from the slow cooker and use two forks to shred it. Return the meat to the sauce, stirring it in to combine, and remove and discard the bay leaves. Serve the chicken mole at the table with the tortillas, lettuce, sour cream, guacamole, and rice.

VARIATIONS

For serving, replace the sour cream with tofu sour cream or leave it out altogether to make this dish milk-free. Since tofu contains soy, this variation will not be soy-free.

For serving, use corn tortillas, but know that this variation will not be corn-free. Some corn tortillas contain wheat, so be sure to purchase 100% corn tortillas or certified gluten-free corn tortillas.

MAKES ONE 9-INCH DOUBLE-CRUST PIE OR
6 MINI PIES; SERVES 6 TO 8
Nutrition information per serving (based on 8 servings): Calories: 512.9, Total Fat: 31.5g, Cholesterol:
80.4mg, Sodium: 874.8mg, Total Carbohydrates: 45g,
Dietary Fiber: 3.2g, Sugars: 4.8g, Protein: 14.3g

Turkey Pot Pie

FOR THE PIE CRUST

2½ cups unbleached
   all-purpose flour (read
   ingredient statement),
   plus more as needed

1 teaspoon kosher salt

1 teaspoon sugar

1 cup (2 sticks) chilled
   unsalted butter, cut
   into pieces

½ cup ice water

FOR THE FILLING

4 tablespoons olive oil

1 small onion, minced

2 stalks celery, chopped

2 medium carrots, diced

3 tablespoons dried
   parsley

1 teaspoon dried oregano

Kosher salt and freshly
   ground black pepper

1 tablespoon chicken
   bouillon granules (read
   ingredient statement)

3 Yukon Gold potatoes,
   peeled and cut into
   1-inch cubes

1½ cups cooked turkey,
   cut into 1-inch cubes

3 tablespoons unbleached
   all-purpose flour (read
   ingredient statement)

½ cup milk

This is a great recipe for using up Thanksgiving leftovers. You can replace the vegetables and herbs called for in the ingredients list and use what you have instead. If you use leftovers, skip step 1 of making the filling too.

When short on time, use store-bought crusts for the top and bottom of the pie. Be sure to allow for thawing time for easy reshaping prior to prep and cooking.

MAKE THE CRUST

1. Mix the flour, salt, and sugar in a large bowl. Drop in the butter pieces. Using your hands, a fork, a pastry cutter, or a mixer, work the butter into the flour mixture until you get pea-size pieces.

2. Using a fork, quickly stir in the ½ cup ice water. Turn out the dough and crumbs onto a clean surface. Knead until the dough just starts to hold together but some bits still fall away, 5 to 10 times. Cut the dough in half and pat each half into a 6-inch disk. Wrap each disk in plastic wrap and refrigerate for at least 20 minutes.

MAKE THE FILLING

1. Heat 2 tablespoons of the olive oil in a large skillet over medium high. Add the onions, celery, carrots, parsley, and oregano; season with salt and pepper. Cook the vegetables until soft, 5 to 7 minutes. Stir in the bouillon and 2 cups water and bring the mixture to a boil. Add the potatoes and cook until fork-tender, 15 to 20 minutes.

2. In a medium saucepan, heat the remaining 2 tablespoons olive oil. Stir in the turkey, flour, and milk and heat through. Stir the turkey mixture into the vegetable mixture and cook until the sauce has thickened.

(continued)

Turkey Pot Pie *(continued)*

COOK'S TIP

When rolling out dough, roll out from the center, working out to the edge in all directions. It's not only easier for rolling, but will help ensure the thickness is consistent across the entire piece of dough.

ASSEMBLE THE PIES

1. Position a rack in the center of the oven and heat the oven to 425°F.

2. Lightly flour your work surface, then roll out one disk of dough for the bottom pie crust to ⅛ inch thick. Cut out six 6-inch rounds if making mini pies; press the dough into the bottom and up the sides of six 4-inch ramekins. If making a 9-inch pie, drape the rolled-out dough over the pie plate and press it into the bottom and up the sides. Trim any excess dough from the edge, leaving a 1-inch overhang.

3. If making mini pies, evenly portion the filling among the ramekins. Flour your work surface, then roll out the other dough disk to ⅛ inch thick, then cut out six 6-inch rounds. Place one round on top of each mini pie. Secure the top and bottom crust together by fluting the edges, and make 2 slits in the top of the crust for steam to release. If making a 9-inch pie, transfer the filling to the pie plate. Roll out the second dough disk to ⅛ inch thick, then place it on top of the filling. Trim the edges so they're even with the bottom crust, then flute the edges. Make 4 slits in the top of the pie for steam to release.

4. Bake for 15 minutes, then reduce the oven temperature to 350°F and continue baking for 15 minutes, or until the crust is golden brown.

VARIATIONS

 Make the crust and the filling milk-free by substituting Earth Balance or another butter substitute for the same amount of butter. Replace the cow's milk with soy milk (contains soy) or almond milk (contains almonds, a tree nut). Don't use rice milk as the sauce won't thicken properly. Read the ingredient statement for the butter substitute to check for other allergens such as corn or soy.

 Use the gluten-free flour recipe on p. 20 or a gluten-free flour blend like Bob's Red Mill in place of the all-purpose flour. If you're making the 9-inch pie, you can even use a frozen store-bought gluten-free crust to save time and hassle.

 To make the pot pie vegetarian, eliminate the turkey and instead add more diced carrots and cubed potatoes. Use vegetarian bouillon instead of chicken bouillon (check ingredient statement).

SERVES 2 TO 4
Nutrition information per serving (based on
4 servings): Calories: 445.3, Total Fat: 10.2g,
Cholesterol: 260mg, Sodium: 720.3mg,
Total Carbohydrates: 1g, Dietary Fiber: 0.8g,
Sugars: 0g, Protein: 92.1g

Perfect Roast Chicken

One 4-pound chicken

4 large fresh sage leaves

4 sprigs fresh thyme

4 sprigs fresh rosemary

1 tablespoon olive oil

Kosher salt and freshly
ground black pepper

1 lemon, quartered

1 teaspoon crushed red
pepper flakes

To make a complete one-pot meal, add vegetables to the pan just before roasting and drizzle them with 1 tablespoon olive oil, salt, pepper, and herbs. For a full menu suggestion, serve on a bed of Creamy Polenta (recipe on p. 179) and top the entire dish with Balsamic Figs (recipe on p. 246). Be aware that polenta is made from corn, so this dish would not be corn-free.

1. Position a rack in the center of the oven and heat the oven to 300°F.

2. Using your fingers, loosen the skin from the chicken breasts. Rub half of the herbs and half of the olive oil under the skin of each chicken breast. Sprinkle 2 teaspoons salt inside the chicken cavity and stuff it with the lemon quarters; tie the legs together with kitchen twine. Sprinkle the outside of the chicken all over with the red pepper flakes, 1 tablespoon salt, and pepper. Place the chicken, breast side up, in a roasting pan.

3. Roast the chicken for 3 hours, basting with the liquid every hour. Let rest for 15 minutes before carving.

SERVES 6 TO 8
Nutrition information per serving (based on 8 servings): Calories: 323.1, Total Fat: 15.5g, Cholesterol: 65mg, Sodium: 43.8mg, Total Carbohydrates: 20.1g, Dietary Fiber: 2.9g, Sugars: 13.8g, Protein: 27.7g

Moroccan Tagine with Apricots and Almonds

1 tablespoon ground cinnamon

1 tablespoon ground ginger

1 teaspoon turmeric

1 teaspoon freshly ground black pepper

1 tablespoon kosher salt

Olive oil

8 boneless, skinless chicken breast halves, cut into thirds lengthwise

1 large red onion, cut into 1/4-inch-thick slices

8 large cloves garlic, finely chopped

6 sprigs fresh cilantro, plus 3 tablespoons chopped cilantro, for serving

8 sprigs fresh flat-leaf parsley, plus 3 tablespoons chopped flat-leaf parsley, for serving

4 tablespoons honey

2 cinnamon sticks

1 cup dried apricots, halved

1/2 cup almonds, chopped

This wonderful stew is easy to make. It's traditionally cooked in a tagine, which makes a really nice presentation. If you don't have one, use a large Dutch oven—you'll get the same results.

1. In a large bowl, combine the cinnamon, ginger, turmeric, pepper, 2 teaspoons of the salt, and 4 tablespoons oil. Add the chicken and toss to coat; let sit for at least 20 minutes and up to 1 hour to marinate.

2. Heat 3 tablespoons olive oil in the base of a tagine or in a large Dutch oven over medium-high heat until hot but not smoking. Add half of the chicken and cook, uncovered, for 6 to 8 minutes total, turning over halfway through cooking, until browned. Transfer to a plate and repeat with the remaining chicken, adding another 3 tablespoons oil for cooking. Transfer the second batch of chicken to the plate.

3. Add the onions and the remaining 1 teaspoon salt to the tagine or Dutch oven and cook, uncovered, stirring frequently, until the onions are soft and translucent, about 8 minutes. Add the garlic and cook, stirring occasionally, for 3 minutes. Tie the cilantro and parsley sprigs into a bundle with kitchen twine and add to the pot along with 1 cup water, the cooked chicken, and any juices that have accumulated on the plate. Reduce the heat and simmer, covered, for 30 minutes.

4. While the chicken is simmering, bring the honey, 1 cup water, the cinnamon sticks, and apricots to a boil in a small saucepan. Reduce the heat and simmer, uncovered, until the apricots are tender and plump and the liquid is reduced to a glaze, 10 to 15 minutes.

5. While the apricots are simmering, heat 1/4 cup olive oil in a small skillet over medium heat and cook the almonds, stirring occasionally, until just golden, 1 to 2 minutes. Using a slotted spoon, transfer the almonds to paper towels to drain; let the oil cool before discarding.

(continued)

Moroccan Tagine *(continued)*

WINE PAIRING

A crisp rosé would be the best choice for this meal and would complement the dried fruits and nuts, which are the main attraction in most mildly spicy Moroccan dishes.

SERVING SUGGESTION

See the Moroccan Dinner menu option on p. 250 for a fun themed dinner.

6. Ten minutes before the chicken is done cooking, add the apricot mixture to the pot but remove and discard the cinnamon sticks. Finish cooking the chicken.

7. Serve the chicken (if cooked in a tagine, serve it at the table if you like), topped with the toasted almonds and more freshly chopped herbs.

VARIATIONS

 To make this dish nut-free, leave out the almonds when serving.

 Replace the chicken with 1 to 2 blocks of extra-firm tofu. To prepare the tofu, cut into ½-inch strips, then place on several layers of paper towels; cover with more paper towels and top with a cutting board to drain excess liquid. Let stand for several minutes, pressing down occasionally. Tofu contains soy, so this variation will not be soy-free.

 To make this dish vegan, replace the chicken with tofu (follow the preparation instructions for the vegetarian option above) and replace the honey with agave nectar. Tofu contains soy, so this variation will not be soy-free.

SERVES 14
Nutrition information per serving (based on 14 servings): Calories: 601.1, Total Fat: 26.2g, Cholesterol: 296.8mg, Sodium: 790.2mg, Total Carbohydrates: 9g, Dietary Fiber: 0.4g, Sugars: 7.3g, Protein: 77.9g

Oven-Roasted Herb and Ginger Turkey

One 14- to 18-pound whole turkey

2 tablespoons dried parsley

2 tablespoons dried onions

2 tablespoons dried oregano

2 tablespoons kosher salt, plus more as needed

1 tablespoon freshly ground black pepper, plus more as needed

6 tablespoons olive oil

Three 12-ounce cans ginger ale

COOK'S TIP

To roast a larger turkey (from about 18 to 22 pounds), simply double the spices and oil and follow the same preparation technique. Use another can of ginger ale and adjust the roasting time. To add extra flavor, replace the olive oil with butter.

WINE PAIRING

The traditional Thanksgiving wine pairing with turkey is a Pinot Noir. It has great earthy undertones that pair well with the flavors of the holiday's classic dishes.

SERVING SUGGESTION

See the New England Thanksgiving Harvest menu option on p. 252 to make a delicious holiday meal.

Whenever I prepare a roast, I always use a disposable roasting pan. Regardless of how nice your roasting pan may be, you should use disposable, too. It will save you a ton of messy cleanup later.

1. Position a rack in the oven so the turkey will fit and heat the oven to 350°F.

2. Rinse and wash the turkey and remove all excess parts. (Save the parts if you're going to make gravy, or discard if not.) Place the turkey in a large roasting bag inside of a large roasting pan; this will trap the steam while cooking to prevent the turkey from drying out.

3. Mix the herbs and spices in a small bowl. Using your fingers, loosen the skin from the breasts. Rub half of the herb mixture and half of the olive oil under the skin of each breast.

4. Pour the ginger ale over the top of the turkey inside the bag, sprinkle the outside of the turkey with salt and pepper, and seal the bag with the ties provided.

5. Cover the turkey with foil and roast for 3 hours. Remove the foil so the turkey will brown nicely (still in the bag) and roast for another 45 to 60 minutes, until the outside is golden brown and the internal temperature of the thickest part of the thigh registers 180°F on an instant-read thermometer. Let rest for 30 minutes before carving.

SERVES 4 TO 6

Nutrition information per serving (based on 6 servings): Calories: 261.9, Total Fat: 12.5g, Cholesterol: 86.7mg, Sodium: 55.4mg, Total Carbohydrates: 4.1g, Dietary Fiber: 0.8g, Sugars: 0.2g, Protein: 38.8g

Greek Chicken Skewers

FOR THE MARINADE

2 pounds boneless, skinless chicken breasts, cut into 1-inch cubes

2 tablespoons olive oil, plus more for the grill

4 cloves garlic, crushed

1 lemon

2 sprigs fresh mint, cut in half if large

1 teaspoon dried oregano

1 teaspoon coarse salt

1 teaspoon freshly ground black pepper

FOR THE SKEWERS

Eight 8-inch wooden skewers, soaked for at least 30 minutes

1 cup whole fresh mint leaves

1 red onion, quartered

Kosher salt and freshly ground black pepper

TO SERVE

1 lemon, juiced

Sea salt

This is a fun grill dish to accompany a Mediterranean-style tapas meal. Invite some friends over, break out the ouzu, and serve with several other classically Mediterranean dishes (see the serving suggestions below).

1. Combine the chicken, olive oil, garlic, 2 tablespoons fresh lemon juice, the squeezed lemon halves, the mint, oregano, salt, and pepper in medium bowl. Cover and let the chicken marinate for 30 minutes.

2. Heat a grill or grill pan on medium high (oil the grill pan, if using). Thread the skewers with the chicken pieces, mint leaves, and red onions, alternating their placement. Sprinkle the skewers with salt and pepper. Lay the skewers on the grate and grill until the chicken is just cooked through, turning halfway through cooking, 3 to 5 minutes per side. If using a grill pan, add more oil as needed to prevent sticking and burning.

3. Drizzle with lemon juice and sea salt, and serve.

VARIATION

Use 1 to 2 blocks of extra-firm tofu instead of chicken. To prepare the tofu, cut into 1-inch cubes, then place on several layers of paper towels; cover with more paper towels and top with a cutting board to drain excess liquid. Let stand for several minutes, pressing down occasionally. Tofu contains soy, so this variation will not be soy-free.

COOK'S TIP

Instead of grilling the skewers for the entire cooking time, sear the prepared skewers on a grill pan until the chicken is marked, then finish cooking in a 375°F oven.

SERVING SUGGESTIONS

Make the meal Greek! Start with the Greek Salad Cucumber Cups on p. 37. Serve the skewers over the Pine Nut and Olive Orzo Salad on p. 80. Top it all off with an ouzo cocktail, a classic Greek drink.

SERVES 4 TO 6; MAKES ABOUT 2 CUPS CHUTNEY

Chicken Tikka nutrition information per serving (based on 6 servings): Calories: 107.8, Total Fat: 2.9g, Cholesterol: 43.3mg, Sodium: 55.3mg, Total Carbohydrates: 2.6g, Dietary Fiber: 0.1g, Sugars: 1.1g, Protein: 17.2g

Cilantro–Mint Chutney nutrition information per serving (based on 16 servings): Calories: 3.5, Total Fat: 0.1g, Cholesterol: 0mg, Sodium: 55.3mg, Total Carbohydrates: 1.5g, Dietary Fiber: 0.3g, Sugars: 0.3g, Protein: 6g

Chicken Tikka with Cilantro–Mint Chutney

FOR THE CHICKEN TIKKA

½ cup soy yogurt (read ingredient statement)

1 lime, juiced

1 teaspoon finely grated fresh ginger

1 large clove garlic, finely minced

1 teaspoon garam masala (read ingredient statement)

1 teaspoon kosher salt

¼ teaspoon cayenne

1 pound boneless, skinless chicken breasts, cut into 1-inch cubes

FOR THE CILANTRO–MINT CHUTNEY

2 packed cups fresh cilantro

1 packed cup fresh mint

½ cup chopped onions

2 teaspoons finely chopped serrano chiles

1 teaspoon sugar, plus more as needed

1 teaspoon kosher salt, plus more as needed

1 to 2 limes

Eight to ten 8-inch skewers, soaked in warm water for at least 30 minutes

Vegetable oil, for the grill (read ingredient statement)

This is a great mild Indian dish, so if you've never had Indian food, it's a good one to start with. If you don't like spicy food, simply omit the serrano chiles from the chutney and you will still experience the exciting flavors.

If you don't like cilantro, replace it with basil or more mint in the chutney. If you can't find a serrano chile or want a little heat but not as much as a serrano, replace it with another small green chile.

1. In a medium bowl, combine the yogurt, lime juice, ginger, garlic, garam masala, salt, and cayenne; add the chicken and toss to coat. Cover and refrigerate for at least 30 minutes.

2. While the chicken is marinating, purée all the chutney ingredients, including the juice of just 1 lime and ⅓ cup water, in a blender until smooth. Season to taste with more salt, sugar, and lime juice. Set aside.

3. Thread 3 or 4 pieces of chicken onto each skewer and transfer to a baking sheet.

4. Heat a grill or grill pan on medium high. Oil the grill or pan, lay the skewers on the grate, and cook the chicken until it's browned and just cooked through, 5 to 7 minutes total. Serve topped with the chutney.

SERVING SUGGESTION

Due to the strong flavors in this dish, serve with a simple jasmine rice or the Thai Coconut Rice on p. 178. The coconut rice should be avoided by those with tree nut allergies.

WINE PAIRING

German Rieslings pair best with the rich spices of Indian food and offer a more balanced experience for the palate.

VARIATION

Substitute 1 to 2 blocks of extra-firm tofu for the chicken. To prepare the tofu, cut into 1-inch cubes, then place on several layers of paper towels; cover with more paper towels and top with a cutting board to drain excess liquid. Let stand for several minutes, pressing down occasionally. Tofu contains soy, so this variation will not be soy-free.

COOK'S TIP

Although some chefs say you don't need to soak wooden skewers before putting them on the grill there's really no reason not to. Sure they will still get a bit charred even if soaked, but wet skewers are less likely to go up in flames, particularly if they're thin. So soak to be on the safe side.

SERVES 6 TO 8
Nutrition information per serving (based on 8 servings): Calories: 333.5, Total Fat: 13.5g, Cholesterol: 32.5mg, Sodium: 197.2mg, Total Carbohydrates: 34.2g, Dietary Fiber: 4.7g, Sugars: 13.8g, Protein: 17.4g

Coconut Chicken Curry

3 tablespoons vegetable oil (read ingredient statement)

1 medium onion, thinly sliced

1 large carrot, cut into ½-inch slices

2 tablespoons fresh ginger, thinly sliced

6 cloves garlic, thinly sliced

1 stalk lemongrass, cut into 2-inch pieces

¼ cup firmly packed brown sugar

2 tablespoons ground cumin

2 tablespoons chili powder (read ingredient statement)

1 teaspoon ground cinnamon

1 teaspoon kosher salt, plus more as needed

1 teaspoon freshly ground black pepper, plus more as needed

One 28-ounce can diced tomatoes, with their juices

Two 14-ounce cans coconut milk

3 medium Yukon Gold potatoes, cut into medium dice

2 cups fresh shiitake mushrooms, quartered

1 cup pearl onions, peeled

2 red bell peppers, cut into medium dice

1 pound boneless, skinless chicken breasts, cut into 1-inch cubes

1 lemon, juiced

1 bunch fresh cilantro, chopped

If you like your food hot and spicy, then double the chili powder; if spicy isn't your thing, then leave it out. If you don't like cilantro, use a mix of mint and flat-leaf parsley instead.

1. Heat the oil in a large pot over medium-high heat. Add the onions and sauté until they're lightly golden and translucent, 3 to 5 minutes. Add the carrots, ginger, garlic, and lemongrass and sauté for about 5 minutes. Reduce the heat to medium, then add the brown sugar, cumin, chili powder, cinnamon, salt, and black pepper; cook for another 5 minutes. Add the tomatoes and cook until the sauce reduces and thickens, 3 to 5 minutes.

2. Once the tomatoes have reduced to almost a paste, stir in the coconut milk and bring the mixture to a boil. Add the potatoes, mushrooms, pearl onions, and bell peppers and cook, partially covered, for 7 to 10 minutes, until the potatoes are fork-tender. Add the chicken and cook until it is cooked through, 5 to 7 minutes. Season to taste with salt, black pepper, and fresh lemon juice.

3. Portion into individual bowls, sprinkle with chopped cilantro, and serve.

VARIATION

Substitute the chicken with 1 to 2 blocks of extra-firm tofu. To prepare the tofu, cut into 1-inch cubes, then place on several layers of paper towels; cover with more paper towels and top with a cutting board to drain excess liquid. Let stand for several minutes, pressing down occasionally. Tofu contains soy, so this variation will not be soy-free.

SERVING SUGGESTION

Serve the chicken over plain basmati rice or Thai Coconut Rice (recipe on p. 178). Coconut is considered a tree nut.

SERVES 2

Nutrition information per serving: Calories: 370.5, Total Fat: 11.9g, Cholesterol: 50.5mg, Sodium: 481.9mg, Total Carbohydrates: 39.2g, Dietary Fiber: 7.6g, Sugars: 5.5g, Protein: 28.1g

One-Pot Mediterranean Chicken

2 boneless, skinless chicken breast halves, cut into 2-inch strips

1 tablespoon olive oil

2 tablespoons finely chopped fresh flat-leaf parsley

2 cloves garlic, crushed

3 scallions, thinly sliced

One 16-ounce can chickpeas, rinsed and drained

1 pint cherry tomatoes

1/2 cup chicken stock (read ingredient statement)

2 tablespoons lemon juice

Kosher salt and freshly ground black pepper

1 cup baby arugula

1 lemon, quartered

A cast-iron pan allows for more even cooking and makes a nice from-the-pan serving presentation. If you don't have cast iron, though, you can use any large heavy-based frying pan. If you like, replace the chickpeas with white beans or kidney beans.

1. Combine the chicken, olive oil, parsley, and garlic in a glass bowl; cover and refrigerate for 30 minutes.

2. Heat a 12-inch cast-iron pan over medium-high heat. Cook the chicken, in batches if necessary, for 3 to 5 minutes on each side until browned; transfer to a plate. Add the scallions, chickpeas, and tomatoes to the pan and cook for 2 minutes; add the chicken stock and lemon juice and bring to a boil. Cook until the tomatoes begin to shrivel and burst, about 5 minutes. Keep an eye on them.

3. Return the chicken to the pan, placing it on top of the chickpea mixture. Reduce the heat to medium and simmer for 5 minutes. Season with salt and pepper to taste.

4. Serve with a side of arugula and lemon wedges for squeezing.

SERVING SUGGESTION

Serve with Bulgur Wheat Tabbouleh Salad on p. 86.

VARIATION

Substitute the chicken with 1 to 2 blocks of extra-firm tofu. To prepare the tofu, cut into 2-inch slices, then place on several layers of paper towels; cover with more paper towels and top with a cutting board to drain excess liquid. Let stand for several minutes, pressing down occasionally. Tofu contains soy, so this variation will not be soy-free.

SERVES 4 TO 6

Nutrition information per serving (based on 6 servings): Calories: 344.5, Total Fat: 7.6g, Cholesterol: 57.3mg, Sodium: 61.8mg, Total Carbohydrates: 51.3g, Dietary Fiber: 4.4g, Sugars: 7.1g, Protein: 19.2g

Rosemary Skillet Chicken with Mushrooms and Potatoes

1 pound fingerling potatoes, halved

Kosher salt

2 sprigs fresh rosemary, plus 1½ tablespoons rosemary leaves, plus more sprigs, for garnish (optional)

2 cloves garlic

1 teaspoon crushed red pepper flakes

2 lemons, juiced and rinds reserved

3 tablespoons extra-virgin olive oil

4 to 6 bone-in, skin-on chicken thighs

2 cups cremini mushrooms, halved

SERVING SUGGESTION

Serve with Sautéed Kale with Pine Nuts (recipe on p. 168). Note that this dish is not nut-free.

This recipe is naturally allergen-free but feel free to experiment with other flavors and cuts of chicken or meat. The recipe is very forgiving. As far as a "skillet," I prefer to use cast iron because I love the way it cooks and because it makes a nice serving presentation. If you don't own a cast-iron skillet, just be sure you use something that has an oven-safe handle.

1. Position a rack in the center of the oven and heat the oven to 450°F.

2. Put the potatoes in a large saucepan, cover with water, and add 1 teaspoon salt. Bring to a boil over medium-high heat and cook until the potatoes are easily pierced with a fork, about 8 minutes; drain the potatoes and set aside.

3. In the bowl of a food processor, combine the rosemary leaves, garlic, 2 teaspoons salt, the red pepper flakes, lemon juice, and 2 tablespoons of the olive oil. Process to a coarse paste, then scrape out into a large bowl, add the chicken, and toss to coat.

4. Heat the remaining 1 tablespoon olive oil in a large cast-iron skillet over medium-high heat. Add the chicken, skin side down, and brown, about 5 minutes. Remove the chicken from the pan; add the mushrooms and potatoes, stir to combine, then return the chicken to the pan, nestling it among the vegetables. Drizzle the chicken with any marinade remaining in the bowl.

5. Add the rosemary sprigs and the reserved lemon rinds to the skillet; transfer to the oven and roast, uncovered, until the chicken is cooked through and the skin is crisp, 20 to 25 minutes. Garnish with more rosemary sprigs, if you like, and serve.

MAKES 20 TO 25 DUMPLINGS;
SERVES 8 TO 10
Nutrition information per serving (based on 8 servings): Calories: 50.4, Total Fat: 2.4g, Cholesterol: 16.9mg, Sodium: 252.4mg, Total Carbohydrates: 2.5g, Dietary Fiber: 0.6g, Sugars: 0.3g, Protein: 4.7g

Persian Gondi (Dumplings)

8 to 10 quarts chicken broth (read ingredient statement)

1/2 to 1 cup chickpea flour (read ingredient statement), plus more as needed

1 pound ground chicken breast

2 large onions, finely grated in the food processor until a liquid

1 teaspoon turmeric

1 to 2 tablespoons ground cardamom

2 teaspoons kosher salt

1 teaspoon freshly ground black pepper

FOR SERVING

Cooked rice (read ingredient statement; optional)

Fresh basil (optional)

Arugula (optional)

I was lucky enough to be taught this recipe by dear friends who are Persian, and what an honor it is to learn this deep-rooted Donay family tradition. The classic way to eat gondi is to serve it over Persian rice, pausing to take the occasional bite of bitter herbs or arugula for freshness. Some people add the rice to the broth and eat it like soup; how you serve it is a matter of preference and tradition.

This gondi recipe is naturally gluten-free because it uses chickpea flour instead of regular flour. The chickpea flours gives the dish its traditional flavor and texture.

1. Bring the chicken broth to a boil, then reduce the heat and continue cooking on a steady simmer.

2. Combine the remaining ingredients in a large bowl and mix well, kneading with your hands; start with 1/2 cup flour and add more, 1 tablespoon at a time, if the dumpling mixture is too wet and doesn't hold together. Scoop out a portion of the dumpling mixture and roll into a golf ball–sized ball; add the dumpling to the stock. Continue making dumplings until all of the mixture has been used (you should have 20 to 25 dumplings), adding them to the broth as they are shaped.

3. Once all the dumplings have been added to the broth, simmer, covered, for 45 minutes.

4. Serve the dumplings over rice, if you like, with the basil and arugula on the side.

SERVES 6 TO 8

Nutrition information per serving (based on 8 servings): Calories: 190.2, Total Fat: 10.6g, Cholesterol: 58.4mg, Sodium: 701.6mg, Total Carbohydrates: 8.8g, Dietary Fiber: 0.9g, Sugars: 0.4g, Protein: 14.3g

Slow-Cooker Provençal Lemon and Olive Chicken

2 cups chopped onions

8 skinless chicken thighs (bone-in or boneless)

1 lemon, thinly sliced and seeded

1 cup green olives, pitted

1 tablespoon white-wine vinegar

2 teaspoons herbes de Provence

1 bay leaf

½ teaspoon kosher salt

1 teaspoon freshly ground black pepper

1 cup chicken stock (read ingredient statement)

½ cup chopped fresh flat-leaf parsley

This is a great dish if you want a fast dinner. You can throw everything in the slow cooker before you leave for work and come home to a lemony aroma and a delicious dinner.

1. Arrange the onions in the bottom of a slow cooker and top with the chicken thighs. Place a lemon slice on each thigh. Add the olives, vinegar, herbs de Provence, bay leaf, salt, pepper, and chicken stock.

2. Cook on low heat for 5 to 6 hours. Remove and discard the bay leaf. Serve each portion sprinkled with the chopped parsley.

SERVING SUGGESTIONS

Serve over a bed of simple steamed rice, the Sweet Potatoes with Honey Mustard Vinaigrette on p. 160, or the Oven-Roasted Fingerling Potatoes on p. 172. Finish off the meal with a chocolaty dessert to cut the acidity of the main course.

SERVES 4 TO 6
Nutrition information per serving (based on 6 servings): Calories: 395.1, Total Fat: 19.1g, Cholesterol: 105.5mg, Sodium: 120.9mg, Total Carbohydrates: 34.5g, Dietary Fiber: 8.7g, Sugars: 21.3g, Protein: 24.5g

Coconut- and Almond-Crusted Chicken Topped with Raspberry Basil Jam

If you like your chicken really crispy, fry the chicken strips instead of baking them. Heat ¼ inch of oil in a large frying pan over medium-high heat, cook the chicken until golden brown and crispy, then drain on a baking sheet lined with paper towels.

A fun trick that my Moroccan in-laws taught me is to add a baby carrot to the frying pan while frying: It will soak up all the burnt bits, leaving you with perfectly golden chicken every time.

2 eggs, beaten

1 tablespoon prepared mustard (read ingredient statement)

1 pound boneless, skinless chicken breasts, cut into strips about 1½ inches wide

1 cup almonds

½ cup unsweetened shredded coconut

1 teaspoon kosher salt

1 teaspoon freshly ground black pepper

½ teaspoon garlic powder

½ teaspoon chili powder (read ingredient statement)

Raspberry Basil Jam (recipe on p. 247)

1. Position a rack on the center of the oven and heat the oven to 375°F.

2. Line a large baking sheet with parchment.

3. Combine the eggs and mustard in a medium bowl, then add the chicken and toss to coat.

4. Combine the almonds, coconut, salt, pepper, and spices in the bowl of a food processor and pulse until the almonds are finely ground. Be careful not to process for too long or you will be left with coconut almond butter. Transfer the almond mixture to a large shallow dish.

(continued)

Coconut- and Almond-Crusted Chicken *(continued)*

5. Working with one chicken strip at a time, place it in the almond mixture and turn to coat both sides. Try to use the same hand with coating the chicken so you don't coat your hands as well. Place each coated chicken strip on the prepared baking sheet.

6. Bake the chicken for a total of 30 minutes, flipping halfway through, until cooked through.

7. Serve hot, topped with Raspberry Basil Jam.

VARIATION

 Substitute the chicken with 1 to 2 blocks of extra-firm tofu. To prepare the tofu, cut into 1½-inch slices, then place on several layers of paper towels; cover with more paper towels and top with a cutting board to drain excess liquid. Let stand for several minutes, pressing down occasionally. Tofu contains soy, so this variation is not soy-free.

SERVING SUGGESTIONS

Serve with Green Beans with Toasted Walnuts and Dried Cherry Vinaigrette (p. 175) or Brussels Sprouts with Lemon and Sage (p. 181). Note that the green beans side is not nut-free.

Balsamic Herb Skirt Steak

Two 1½-pound skirt steaks

4 packed teaspoons dark brown sugar

2 teaspoons paprika

2 tablespoons balsamic vinegar

1 teaspoon kosher salt

1 teaspoon freshly ground black pepper

Vegetable oil, for the pan (read ingredient statement)

SERVING SUGGESTIONS
Serve with the Bloody Mary Salad on p. 77 and Garlic Mashed Potatoes on p. 164.

After cooking, allow time for your steak to rest before cutting into it. If you cut into your meat too early, all the juices will pour out, causing the steak to dry up quickly.

1. Arrange the steaks on a large rimmed baking sheet or cutting board. In a shallow dish, combine the brown sugar, paprika, balsamic vinegar, salt, and pepper. Coat both sides of the steaks with the seasoning mixture and let sit for at least 20 minutes at room temperature, or 1 to 3 hours covered in the refrigerator. (If refrigerating the steaks, let them sit on the counter for 1 hour before cooking to bring them to room temperature.)

2. Heat a large cast-iron skillet over medium-high heat and brush the pan with oil. Put one steak in the skillet to sear; don't move it for 5 minutes. Flip the steak and cook for another 3 minutes for medium rare. Repeat with the second steak. If your steaks are too large to cook in one piece, cut them in half to fit the pan.

3. Let the steaks rest for 10 minutes before slicing into ¼-inch-thick slices.

MAKES 24 MEATBALLS; SERVES 8 WITH 3 MEATBALLS PER SERVING
Nutrition information per serving: Calories: 455.2, Total Fat: 24.1g, Cholesterol: 86.3mg, Sodium: 364.4mg, Total Carbohydrates: 41.7g, Dietary Fiber: 4.8g, Sugars: 27g, Protein: 23.9g

Unstuffed Cabbage Meatballs

1 large head cabbage, thinly sliced

One 28-ounce can tomato purée (read ingredient statements)

½ cup dark brown sugar

2 cups chicken stock (read ingredient statement)

½ cup raisins

Kosher salt and freshly ground black pepper

2½ pounds ground beef (80% lean)

½ cup uncooked rice

This recipe came as inspiration from my younger foodie self. I have been told that I hated jarred baby food, so my parents would take whatever they were eating and throw it into the food processor; apparently, I couldn't get enough of stuffed cabbage. Here I've turned the traditional recipe into something a bit more family-friendly.

1. Rinse the cabbage under cold water, then put it in a large pot. Stir in the tomato purée, brown sugar, stock, and raisins and bring to a simmer over medium-high heat. Reduce the heat to low and simmer the sauce gently, uncovered, for about 10 minutes. Add salt and pepper to taste.

2. While the sauce is cooking, combine the ground beef and uncooked rice in a large bowl; season with salt and pepper. Shape walnut-sized (about 1½ inches) meatballs and drop them into the simmering sauce.

3. Once all the meatballs are added, cover the sauce and simmer gently over low heat, stirring occasionally, for 1 to 2 hours, or until the cabbage is tender and the meatballs are cooked though.

VARIATION

Use precooked lentils in place of the ground beef and use vegetable stock in place of the chicken stock. Be sure to check ingredient statements for unwanted allergens for the precooked lentils and the broth, both vegetable and chicken.

SERVING SUGGESTION

Serve with the Basic Baguette on p. 216. Note that this recipe contains wheat and gluten.

SERVES 2 TO 4

Nutrition information per serving (based on 4 servings, without bun): Calories: 416.2, Total Fat: 24.8g, Cholesterol: 85.1mg, Sodium: 849.8mg, Total Carbohydrates: 26.5g, Dietary Fiber: 1.7g, Sugars: 21.1g, Protein: 21.6g

Sloppy Joes

1 tablespoon olive oil

1 medium onion, finely diced

2 cloves garlic, minced

2 teaspoons kosher salt, plus more as needed

Freshly ground black pepper

1 pound ground beef (80% lean)

One 14-ounce can tomato sauce (read ingredient statement)

1 teaspoon crushed red pepper flakes (optional)

½ cup ketchup (read ingredient statement)

1 tablespoon gluten-free Worcestershire sauce (read ingredient statement)

2 tablespoons dark brown sugar

1 tablespoon cider vinegar

Brioche Buns (recipe on p. 228), for serving

If you want to make your loved ones love you forever, make this easy and delicious meal. It is key to serve the sloppy Joes with the brioche bun recipe on p. 228. This recipe also freezes well, so make a double batch and save half for later in the month when you don't have time to cook.

Turn this recipe into shepherd's pie by transferring the beef to a Dutch oven and topping it with Garlic Mashed Potatoes (recipe on p. 164). Bake the dish at 350°F for 40 to 50 minutes, until the potatoes are golden brown and the sauce is bubbling up the sides.

1. Heat the oil in a large saucepan over medium heat. Add the onions and garlic, season with the salt and black pepper to taste, and cook until the onions are softened, stirring occasionally, 5 to 8 minutes.

2. Add the ground beef to the onions, breaking it up with a wooden spoon, and cook until the meat is no longer pink, about 5 minutes. Add the tomato sauce, red pepper flakes (if using), ketchup, Worcestershire sauce, brown sugar, and vinegar. Cook for 8 to 10 minutes, until the sauce is slightly thickened. Season to taste with more salt and black pepper.

3. Split the buns open. Spoon meat over top of the insides and serve open-faced or as a sandwich.

VARIATION

To make this recipe corn-free, use ketchup made without corn syrup. Many markets sell this year-round, but you're especially likely to find it before Passover (so be sure to stock up!).

SERVES 4
Nutrition information per serving: Calories: 409.7, Total Fat: 25.9g, Cholesterol: 59.1mg, Sodium: 120.7mg, Total Carbohydrates: 3g, Dietary Fiber: 0.4g, Sugars: 0.7g, Protein: 37.5g

Strip Steak with Red Wine–Mushroom Pan Sauce

¼ cup extra-virgin olive oil

12 ounces assorted mushrooms, quartered

Kosher salt and coarsely ground black pepper

One 1½-pound strip steak, trimmed, pounded to ½ inch thick

3 large cloves garlic, lightly crushed

One 6-inch sprig fresh rosemary

½ cup dry red wine

⅓ cup chicken stock (read ingredient statement)

2 tablespoons fresh tarragon, finely chopped

SERVING SUGGESTION

This steak is delicious paired with Green Beans with Toasted Walnuts and Dried Cherry Vinaigrette on p. 175. Note that this side is not nut-free.

Don't think that just because you're making a beef dish that you need to use beef stock. Stocks provide flavor variation to a recipe, sometimes adding more complexity to a dish. Experiment with chicken and beef stock to see which you prefer.

1. Heat 2 tablespoons of the oil in a large heavy skillet over medium-high heat. Add the mushrooms and cook, stirring occasionally, until they're soft and golden, about 7 minutes. Season to taste with salt and pepper. Transfer to a bowl and set aside.

2. Heat the remaining 2 tablespoons oil in the same skillet over medium heat. Season the steak with salt and pepper, then add it to the skillet, along with the garlic and rosemary. Cook the steak for 3 minutes per side for medium rare (adjust the time to get your preferred doneness). Transfer the steak to a cutting board, cover with foil, and let rest while you prepare the sauce.

3. Remove the garlic and rosemary from the skillet and discard. Add the wine and stock to the skillet and cook over medium-low heat until reduced, about 3 minutes. Stir in the mushrooms and 1 tablespoon of the tarragon. Season with salt and pepper to taste.

4. Thinly slice the steak and arrange on a serving platter. Carefully spoon the red wine–mushroom sauce over the steak and garnish with the remaining 1 tablespoon tarragon.

SERVES 4 TO 6

Nutrition information per serving (based on 6 servings): Calories: 438.5, Total Fat: 14.7g, Cholesterol: 46.8mg, Sodium: 260.5mg, Total Carbohydrates: 51.6g, Dietary Fiber: 10g, Sugars: 2.1g, Protein: 25.5g

Seared Steak Fusilli with Broccoli and Sun-Dried Tomato Sauce

1 pound skirt steak

Kosher salt and freshly ground black pepper

Olive oil

1 pound whole wheat fusilli (check ingredient statement)

1 head broccoli, cut into florets

1 small onion, diced

1 cup cremini mushrooms, roughly chopped

1/2 cup sun-dried tomatoes

1/2 teaspoon crushed red pepper flakes

8 large cloves garlic, minced

2 teaspoons whole-grain mustard (check ingredient statement)

1 cup dry red wine

1 cup beef stock (check ingredient statement)

1 tablespoon unbleached all-purpose flour (check ingredient statement)

1/2 cup finely chopped fresh basil

This recipe can be made with chicken instead of beef; simply substitute 2 boneless, skinless chicken breasts for the skirt steak and use white wine instead of red wine for the sauce.

1. Sprinkle the steak with salt and black pepper. In a large nonstick skillet over medium-high heat, heat 1 teaspoon olive oil. Add the steak and cook for 3 minutes on each side for medium rare. Transfer the steak to a cutting board, cover with foil, and let rest for 5 minutes; cut into thin slices and set aside.

2. Bring a large pot of salted water to a boil. Add the pasta and cook according to the package directions for al dente. Put the broccoli florets in a steamer basket, set over the boiling pasta water, and cover. Steam the broccoli for 3 minutes until crisp-tender, then remove from the heat. Finish cooking the pasta, then drain and set aside.

3. Meanwhile, heat 1 tablespoon olive oil in a large saucepan over medium-high heat. Add the onions, mushrooms, sun-dried tomatoes, red pepper flakes, and 1/2 teaspoon salt and cook until the vegetables are soft, stirring often, 5 to 7 minutes. Stir in the garlic and mustard and cook for another minute. Add the wine and stock and bring to a boil; reduce the heat and let the mixture simmer until it's reduced by about half, 5 to 6 minutes, stirring occasionally. Add the flour and stir the mixture over low heat until thickened slightly. Season generously with black pepper.

4. Return the pasta to the pot it was cooked in, then add the steak, broccoli, sauce, and 1 teaspoon salt. Heat briefly over low heat until warm, about 3 minutes. Transfer to a serving bowl, sprinkle with the basil, and serve warm.

VARIATIONS

 Use a gluten-free pasta. I prefer Heartland® brand, but use whichever you prefer. Heartland gluten-free pastas contain corn, so if you use this brand, the recipe will no longer be corn-free. Whatever brand you use, check for other allergens. Also, leave out the flour and let the sauce simmer for another 2 minutes to thicken.

 To make this dish suitable for vegetarians and vegans, replace the beef stock with water or vegetable stock and replace the steak with 1 to 2 blocks of extra-firm tofu, cut into 1-inch cubes. To prepare the tofu, place the cubes on several layers of paper towels; cover with more paper towels and top with a cutting board to drain excess liquid. Let stand for several minutes, pressing down occasionally. Tofu contains soy, so this variation will no longer be soy-free. Be sure to check the ingredient statement for vegetable stock to check for other allergens.

SERVES 8 TO 10
Nutrition information per serving (based on 10 servings): Calories: 465.8, Total Fat: 20.3g, Cholesterol: 126.5mg, Sodium: 747.1mg, Total Carbohydrates: 26.6g, Dietary Fiber: 1.1g, Sugars: 21.3g, Protein: 41.9g

Coffee-Glazed Braised Beef

3 pounds beef brisket

Coarse salt and freshly ground black pepper

2 tablespoons olive oil

2 medium carrots, sliced thin

2 cups white button mushrooms, quartered

2 medium onions, quartered

½ cup freshly brewed black coffee (regular or decaf) (read ingredient statement)

½ cup ketchup (read ingredient statement)

½ cup chili sauce (read ingredient statement)

½ cup honey

⅓ cup gluten-free Worcestershire sauce (read ingredient statement)

½ cup dry red wine

4 cloves garlic, minced

3 tablespoons gluten-free soy sauce

SERVING SUGGESTIONS
Serve the brisket over boiled egg noodles or with Oven-Roasted Fingerling Potatoes (recipe on p. 172) for a hearty winter meal.

My friends who are trying to woo that special man ask me for this recipe, which we've jokingly dubbed "man killer." I'm not sure what makes this dish so appealing to guys (maybe the overload of meat in a rich sauce), but it works every time, hence the name. (P.S. I made this for my husband on the first night we met . . . and he never left!)

1. Season the brisket with salt and pepper. Warm the oil in a large, heavy-based skillet over high heat. Add the brisket, fat side down, and cook until it's well browned, 4 to 5 minutes per side. Transfer the brisket to a plate.

2. Pour the meat drippings into a slow cooker. Add the carrots, mushrooms, and onions. Put the browned brisket on top of the vegetables.

3. In a medium bowl, combine the coffee, ketchup, chili sauce, honey, Worcestershire sauce, wine, garlic, and soy sauce. Pour the mixture over the brisket. Cover the slow cooker and cook on low for 8 to 10 hours.

4. Remove the meat from the slow cooker and use two forks to pull it apart. Return the meat to the sauce, stirring it in to combine.

VARIATION

 To make this recipe corn-free, use ketchup made without corn syrup. Many markets sell this year-round, but you're especially likely to find it before Passover.

SERVES 4 TO 6
Nutrition information per serving (based on 6 servings): Calories: 221.3, Total Fat: 14.3g, Cholesterol: 50.7mg, Sodium: 1,239.1mg, Total Carbohydrates: 7.5g, Dietary Fiber: 0.5g, Sugars: 4.9g, Protein: 16.7g

Yakitori Beef Skewers

½ cup gluten-free soy sauce (read ingredient statement)

2 tablespoons vegetable oil, plus more for the grill (read ingredient statement)

1 lemon, juiced

1 tablespoon sesame seeds, plus more for garnish

2 tablespoons sugar

½ teaspoon kosher salt, plus more as needed

2 scallions, thinly sliced

1 large clove garlic, minced

½ teaspoon ground ginger

1 pound sirloin steak, cut into 1-inch cubes

Ten to twelve 8-inch wooden skewers, soaked for at least 30 minutes

Freshly ground black pepper

SERVING SUGGESTIONS
Serve over Thai Coconut Rice (recipe on p. 178) or with a seaweed salad. If you have a nut allergy avoid the coconut rice.

If you eat gluten-free, be sure to choose a soy sauce that is gluten-free. If not, use whatever kind of soy sauce you'd like. Some people with a nut allergy avoid sesame seeds. If you like, omit the sesame seeds from this recipe.

1. In a small bowl, whisk the soy sauce, oil, lemon juice, sesame seeds, sugar, salt, scallions, garlic, and ginger.

2. Thread 4 to 5 cubes of steak onto each skewer. Put the skewers in a large shallow dish and pour the marinade over the meat, turning to coat well. Cover and refrigerate for 1 to 2 hours to marinate.

3. Heat a grill or grill pan on high and brush the grill grates with olive oil. Sprinkle the beef with salt and pepper and cook the skewers on the grill, making sure not to crowd them, for about 3 minutes per side for medium (adjust the cooking time based on the size of your steak cubes or for doneness). Repeat with the remaining skewers. Sprinkle with more sesame seeds and serve.

VARIATION

Replace the beef with 1 to 2 blocks of extra-firm tofu, cubed. To prepare the tofu, place the cubes on several layers of paper towels; cover with more paper towels and top with a cutting board to drain excess liquid. Let stand for several minutes, pressing down occasionally. Marinate the cubed tofu and continue with the recipe as written. Cook the tofu until golden brown and well seared, 5 to 10 minutes.

SERVES 12 TO 14
Nutrition information per serving (based on 14 servings): Calories: 594.9, Total Fat: 34.4g, Cholesterol: 121.5mg, Sodium: 917.3mg, Total Carbohydrate: 36g, Dietary Fiber: 6.4g, Sugars: 19.g, Protein: 35.2g

6-Hour Chili

FOR THE CHILI

5 pounds ground beef (80% lean)

5 large cloves garlic, minced

1 large yellow onion, chopped

Three 14-ounce cans diced tomatoes, with their juices

Two 14-ounce cans tomato sauce (read ingredient statement)

3/4 cup ketchup (read ingredient statement)

2 cups beef stock (read ingredient statement)

One 14-ounce can black beans, rinsed and drained

One 14-ounce can kidney beans, rinsed and drained

1/3 cup cornmeal

1/4 cup unsweetened cocoa powder (read ingredient statement)

6 tablespoons chili powder (read ingredient statement)

2 teaspoons dried oregano

3 teaspoons ground cumin

1/2 cup brown sugar

Kosher salt and freshly ground black pepper

FOR THE GARNISH

Cilantro

Guacamole (recipe on p. 155)

This chili has a bit of a bite if you use all the chili powder. You might want to cut the amount in half the first time you make the recipe and add more at the end of cooking, once you've tasted the chili. This dish freezes well, so put some away for another meal.

Adjust the garnishes based on your allergies.

1. Brown the beef in a large skillet over medium-high heat, then transfer to a slow cooker. Add the remaining chili ingredients and stir to blend. Cover and cook for on low for 6 to 8 hours.

2. Serve with the garnishes.

SERVING SUGGESTIONS

Serve with sour cream, Lemon and Olive Oil Muffins on p. 223, or lots of chips and salsa. The muffins contain wheat and gluten as well as soy, milk, and eggs. Be mindful if you have any of those allergies. Check ingredient statements for chips and salsa for allergens. Sour cream contains milk.

SERVES 8

Nutrition information per serving: Calories: 520.8, Total Fat: 20.7g, Cholesterol: 0mg, Sodium: 873.1mg, Total Carbohydrates: 9.3g, Dietary Fiber: 0.7g, Sugars: 0.4g, Protein: 73.2g

Individual Braised Beef and Potato-Crusted Pot Pies

FOR THE FILLING

$1/3$ cup unbleached all-purpose flour (check ingredient statement)

4 pounds stewing beef, (such as boneless beef chuck), cut into 1-inch pieces

Kosher salt and freshly ground black pepper

$1/4$ cup vegetable oil (read ingredient statement)

1 medium yellow onion, halved and thinly sliced

6 cloves garlic, thinly sliced

2 cups dry red wine

3 sprigs fresh rosemary

FOR THE TOPPING

10 fingerling potatoes, peeled, thinly sliced, and soaked for 30 minutes

Olive oil, for brushing

Kosher salt and freshly ground black pepper

Soaking cut potatoes for 30 minutes and up to 2 hours greatly reduces acrylamide, a chemical that occurs when starch-rich foods are cooked at high temperatures without soaking off the starch first.

To make 1 large pot pie instead of minis, fill a 9-inch pie plate instead of ramekins and bake for 1 hour after assembling the potato crust topping.

MAKE THE FILLING

1. Position a rack in the center of the oven and heat the oven to 300°F.

2. Put the flour in a shallow bowl. Season the beef with salt and pepper and coat in the flour. Heat the oil in a large oven-safe pot over high heat, add the beef (in batches if necessary), and brown, about 1 minute per side. Transfer to a plate.

3. Reduce the heat to medium and add the onions and garlic. Cook until the vegetables are golden brown, 6 to 8 minutes. Return the meat to the pot and add the red wine and rosemary. Bring to a simmer, then cover and transfer the pot to the oven and cook for $2^{1}/2$ hours.

4. Remove the pot from the oven (leave the oven on and raise the temperature to 375°F) and return to the stovetop over low heat until the meat is tender about 30 minutes. Remove the rosemary sprigs, shred the meat using two forks, and season with salt and pepper. Portion the filling among eight 6-inch ramekins.

MAKE THE TOPPING

1. Drain the potatoes and pat dry. Arrange the potatoes on top of the meat in concentric circles, working around the edge and overlapping each slice. Brush the tops with olive oil and sprinkle with salt and pepper.

2. Put the ramekins on a baking sheet and bake until the topping is golden and the filling is bubbling at the edges, 35 to 45 minutes.

VARIATION

  Use the gluten-free flour recipe on p. 20 or a gluten-free flour blend; I like Bob's Red Mill.

SERVES 6 TO 8
Nutrition information per serving
(based on 8 servings): Calories: 555.7,
Total Fat: 28g, Cholesterol: 185.4mg,
Sodium: 199mg, Total Carbohydrates:
13.7g, Dietary Fiber: 3.3g, Sugars: 7.2g,
Protein: 67.9g

Lamb Shawarma with Pomegranate–Mint Salsa

If you don't like lamb or can't find it at your local grocery store, try this recipe with boneless, skinless chicken or turkey breasts. If you like, serve the shawarma with flatbread, though be sure to check the ingredient statement for allergens.

The salsa is delicious on top of the Israeli Meatballs (without the tahini glaze) on p. 49.

FOR THE MEAT

- ½ cup plain yogurt
- 1 lemon, juiced
- 1 tablespoon distilled white vinegar (read ingredient statement)
- 1 tablespoon olive oil
- ½ cup chopped onions
- 2 cloves garlic, minced
- 1 tablespoon kosher salt
- 1 teaspoon freshly ground black pepper
- 1 teaspoon ground cumin
- ½ teaspoon ground nutmeg
- ½ teaspoon ground cloves
- 1 teaspoon cayenne
- 5 pounds boneless shoulder lamb or lamb loin, cut into ¼-inch strips

FOR THE SALSA

- 1½ cups pomegranate seeds
- 1 cup pistachios, coarsely chopped
- ½ cup coarsely chopped fresh mint leaves
- 2 tablespoons olive oil
- 1 lemon, juiced
- Kosher salt and freshly ground black pepper

PREPARE THE MEAT

1. Combine the yogurt, ¼ cup water, the lemon juice, vinegar, olive oil, onions, and garlic in a large bowl. Whisk in the salt, pepper, cumin, nutmeg, cloves, and cayenne. Add the lamb strips and toss to coat.

2. Cover the bowl with plastic wrap and marinate in the refrigerator for 12 to 24 hours (the longer you allow the meat to marinate, the more tender and flavorful it will be).

(continued)

MAKE THE SALSA

While the meat is marinating, prepare the salsa for serving and keep covered at room temperature for up to 2 hours (or refrigerate if making more than 2 hours ahead). Mix all of the ingredients in a medium bowl. Season to taste with salt and pepper.

FINISH THE DISH

1. Heat a large skillet over high heat. Drain the marinade off the lamb and cook the lamb strips in a single layer in batches until the meat has browned and cooked through, about 5 minutes. (The lamb will give off liquid as it cooks, so let it cook until the liquid is absorbed and the meat is brown.) Transfer the cooked lamb to a plate and cover to keep warm.

2. Arrange the lamb strips on a platter, top with pomegranate–mint salsa, and serve.

VARIATION

 Substitute the yogurt with soy yogurt or tofu sour cream. Either option means the recipe will no longer be soy-free.

SERVES 4

Nutrition information per serving: Calories: 581.3, Total Fat: 32g, Cholesterol: 112mg, Sodium: 890.3mg, Total Carbohydrates: 41.6g, Dietary Fiber: 3.7g, Sugars: 28g, Protein: 48.6g

Roasted Pomegranate and Pistachio Rack of Lamb

1 cup pomegranate juice

⅓ cup golden raisins

1 large clove garlic

3 tablespoons olive oil

1 teaspoon ground cinnamon

½ teaspoon ground cumin

1 teaspoon kosher salt

1 teaspoon freshly ground black pepper

1 large rack of lamb (about 2½ pounds)

½ cup unsalted pistachios, finely chopped

⅓ cup panko breadcrumbs (read ingredient statement)

½ cup finely chopped fresh mint leaves

For a richer flavor, replace the olive oil with 4 tablespoons chilled unsalted butter. If you do this, the recipe will no longer be milk-free.

1. Position a rack in the center of the oven and heat the oven to 400°F.

2. In a medium skillet over medium-high heat, combine the pomegranate juice, raisins, and garlic and bring to a boil until thickened, about 10 minutes. Let cool, then transfer to a food processor, along with the olive oil, cinnamon, cumin, salt, and pepper. Blend until a purée forms, then let the mixture cool completely.

3. Line a large roasting pan with foil and place the rack of lamb bone side down. Spread the pomegranate mixture over the lamb, then sprinkle with the pistachios and panko, pressing on them so they adhere.

4. Roast the lamb for 30 to 35 minutes for medium rare. Let the lamb rest on the counter for at least 10 minutes to allow the meat to settle.

5. To serve, cut the rack of lamb between the bones and sprinkle with the chopped mint.

SERVING SUGGESTION

Serve with Garlic-Seared Tomatoes and Asparagus on p. 161.

VARIATION

  Leave out the panko or replace with ⅓ cup gluten-free breadcrumbs (store-bought or made from toasting gluten-free bread and crumbling in a food processor). Check ingredient statement for other allergens.

SERVES 4 TO 6
Nutrition information per serving (based on 6 servings): Calories: 508.6, Total Fat: 20.1g, Cholesterol: 175.4mg, Sodium: 403.6mg, Total Carbohydrates: 27.4g, Dietary Fiber: 1.9g, Sugars: 3.3g, Protein: 51.5g

Breaded Veal with Truffle Oil and Sage

1½ cups milk

1 tablespoon spicy brown mustard (read ingredient statement)

Coarse salt and freshly ground black pepper

2 pounds boneless, skinless veal cutlets, pounded thin

2 cups plain dried breadcrumbs (read ingredient statement)

½ cup finely chopped fresh sage, divided

Canola oil, for frying

1 tablespoon truffle oil

Sea salt

My husband and I tried a variation of this dish while on our honeymoon to Italy, and it's the only meal the two of us can remember (especially after all the wine we drank!). After several failed attempts to recreate the recipe, we think this closely represents the authentic Italian flavor we experienced.

If you don't eat veal, use boneless and skinless chicken breasts instead.

1. Position a rack in the center of the oven and heat the oven to 200°F.

2. In a medium bowl, combine the milk, mustard, 1 tablespoon salt, and ½ teaspoon pepper. Add the veal and toss to coat. Let sit for about 15 minutes.

3. Meanwhile, mix the breadcrumbs and ⅓ cup of the chopped sage in a shallow baking dish; set aside.

4. Heat 1 inch of canola oil in a large skillet. Working with one cutlet at a time, dredge the veal in the breadcrumb mixture, coating both sides completely. Gently place each cutlet in the hot oil. You don't want to crowd the pan, so cook in batches if necessary. Fry the cutlets, flipping them halfway through cooking, until dark golden, 2 to 3 minutes on each side. Transfer to paper towels to drain, then keep warm in the oven. Repeat with the remaining veal cutlets.

5. Drizzle the fried cutlets with the truffle oil, sprinkle with the remaining sage and sea salt, and serve.

SERVING SUGGESTIONS

This dish pairs well with any fresh tomato salad (try the Bloody Mary Salad on p. 77) and the Oven-Roasted Fingerling Potatoes on p. 172. If you want to create the perfect Tuscan meal, start with a classic Italian vegetable bean stew.

WINE PAIRING

Pair this dish with an Italian Chianti. The richness of the wine will bring out the flavors of the truffle oil and sage.

VARIATIONS

Replace the cow's milk with soy milk or almond milk. Using soy milk means the recipe is no longer soy-free. If using almond milk, the recipe is no longer nut-free.

Replace the regular breadcrumbs with gluten-free breadcrumbs (store-bought or made from toasting gluten-free bread and crumbling in a food processor). Check ingredient statement for other allergens.

Sweet and Spicy Meatballs

FOR THE SAUCE

¼ cup olive oil

1½ cups small-diced onions

5 cloves garlic, chopped

¼ cup chili powder (read ingredient statement)

1 tablespoon crushed red pepper flakes

¼ cup dark brown sugar

¼ cup apple cider vinegar

2 cups tomato sauce (read ingredient statement)

¼ cup sweet chili sauce (read ingredient statement)

One 14-ounce can whole-berry cranberry sauce (read ingredient statement)

3 bay leaves

4 sprigs fresh thyme

Kosher salt and freshly ground black pepper

FOR THE MEATBALLS

1 pound ground beef (80% lean)

1 egg yolk

½ cup plain dried breadcrumbs (read ingredient statement)

2 teaspoons kosher salt

Freshly ground black pepper

2 teaspoons finely chopped fresh flat-leaf parsley

Pasta or rice, for serving

I have to give credit where credit is due. Much of my cooking knowledge came from chef Jonathan Lindenauer, the former chef de cuisine at *Bon Appétit* magazine. While working together at *Bon Appétit*, Jonathan taught me not only some essential kitchen skills and techniques, but also how to combine ingredients for the best flavor and create inspiring presentations when serving a dish.

Jonathan also shared a variation of this recipe with me, although I am pretty sure it was created by his mother, who actually taught me how to make this delicious dish.

MAKE THE SAUCE

Heat the olive oil in a large pot over medium heat. Add the onions and cook until they're translucent and starting to brown on the edges, about 8 minutes. Add the garlic and cook for 2 minutes. Add the chili powder, red pepper flakes, brown sugar, and vinegar. Cook for 2 minutes. Stir in the remaining ingredients and season with salt and pepper to taste. Let simmer on low heat while you make the meatballs.

MAKE THE MEATBALLS

1. Combine the ground beef, egg yolk, breadcrumbs, salt, a pinch of black pepper, and the parsley. Shape the mixture into tablespoon-size meatballs and carefully add them to the simmering sauce. Cook the meatballs for 30 minutes.

2. Turn off the heat and allow the meatballs and sauce to cool. Serve over pasta or rice.

VARIATION

  Use gluten-free breadcrumbs made from toasting your choice of gluten-free bread; place hunks of the bread in a food processor and process until crumbly. If serving with pasta, use a gluten-free brand and read the ingredient statement for other allergens.

SERVES 10 TO 12
Nutrition information per serving (based on 12 servings): Calories: 506.3, Total Fat: 23.9g, Cholesterol: 140.5mg, Sodium: 596.5mg, Total Carbohydrates: 20.3g, Dietary Fiber: 0.9g, Sugars: 7.1g, Protein: 47.4g

Slow-Roasted Oven-Braised Apricot Beef

FOR THE BRISKET

1 tablespoon plus 1 teaspoon kosher salt

1 teaspoon freshly ground black pepper

1/2 teaspoon smoked paprika

1/8 teaspoon ground cinnamon

One 5-pound trimmed flat-cut brisket with about 1/3 inch top layer of fat

2 tablespoons olive oil, divided

1 cup chopped onions

4 cloves garlic, smashed

4 cups chicken stock (read ingredient statement)

One 12-ounce bottle Guinness®

1/2 cup bourbon

1/4 packed cup light brown sugar

1/4 cup gluten-free soy sauce (read ingredient statement)

6 large sprigs fresh thyme

4 celery stalks, chopped

2 plum tomatoes, cored and chopped

2 large carrots, chopped

2 tablespoons balsamic vinegar

If you like to cook ahead, then this is the recipe for you! The brisket can be made 2 days ahead and refrigerated. When ready to serve, put the cooked brisket and all of the liquid in a large pot, cover, and bring to a simmer to warm. Make the apricot glaze just before serving.

Most stout beers contain gluten, so if you have celiac disease or gluten sensitivity, be sure to look for a gluten-free brand.

PREPARE THE BRISKET

1. Mix the salt, black pepper, paprika, and cinnamon in a small bowl. Rub the brisket all over with the spice rub. Cover and chill for at least 2 hours or overnight, then let stand at room temperature for 1 hour.

2. Position a rack in the center of the oven and heat the oven to 325°F.

3. Heat 1 tablespoon of the oil in a large Dutch oven over high heat. Add the brisket, fat side down, and cook until browned, 3 to 5 minutes per side. Using tongs, transfer the brisket to a plate.

4. Reduce the heat to medium and add the remaining 1 tablespoon oil. Add the onions and garlic and cook, stirring occasionally, until the onions are slightly golden, about 5 minutes. Add the stock and the remaining ingredients. Bring the liquid to a simmer, then return the brisket to the pot, cover, and transfer to the oven.

5. Braise the brisket in the oven until it's very tender to the touch but still holds its shape, about 4 1/2 hours. Return the pot to the stovetop and simmer over medium heat for another 15 minutes until the liquid begins to reduce.

FOR THE GLAZE

½ cup apricot jam

Kosher salt and freshly
ground black pepper

SERVING SUGGESTIONS

The beef is delicious served
with the Bloody Mary Salad
(recipe on p. 77), Creamy
Polenta (recipe on p. 179),
and Brussels Sprouts with
Lemon and Sage (recipe on
p. 181).

COOK'S TIP

You can also make this dish
in a slow cooker. Braise
the beef on the stovetop
(through step 2 in Prepare
the Brisket), then put everything in the slow cooker and
cook on low for 10 hours.

MAKE THE GLAZE AND FINISH THE DISH

1. Transfer ¼ cup of the braising liquid to a blender. Add the jam and purée until smooth. Season with salt and pepper.

2. Drizzle the glaze on top of the brisket, then move the brisket to a cutting board. Slice the meat against the grain and transfer to a large platter. Ladle the remaining braising liquid over the top.

VARIATIONS

  Make this gluten-free by using gluten-free stout beer.

 Use a brand of apricot jam that doesn't contain corn syrup to make this dish corn-free.

SERVES 4
Nutrition information per serving: Calories: 315.9,
Total Fat: 11.1g, Cholesterol: 65.7mg, Sodium:
473.8mg, Total Carbohydrates: 16.4g, Dietary Fiber:
2.1g, Sugars: 5.4g, Protein: 37g

Sesame Tuna with Ginger–Miso Dipping Sauce

FOR THE DIPPING SAUCE

2 tablespoons mirin
(Japanese rice wine)

2 teaspoons white miso

2 teaspoons grated fresh
ginger

1/3 cup carrot juice

2 tablespoons fresh
orange juice

2 teaspoons gluten-
free soy sauce (check
ingredient statement)

2 tablespoons distilled
white vinegar

1 teaspoon crushed red
pepper flakes

1 teaspoon Asian
sesame oil

FOR THE TUNA

2 tablespoons black
sesame seeds

3 tablespoons white
sesame seeds

Four 4-ounce yellowfin
tuna steaks

1 tablespoon grape
seed oil

1 bunch fresh cilantro,
finely chopped
(optional)

This preparation leaves the tuna partially raw in the middle. Feel free to cook it longer to your preferred level of doneness; just be sure to flip the tuna halfway through cooking and lower the heat slightly so it doesn't burn.

If you have a tree nut allergy you might want to consider eliminating the sesame seeds in the recipe. Although not a nut, some people with a nut allergy experience similar symptoms when they eat sesame seeds.

MAKE THE DIPPING SAUCE

Combine the mirin, miso, ginger, carrot juice, orange juice, soy sauce, vinegar, red pepper flakes, and sesame oil in a small bowl, whisking until everything is fully dissolved. Set aside.

PREPARE THE TUNA AND SERVE

1. Combine the black and white sesame seeds in a shallow dish and press the tuna steaks into them, turning to coat each side.

2. Heat the oil in a medium sauté pan over medium-high heat. Cook the tuna on both sides until the white seeds have browned slightly, about 30 seconds per side. Transfer the tuna to a paper towel–lined plate for a minute to drain and cool.

3. Cut each tuna steak into ¼-inch-thick slices and serve with the dipping sauce and chopped cilantro, if using.

VARIATION

 Substitute the tuna with 1 to 2 blocks of extra-firm tofu. To prepare the tofu, place the blocks on several layers of paper towels; cover with more paper towels and top with a cutting board to drain excess liquid. Let stand for several minutes, pressing down occasionally. Cut into serving-size portions.

SERVING SUGGESTIONS

The tuna is delicious served with cold aspara-gus or a watercress salad. Serve with Sriracha on the side.

SERVES 4

Nutrition information per serving: Calories: 353.5, Total Fat: 18g, Cholesterol: 90.1mg, Sodium: 270.1mg, Total Carbohydrates: 5.3g, Dietary Fiber: 1.2g, Sugars: 2.4g, Protein: 41.2g

Spicy Italian Poached Sea Bass

¼ cup olive oil, plus more for the pan

1 small onion, chopped

¼ teaspoon crushed red pepper flakes

Two 14-ounce cans diced tomatoes with herbs, drained (read ingredient statement)

2 teaspoons kosher salt, plus more as needed

Freshly ground black pepper

1 tablespoon finely chopped fresh basil

1½ pounds sea bass, skinned and boned, cut into four 6-ounce portions

For an extra Italian kick, top this spicy dish with some shredded mozzarella or freshly grated Parmesan prior to baking. However, the recipe will no longer be milk-free. To keep this dish gluten-free, serve over gluten-free pasta.

1. Position a rack in the center of the oven and heat the oven to 350°F. Grease a 9-inch-square glass baking dish with olive oil.

2. Heat the olive oil in a large saucepan over medium-high heat. Add the onions and red pepper flakes and sauté until the onions are tender, about 10 minutes. Stir in the tomatoes and season with the salt and a pinch of black pepper; cook until the mixture forms a sauce-like consistency, about 5 minutes. Stir in the basil.

3. Arrange the fish in the prepared dish and pour the sauce over the top. Bake until the fish is cooked through and the top is golden, about 25 minutes.

VARIATION

Substitute the sea bass with 1 to 2 blocks of extra-firm tofu. To prepare the tofu, place the blocks on several layers of paper towels; cover with more paper towels and top with a cutting board to drain excess liquid. Let stand for several minutes, pressing down occasionally. Cut into serving-size portions. Tofu contains soy, so this variation is not soy-free.

SERVES 4

Nutrition information per serving: Calories: 226.8, Total Fat: 6.8g, Cholesterol: 46.5mg, Sodium: 78.6mg, Total Carbohydrates: 9.5g, Dietary Fiber: 0.1g, Sugars: 9.1g, Protein: 30.5g

Broiled Rosemary and Orange Halibut en Papillote

2 oranges, zested and juiced (about ½ cup juice)

2 sprigs fresh rosemary

2 tablespoons sugar

1 teaspoon coarse salt, plus more as needed

Four 4- to 6-ounce halibut fillets, skinned

1 tablespoon olive oil

Freshly ground black pepper

SERVING SUGGESTIONS

Serve with blanched baby bok choy tossed with olive oil and sea salt, and jasmine rice, and Roasted Lime Carrots on p. 170.

En papillote is a fancy French term for "in paper." Cooking in paper is a classic technique of baking with moist heat. You might find making the parchment pouches a bit difficult at first, but it won't take long to get the hang of it. Check out YouTube tutorials for advice (or stick to aluminum foil instead of parchment for no-fail folding).

1. Position an oven rack 4 inches from the heating element and heat the broiler.

2. Combine the orange zest and juice, rosemary sprigs, sugar, and 1 teaspoon of the salt in a small saucepan and bring to a boil. Cook until the mixture becomes syrupy, 8 to 10 minutes, stirring occasionally. Discard the rosemary sprigs.

3. Meanwhile, prepare four pieces of parchment or foil. Cut four 12x14-inch pieces and fold in half lengthwise, then cut each piece of parchment into a heart shape (you don't need to cut a heart if using foil). Place one fish fillet in the center of one side of each heart. Rub the fillets with the olive oil and season generously with salt and pepper. Drizzle the orange syrup evenly over each fillet. Fold over the other side of the heart, then work from one end to fold up and seal the parchment or foil tightly.

4. Arrange the packages on a rimmed baking sheet and broil until cooked, 7 to 10 minutes. Let the parchment pouches rest for 3 minutes before opening. Serve the fish in its pouch, if you like.

SERVES 6; MAKES 1¼ CUPS PESTO
Nutrition information per serving: Calories: 516.2, Total Fat: 37.7g, Cholesterol: 113.5mg, Sodium: 93.3mg, Total Carbohydrates: 2.5g, Dietary Fiber: 0.6g, Sugars: 0.8g, Protein: 42.4g

Seared Salmon Topped with Pine Nut–Arugula Pesto

FOR THE PESTO

1 clove garlic, peeled

⅓ cup pine nuts

4 packed cups baby arugula

2 teaspoons finely grated lemon zest

1 tablespoon fresh lemon juice, plus more as needed

⅓ cup olive oil

Kosher salt and freshly ground black pepper

FOR THE FISH

Six 6-ounce salmon fillets (skin left on or removed)

2 tablespoons olive oil

1 teaspoon kosher salt

½ teaspoon freshly ground black pepper

1 lemon, cut into wedges, for serving

SERVING SUGGESTIONS
The salmon is delicious served over the Pine Nut and Olive Orzo Salad (recipe on p. 80) or simply seasoned couscous.

The seared salmon is very versatile and can be paired with several sauces and salads for a filling and delicious meal.

MAKE THE PESTO

1. Put the garlic, pine nuts, arugula, lemon zest, and lemon juice in a blender or food processor. Process until the nuts are finely chopped, then blend to a coarse paste. Add the olive oil and process to combine. Season the pesto with salt and pepper and more lemon juice if needed.

2. Transfer to an airtight container, cover, and refrigerate for 3 to 5 days.

COOK THE FISH

Heat a large skillet over medium heat for 3 minutes. If you've left the skin on the salmon, lightly score it before cooking to help the fish lay flat and cook through. Drizzle the salmon fillets with olive oil, then season with the salt and pepper. Put the salmon in the skillet and increase the heat to high. Sear the salmon fillets for 7 minutes total, flipping them halfway through cooking, until browned.

TO SERVE

Plate each salmon fillet and top with a heaping tablespoon of the pesto on one end of the fish and, using the back of a spoon, spread to the other end. Serve with lemon wedges.

VARIATION

 To make the pesto nut-free, replace the pine nuts with more arugula. Once blended, be sure to adjust for consistency using olive oil so it isn't too thick and can be easily spread.

SERVES 4
Nutrition information per serving: Calories: 228.3,
Total Fat: 9g, Cholesterol: 78.3mg, Sodium: 73.8mg,
Total Carbohydrates: 2.3g, Dietary Fiber: 0.5g, Sugars:
0.7g, Protein: 28.5g

White Wine–Poached Salmon

1 tablespoon olive oil

2 cloves garlic, crushed

1 medium carrot, thinly
sliced

2 sprigs fresh thyme

1 bay leaf

3 black peppercorns

1 teaspoon kosher salt

1/2 cup dry white wine

Four 5-ounce salmon
fillets, skin on

SERVING SUGGESTIONS
Serve over a bed of cous-
cous accompanied by
Green Beans with Toasted
Walnuts and Dried Cherry
Vinaigrette (recipe on
p. 175).

Salmon is a healthful source of protein since it's high in omega-3 fatty
acids and vitamin D and low in omega-6 and saturated fats. Look for wild
Pacific salmon, which has better flavor than farm-raised salmon.

1. Heat the oil in a medium sauté pan over medium-high heat. Add the garlic,
   carrots, herbs, peppercorns, salt, and wine and bring to a boil. Once boiling,
   turn off the heat and add the fillets, skin side down.

2. Cover the pan and poach the fillets until they're until slightly underdone in the
   center, 10 to 15 minutes, depending on the thickness of the fillets.

SERVES 4

Nutrition information per serving: Calories: 763.3, Total Fat: 60.8g, Cholesterol: 270.2mg, Sodium: 135.7mg, Total Carbohydrates: 5.4g, Dietary Fiber: 0.1g, Sugars: 0.7g, Protein: 33.2g

Striped Bass with Sage and Red-Wine Butter

2 cups (4 sticks) unsalted butter, at room temperature, divided

1/3 cup fresh sage leaves, plus 1 tablespoon finely chopped sage, for garnish

1 teaspoon freshly squeezed lemon juice, plus 1/2 teaspoon lemon zest

2 cloves garlic

1 teaspoon coarse salt, plus more as needed

2 cups rice flour (read ingredient statement)

Four 5-ounce striped bass fillets, skinned

Freshly ground black pepper

1 1/2 cups dry red wine

3 tablespoons red-wine vinegar

3 medium shallots, finely chopped

1/2 cup canola oil

1/4 cup micro greens, for garnish (optional)

SERVING SUGGESTIONS

Start the meal with the Spiced Butternut Squash and Lentil Salad on p. 78 and pair with Lemon Thyme Potato Gratin on p. 167

This is by no means a "healthy dish," but it is delicious and will impress your pickiest gluten-free guest. If you don't have to make the dish wheat- or gluten-free, feel free to use all-purpose flour instead of the rice flour. When cooking with wine, always remember that if it isn't good enough for you to drink, then it isn't good enough to cook with!

1. Combine 1 cup of the butter, the 1/3 cup sage leaves, lemon juice, lemon zest, garlic, and 1/2 teaspoon of the salt in the bowl of a food processor. Process until puréed. Transfer the sage butter to a small bowl. The butter can be prepared and refrigerated up to 5 days in advance.

2. Put the rice flour in a shallow dish. Spread 2 tablespoons of the sage butter over each bass fillet, then cover the fillets with the flour and sprinkle with salt and pepper; set aside.

3. To make the red-wine butter reduction, pour the wine and vinegar into a large saucepan, add the shallots, and bring to a boil over high heat. Reduce the heat to a simmer and cook the mixture until it becomes syrupy and has reduced to about 2 tablespoons, about 20 minutes. Reduce the heat to low and gradually whisk in the remaining 1 cup butter until combined; season to taste with salt and pepper.

4. Heat the oil in a large skillet over medium-high heat. Add the fillets, butter side up, and cook them for 6 to 8 minutes. Carefully flip the fish and continue cooking for another 1 to 2 minutes.

5. To serve, spoon 3 tablespoons of the red-wine butter reduction onto each of four plates and spread across the plate using the back of a spoon. Top with a fish fillet and garnish with the remaining chopped sage and micro greens, if using; serve immediately.

SERVES 12 TO 24
Nutrition information per serving (based on 24 servings): Calories: 148.3, Total Fat: 5.4g, Cholesterol: 75.5mg, Sodium: 131.9mg, Total Carbohydrates: 4.7g, Dietary Fiber: 0.5g, Sugars: 1.8g, Protein: 19.2g

Tri-Color Fish Terrine

Nonstick cooking spray (read ingredient statement)

One 10-ounce package frozen spinach

One 20-ounce package frozen ground salmon, thawed

Two 20-ounce packages frozen ground whitefish, thawed

3/4 cup seasoned dried breadcrumbs (read ingredient statement)

3 tablespoons sugar

3 eggs

Prepared horseradish, for serving (read ingredient statement)

This recipe is my mom's Ashkenazik twist on classic Jewish gefilte fish, which she made for all High Holidays. While I'm not a fan of traditional gefilte fish, I love this dish. It is a simple but exciting way to start off a traditional meal or even serve as an appetizer at a party.

Packages of frozen ground fish can be found at many grocery stores. If you prefer to use fresh fish, ask your fishmonger for 20 ounces of ground salmon and 40 ounces of ground whitefish, divided.

1. Position a rack in the center of the oven and heat the oven to 350°F. Grease a 9-inch springform pan with cooking spray. Thaw the spinach according to the package directions.

2. Put each package of fish into three separate bowls. To each bowl, add ¼ cup of the breadcrumbs, 1 tablespoon of the sugar, and 1 of the eggs; mix until combined. Add the thawed and drained spinach to one of the whitefish mixtures and mix until combined.

3. One at a time, pour each bowl of fish into the prepared springform pan, flattening each layer as you go. Start with the salmon mixture, then add in the whitefish-spinach mixture, then add the plain whitefish mixture. Cover the springform pan loosely with foil, place it in a larger pan, and fill the larger pan with water to come about halfway up the sides of the springform.

4. Bake for 1 hour, then remove the foil and bake for another 15 minutes, until the top of the terrine is brown. Remove from the oven and let cool. Unclasp the springform and serve chilled with prepared horseradish. The terrine keeps, refrigerated, for up to 1 week and freezes well for up to 3 months.

VARIATION

 Leave out the breadcrumbs, or replace them with ¾ cup gluten-free breadcrumbs (store-bought or made from toasting gluten-free bread and crumbling in a food processor). Read the ingredient statement to check for other allergens.

SERVES 4
Nutrition information per serving: Calories: 350, Total Fat: 23g, Cholesterol: 50mg, Sodium: 323mg, Total Carbohydrates: 9.4g, Dietary Fiber: 0.8g, Sugars: 4.1g, Protein: 26.5g

Seared Tuna Steaks Topped with Basil Olive Relish

½ cup olive tapenade (read ingredient statement)

½ cup finely chopped red onions

½ cup fresh basil, finely chopped

¼ cup fresh flat-leaf parsley, finely chopped

6 tablespoons olive oil

¼ cup white balsamic vinegar

2 teaspoons finely grated lemon zest

2 teaspoons kosher salt, plus more as needed

Freshly ground black pepper

Four 4-ounce tuna steaks

SERVING SUGGESTION
Serve over Oven-Roasted Fingerling Potatoes (recipe on p. 172).

The basil olive relish pairs beautifully with the flavor of tuna. Use this relish to top other fish too.

1. Combine the tapenade, red onions, basil, parsley, 5 tablespoons of the olive oil, the vinegar, and lemon zest in medium bowl; season with the 2 teaspoons salt and pepper to taste. Set the relish aside.

2. Brush the tuna steaks with the remaining 1 tablespoon olive oil. Season generously with salt and pepper.

3. Heat a large skillet over medium-high heat. Add the tuna and cook to your preferred doneness, 1 to 2 minutes per side for medium rare. Cut the tuna into ½-inch-thick slices and top with the prepared olive relish.

SERVES 4
Nutrition information per serving: Calories: 294.3, Total Fat: 18.7g, Cholesterol: 124.7mg, Sodium: 123.4mg, Total Carbohydrates: 2.6g, Dietary Fiber: 1.7g, Sugars: 0.6g, Protein: 29.1g

Rosemary- and Pecan-Crusted Trout

½ cup pecans, finely chopped into a coarse meal for breading

1 teaspoon dried rosemary

1 teaspoon kosher salt

1 teaspoon freshly ground black pepper

½ cup unbleached all-purpose flour (read ingredient statement)

1 egg

1 tablespoon prepared mustard (read ingredient statement)

Four 4-ounce trout fillets

Try different herb and nut combinations to flavor the fish in new ways.

1. Position a rack in the center of the oven and the heat the oven to 400°F. Line a rimmed baking sheet with parchment.

2. Mix the pecans, rosemary, salt, and pepper in a shallow dish. Put the flour in a separate shallow dish. In a medium bowl, beat the egg and mustard.

3. Working with one fillet at a time, dip the fish in the flour and shake off the excess; then dip the fish into the egg mixture and then into pecans. Lightly press the pecan coating onto the fillet. Arrange the fillets on the prepared baking sheet.

4. Bake the fish until it flakes easily with a fork and has browned slightly, 10 to 12 minutes.

WINE PAIRING

The hints of blackberries and mint in a Syrah wine would pair well with the intense rosemary flavors in this dish.

VARIATION

 Leave out the flour and dip the fillets in the egg wash and then the pecan mixture for the coating. Or use a gluten-free flour to replace the all-purpose flour. Be sure the mustard is gluten-free.

SERVING SUGGESTIONS

Serve with Garlic Arugula Crostini Salad on p. 82 or a simple green salad tossed with freshly squeezed lemon juice and salt and pepper.

SERVES 6
Nutrition information per serving: Calories: 243.7,
Total Fat: 7.3g, Cholesterol: 75.8mg, Sodium: 892mg,
Total Carbohydrates: 17.5g, Dietary Fiber: 0.2g,
Sugars: 16.5g, Protein: 29.9g

Barbecue-Glazed Alaskan Salmon

Six 4-ounce salmon fillets,
  skin on

1½ teaspoons kosher salt

1 teaspoon freshly ground
  black pepper

1 teaspoon garlic powder

⅓ cup gluten-free soy
  sauce (check ingredient
  statement)

⅓ cup firmly packed
  brown sugar

3 tablespoons vegetable
  oil, plus more
  as needed (read
  ingredient statement)

While I was cooking as a guest chef on a cruise in Alaska, I found this dish in local Alaskan eateries along the piers we passed through. The very simple preparation lets fish truly shine.

1. Season the salmon fillets with the salt, pepper, and garlic powder.

2. In a small bowl, stir the soy sauce, brown sugar, ⅓ cup water, and vegetable oil until well combined. Put the fish in a large zip-top plastic bag, pour in the soy sauce mixture, seal the bag, and toss to coat. Marinate the salmon for 1 to 2 hours in the refrigerator.

3. Heat a grill or grill pan on medium-high heat. Lightly oil the grill and cook the salmon fillets to your preferred doneness, 6 to 8 minutes per side for medium to fully cooked, depending on the thickness.

SERVING SUGGESTIONS

Serve with rice and
Sautéed Kale with Pine
Nuts (recipe on p. 168).

SERVES 4 TO 6
Nutrition information per serving (based on 6 servings): Calories: 147.4, Total Fat: 3.6g, Cholesterol: 67.6mg, Sodium: 89.2mg, Total Carbohydrates: 1g, Dietary Fiber:0.2g, Sugars: 0.1g, Protein: 25.8g

Broiled Sesame–Tarragon Cod with Garlic–Lemon Butter

Six 4-ounce cod fillets, skinned

1 tablespoon unsalted butter, melted

2 teaspoons lemon juice

2 cloves garlic, finely minced

1 teaspoon dried tarragon

1 teaspoon kosher salt

1 teaspoon freshly ground black pepper

1 tablespoon sesame seeds

SERVING SUGGESTIONS

Serve the fish with the Lemon Thyme Potato Gratin recipe on p. 167 or the Roasted Butternut Squash recipe on p. 169.

A flaky and dense white fish, cod is versatile and responds well to many cooking methods.

While sesame seeds are not a tree nut, some people with a tree nut allergy can have a similar reaction to sesame seeds. Feel free to eliminate the sesame seeds from the recipe.

1. Position an oven rack 4 inches from the heating element and heat the broiler. Line a rimmed baking sheet with aluminum foil.

2. Arrange the cod fillets on the foil and brush with the melted butter. Drizzle the lemon juice on top and sprinkle with the garlic, tarragon, salt, black pepper, and sesame seeds.

3. Broil the fish until it flakes easily, about 10 minutes.

VARIATION

 Replace the butter with 1 tablespoon olive oil.

SERVES 6
Nutrition information per serving: Calories: 364.8, Total Fat: 19g, Cholesterol: 60.1mg, Sodium: 312mg, Total Carbohydrates: 19.7g, Dietary Fiber: 1.6g, Sugars: 0.8g, Protein: 30.9g

Roasted Sea Bass and Potatoes with Olive Dressing

FOR THE POTATOES

1 pound fingerling potatoes

2 tablespoons olive oil

2 tablespoons finely chopped fresh basil

2 tablespoons finely chopped fresh mint

Kosher salt and freshly ground black pepper

FOR THE OLIVE DRESSING

1/2 cup green olives, quartered

2 tablespoons finely minced red onions

1 tablespoon capers, drained

2 tablespoons lemon juice

1 1/2 tablespoons apple cider vinegar

5 tablespoons olive oil

1/4 teaspoon kosher salt

The dressing, although acidic, pairs perfectly with both potatoes and sea bass because they're both very "meaty" in texture and absorb and contrast acidic flavors well.

PREPARE THE POTATOES

In a large saucepan, boil the potatoes until fork-tender, 15 to 20 minutes. Drain, then slice the potatoes in half. In a large bowl, toss the potatoes with the olive oil, herbs, and salt and pepper to taste. Set aside.

MAKE THE OLIVE DRESSING

Combine the olives, onions, capers, lemon juice, vinegar, olive oil, and salt. Let the mixture sit at room temperature while you cook the fish.

FOR THE FISH

Six 4-ounce sea bass fillets, skinned

½ teaspoon cayenne

Kosher salt and freshly ground black pepper

1 tablespoon olive oil

FOR GARNISH

Finely chopped fresh basil

Finely chopped fresh mint

SERVING SUGGESTIONS

Start off this meal with the Garlic Arugula Crostini Salad (recipe on p. 82). For dessert, serve none other than the Lemon Shortbread Tart (recipe on p. 210). The combination will excite your palate!

WINE PAIRING

The citrus and vanilla flavors of a Chablis will complement the savory qualities of the fish and add complexity to your meal.

COOK THE FISH

1. Position a rack in the center of the oven and heat the oven to 450°F.

2. Heat a large oven-safe nonstick skillet over high heat until hot. Season the fillets on both sides with the cayenne, salt, and black pepper. Drizzle the skillet with the olive oil, add the fish, and cook for 3 minutes.

3. Transfer the skillet to the oven and cook the fish for another 3 minutes to finish cooking through.

TO SERVE

Portion the potatoes equally among six plates and top each with a sea bass fillet. Drizzle with the olive dressing just before serving and garnish with more herbs.

SERVES 6 TO 8

Nutrition information per serving (based on 8 servings): Calories: 550.2, Total Fat: 32.5g, Cholesterol: 78.1mg, Sodium: 359.3mg, Total Carbohydrates: 28.6g, Dietary Fiber: 10.3g, Sugars: 1.6g, Protein: 38.1g

Blackened Fish Tacos with Guacamole and Cilantro–Lime Slaw

FOR THE GUACAMOLE

4 ripe avocados

½ red onion, finely chopped

1 serrano chile, minced

1 cup cherry tomatoes, quartered

1 tablespoon lime juice, plus more as needed

1 teaspoon kosher salt

FOR THE CILANTRO– LIME SLAW

½ cup mayonnaise (read ingredient statement)

2 limes, juiced

1 jalapeño, minced

½ teaspoon dried oregano

½ teaspoon ground cumin

1 teaspoon cayenne

1 medium head cabbage, finely shredded

1 bunch fresh cilantro, chopped

(continued)

This is a fun family-style meal. Serve with salsa and any additional vegetables or toppings you like. The guacamole recipe is simple and classic, but for added flavor and a kick, you can add more minced chiles and ½ cup chopped cilantro or parsley. To lighten up the slaw, swap out the full-fat mayonnaise for a lighter or fat-free version. You can also use sour cream instead, although that would make it not milk-free.

MAKE THE GUACAMOLE

Cut the avocados in half, remove the pit, and scoop out the flesh into a large mixing bowl. Slightly mash the avocado using a fork. Add the onions, chile, tomatoes, and lime juice. Stir to combine and season to taste with salt and more lime juice. Cover with plastic wrap and set aside for serving.

MAKE THE CILANTRO–LIME SLAW

In a medium bowl, mix the mayonnaise, lime juice, minced jalapeño, oregano, cumin, and cayenne until well combined. Add the shredded cabbage and cilantro, toss to coat, and set aside.

(continued)

FOR THE FISH

1 tablespoon paprika

2 teaspoons dry mustard

1 teaspoon cayenne

1 teaspoon ground cumin

1 teaspoon dried thyme

1 teaspoon kosher salt

1 teaspoon black pepper

¼ cup olive oil

Six 4-ounce cod fillets

TO SERVE

One 12-ounce package 100% corn tortillas

3 limes, quartered

PREPARE AND COOK THE FISH

1. In a small bowl, mix together the paprika, dry mustard, cayenne, cumin, thyme, salt, and black pepper; set aside.

2. Heat a cast-iron pan on high heat until extremely hot, about 10 minutes. Pour the olive oil into a shallow dish or bowl and dip each fillet, turning once to coat. Remove the fish from the oil and sprinkle both sides with the spice mixture, gently patting the mixture onto the fish.

3. Put the spiced fillets in the pan without crowding them. Cook the fish until it appears charred, about 2 minutes. Flip and continue cooking until the second side is charred, another 2 to 3 minutes. Transfer the cooked fish to a plate (and repeat with the remaining fish, if you cooked in batches).

TO SERVE

Put a portion of fish in a corn tortilla and top with guacamole and Cilantro–Lime Slaw. Garnish each plate with lime wedges.

VARIATION

Replace the cod with 1 to 2 blocks of extra-firm tofu. To prepare the tofu, cut into ½-inch-thick strips, then place on several layers of paper towels; cover with more paper towels and top with a cutting board to drain excess liquid. Let stand for several minutes, pressing down occasionally. Dredge the tofu as you would the fish. Replace the regular mayonnaise with vegan mayonnaise. Tofu contains soy, so this variation will no longer be soy-free. Read the ingredient statement for vegan mayonnaise for additional allergens.

SERVES 4
Nutrition information per serving: Calories: 303.5, Total Fat: 13.9g, Cholesterol: 78.9mg, Sodium: 1297mg, Total Carbohydrates: 14g, Dietary Fiber: 2.8g, Sugars: 1.3g, Protein: 29g

Cajun Wasabi Trout with Buttered Potatoes

Olive oil, for the pan

FOR THE POTATOES

4 medium Yukon Gold potatoes, boiled for 10 to 15 minutes until fork-tender and cut into 1-inch cubes

¼ cup unsalted butter, melted

Kosher salt and freshly ground black pepper

FOR THE FISH

¼ cup gluten-free soy sauce (read ingredient statement)

2 tablespoons olive oil

2 teaspoons wasabi paste (read ingredient statement)

1 teaspoon finely minced garlic

1 teaspoon dried oregano

1 teaspoon kosher salt

1 teaspoon freshly ground black pepper

Four 4-ounce trout fillets

1 tablespoon Cajun seasoning (read ingredient statement)

This dish is an interesting combination of Asian and Creole thanks to the wasabi paste and Cajun seasoning. Neither overpowers the other and instead creates a kickin' blend that works well with the gamey flavor of the trout.

1. Position a rack in the center of the oven and heat the oven to 450°F. Line a baking dish with aluminum foil and grease it with olive oil.

2. Spread the cooked potatoes in a single layer in the bottom of the baking dish, drizzle with the melted butter, and season with salt and pepper. Bake for 10 minutes, until the potatoes are slightly golden.

3. While the potatoes are baking, combine the soy sauce, olive oil, wasabi paste, garlic, oregano, salt, and pepper in a small bowl. Coat each fish fillet with the wasabi mixture.

4. Remove the potatoes from the oven and arrange the fish fillets on top; sprinkle with the Cajun seasoning. Bake the fish and potatoes for 8 to 10 minutes, until the fish is white and flaky.

VARIATIONS

 Substitute ¼ cup olive oil for the butter when preparing the potatoes.

 Replace the soy sauce with ¼ cup lemon juice. It will alter the taste slightly, but the dish will still be delicious.

COOK'S TIP

Unless you're in a pinch for time, resist using prechopped and minced garlic. It doesn't taste nearly as good as fresh garlic and won't keep as long. Plus, mincing or chopping fresh garlic doesn't take long once you know how to do it. First, break the skin on a clove to peel. Cover it with the flat side of a chef's knife and press down on the blade with the heel of your hand. Remove the skin, then use the same knife to mince or chop as your recipe directs.

Chapter 5

Sides

SERVES 2 TO 4

Nutrition information per serving (based on 4 servings): Calories: 211.2, Total Fat: 1.4g, Cholesterol: 0mg, Sodium: 145.6mg, Total Carbohydrates: 47.8g, Dietary Fiber: 6.8g, Sugars: 1.1g, Protein: 2.6g

Sweet Potatoes with Honey Mustard Vinaigrette

3 medium sweet potatoes, peeled and cut into 1-inch cubes

2 teaspoons olive oil

2½ teaspoons kosher salt, plus more as needed

1 teaspoon freshly ground black pepper, plus more as needed

1 tablespoon fresh thyme, finely chopped

¼ cup vegetable stock (read ingredient statement) or water

½ teaspoon capers, plus ½ teaspoon caper juice

1 tablespoon whole-grain mustard (read ingredient statement)

2 teaspoons honey

1½ teaspoons balsamic vinegar

1½ tablespoons chopped fresh flat-leaf parsley

This recipe pairs well with several recipes from this book, among them Perfect Roast Chicken (p. 99) and Balsamic Herb Skirt Steak (p. 117).

1. Position a rack in the center of the oven and heat the oven to 400°F.

2. On a rimmed baking sheet, spread the sweet potato cubes in a single layer and drizzle with 1 teaspoon of the olive oil, 2 teaspoons of the salt, the pepper, and the thyme. Bake the potatoes for 20 to 30 minutes, until golden and tender when pricked with a knife.

3. Whisk together the stock, the remaining 1 teaspoon olive oil, the capers and juice, mustard, honey, vinegar, and remaining ½ teaspoon salt. Toss with the cooked sweet potatoes while still warm, season with salt and pepper, sprinkle with parsley, then serve warm or at room temperature. You can also refrigerate for about an hour and serve cold.

SERVES 4 TO 6

Nutrition information per serving (based on 6 servings): Calories: 48, Total Fat: 2.6g, Cholesterol: 0mg, Sodium: 5.4mg, Total Carbohydrate: 5.8g, Dietary Fiber: 2.2g, Sugars: 0g, Protein: 2.1g

Garlic-Seared Tomatoes and Asparagus

1 pound asparagus, bottoms trimmed, spears cut in half

1 tablespoon extra-virgin olive oil, plus more as needed

2 cloves garlic, finely minced

2 medium tomatoes, seeded and diced

1 teaspoon kosher salt

1/2 teaspoon freshly ground black pepper

1 teaspoon fresh lemon juice

1 tablespoon fresh oregano, picked from the stems

1 teaspoon sea salt

This rustic dish can be served at room temperature as a salad course or hot as a side. I like it paired with the Slow-Cooker Provençal Lemon and Olive Chicken (p. 113).

1. Spread the asparagus in a large skillet, fill with about 1 inch of water, and cover. Let the water come to a boil over high heat, then continue to cook for an additional 2 minutes. Drain, then plunge the asparagus into a bowl of ice water.

2. In a separate skillet, heat the oil over medium heat; add the garlic and cook for about 1 minute, until fragrant. Add the tomatoes and cook for about 2 minutes, until the tomatoes are warmed but still hold their shape a bit. Season with the kosher salt and pepper.

3. Portion the asparagus evenly among serving plates or arrange on a platter and spoon the tomato mixture over the top. Drizzle with more olive oil, if you like, and lemon juice and sprinkle with the fresh oregano and sea salt.

SERVES 4 TO 6
Nutrition information per serving (based on 4 steaks and ½ cup sauce): Calories: 127.4, Total Fat: 5.4g, Cholesterol: 0.8mg, Sodium: 26.7mg, Total Carbohydrates: 17.7g, Dietary Fiber: 1.5g, Sugars: 2.2g, Protein: 3g

Polenta "Steaks" with Spicy Tomato Sauce

1 cup uncooked polenta or coarse-ground cornmeal

1 cup soy milk

2 tablespoons olive oil, plus more for the pan

Kosher salt and freshly ground black pepper

½ recipe Spicy Tomato Sauce (p. 236)

½ cup chopped fresh basil

This is my go-to vegan dish when I entertain. It's hearty and simple and can be served with sautéed greens to round out the meal. This recipe can also be made as "polenta fries" minus the tomato sauce and served with ketchup as well as several other dips from this book. Just be sure to read the ingredient statement or check allergens in the dip recipes before using.

1. In a large pot over medium-high heat, stir together the polenta, milk, and 3 cups water. Continue stirring until the polenta comes to a boil, then reduce the heat to a simmer and cook (continue stirring!) until the polenta is smooth and creamy, 15 to 20 minutes. Stir in the olive oil and season with salt and pepper to taste.

2. Scrape the cooked polenta out of the pot into a lightly oiled 8-inch-square pan, spread evenly, and smooth the top. Chill in the refrigerator until the polenta is set and firm, 1 to 2 hours.

3. Once firm, invert the pan onto a cutting board and cut the polenta into equal portions. (I like to cut the polenta into about 12 logs but you can cut it into squares, wedges, or whatever shape you like.)

4. Position a rack in the center of the oven and heat the oven to 375°F. Lay the polenta "steaks" on a lightly greased rimmed baking sheet and bake until they're browned and crisp, flipping halfway through cooking, 30 to 40 minutes total. To serve, top with the Spicy Tomato Sauce and chopped basil.

VARIATION

Use 1 cup almond milk in place of the soy milk. Don't use rice milk, as it won't have the same consistency and flavor. Using almond milk means this recipe is not nut-free.

SERVES 8 TO 10
Nutrition information per serving (3/4 cup):
Calories: 407.8, Total Fat: 12.5g, Cholesterol:
4.7mg, Sodium: 73mg, Total Carbohydrates: 67.9g,
Dietary Fiber 10.2g, Sugars: 4.8g, Protein: 7.6g

Garlic Mashed Potatoes

5 pounds medium
  Yukon Gold potatoes,
  unpeeled, scrubbed

2 sprigs fresh rosemary

1 tablespoon kosher salt,
  plus more as needed

2 teaspoons freshly
  ground black pepper,
  plus more as needed

½ cup sour cream

½ cup olive oil

4 large cloves garlic,
  peeled and minced

COOK'S TIP

These potatoes won't be
completely smooth—
mashing will leave some
delicious small chunks.
If you like your potatoes
really smooth, incorporate
the sour cream and oil,
then use a hand-held mixer
to whip the potatoes to the
desired smoothness.

I don't peel the potatoes because I like the texture of the skin; plus it packs an additional nutrition punch. Feel free to peel your potatoes if you don't like the skin.

If you make these potatoes in advance of serving, they will harden as they sit. Add a bit of olive oil, sour cream, or milk until you get the right texture and flavor for serving.

1. Put the potatoes in a large stockpot and cover with cold water. Add the rosemary, salt, and pepper. Bring to a simmer over medium heat and cook until a knife inserted into a potato comes out easily, 15 to 25 minutes. Drain the potatoes in a colander, then transfer them back into the original pot.

2. Using a potato masher, mash the potatoes until relatively smooth, leaving some chunks. Stir in the sour cream, olive oil, and garlic. Season the potatoes with more salt and pepper to taste and serve immediately.

VARIATION

Replace the sour cream with tofu sour cream or soy milk. Using tofu sour cream or soy milk makes this variation no longer soy-free.

SERVES 4 TO 6
Nutrition information per serving (based on 6 servings): Calories: 87.5, Total Fat: 5g, Cholesterol: 0mg, Sodium: 5.5mg, Total Carbohydrates: 11.1g, Dietary Fiber: 4.6g, Sugars: 0g, Protein: 1.9g

Fire-Roasted Eggplant

2 whole small eggplants

2 tablespoons olive oil

1$\frac{1}{2}$ teaspoons kosher salt

1 teaspoon freshly ground black pepper

Simple Tahini Dip (p. 244; optional)

The simple preparation lets the flavor of the eggplant shine. Although any variety of eggplant can be cooked this way, you'll have the best luck with the more oval or round types (like the classic Italian or Sicilian varieties) rather than the cylindrical varieties, like Chinese or Japanese.

This dish is nice as part of a Mediterranean tapas meal, accompanied by the Simple Tahini Dip on p. 244 (use as a dressing or dipping sauce). If you have a sensitivity to sesame seeds, use one of the herb pestos (recipes on pp. 238–239) in place of the tahini dressing. Using one of the herb pestos will make the recipe no longer nut-free. Note that sometimes people with a sesame allergy will react to nuts as well.

1. Prepare a charcoal or gas grill or heat the broiler.

2. Prick the eggplant skin with a fork or skewer to allow steam to escape while it's cooking. If broiling the eggplants, set them on a baking sheet; if grilling, the eggplants can sit directly on the grates. Grill or broil the eggplants for 15 to 30 minutes, turning frequently, until they're charred and slightly wrinkled.

3. Let the eggplants cool, then halve each lengthwise, drizzle with olive oil, and sprinkle with the salt and pepper. Serve with the Simple Tahini Dip, if using.

SERVES 4 TO 6
Nutrition information per serving (based on 6 servings): Calories: 127.7, Total Fat: 4.8g, Cholesterol: 0.8mg, Sodium: 20.6mg, Total Carbohydrates: 17.5g, Dietary Fiber: 3.4g, Sugars: 2.1g, Protein: 4.1g

Lemon Thyme Potato Gratin

Nonstick cooking spray (read ingredient statement) or olive oil, for the pan

2 pounds Yukon Gold potatoes, peeled and cut into $\frac{1}{8}$-inch-thick slices

3 teaspoons finely chopped fresh thyme

$\frac{1}{2}$ teaspoon freshly grated nutmeg

1 lemon, zested

Kosher salt and freshly ground black pepper

1 tablespoon olive oil

1 cup soy milk

Potato gratin is comfort food like no other. The little bit of lemon zest in this recipe adds a subtle zing. For a richer flavor, replace the olive oil with small cubes of butter scattered among the layers of potatoes before baking.

1. Position a rack in the center of the oven and heat the oven to 400°F. Spray a 10-inch gratin dish with cooking spray or coat generously with olive oil.

2. Arrange a third of the potato slices on the bottom of the gratin dish in an even layer. Sprinkle with 1 teaspoon thyme, $\frac{1}{8}$ teaspoon nutmeg, $\frac{1}{2}$ teaspoon lemon zest, $\frac{1}{2}$ teaspoon salt, and $\frac{1}{2}$ teaspoon pepper. Drizzle with 1 teaspoon olive oil. Repeat with two more layers, then pour the milk over the gratin and sprinkle with any remaining thyme and nutmeg.

3. Cover with foil and bake for 35 minutes. Remove the foil and continue to bake for another 10 to 20 minutes, until the potatoes are golden brown.

COOK'S TIP

If you haven't used a mandoline, this is the perfect recipe to try it out on since you want the slices of potato to be uniformly thin. Most mandolines come with different blades so you can make decorative or straight slices quickly and easily.

SERVES 6 TO 8
Nutrition information per serving (based on 8 servings): Calories: 123.9, Total Fat: 10.9g, Cholesterol: 0mg, Sodium: 15.8mg, Total Carbohydrates: 6.3g, Dietary Fiber: 1.9g, Sugars: 1g, Protein: 2.3g

Sautéed Kale with Pine Nuts

¼ cup olive oil

½ large red onion, chopped

4 cloves garlic, finely minced

2 pounds (about 4 cups) kale, washed, trimmed, and torn into bite-sized pieces

¼ cup pine nuts, toasted

1½ teaspoons kosher salt, plus more as needed

1 teaspoon freshly ground black pepper, plus more as needed

If you grow kale or subscribe to a CSA (community-supported agriculture program), you know that kale is abundant when in season. If you're tired of the same old sautéed version, try this one—it's simple but flavorful.

If you can't find kale, use spinach or any other dark leafy green that's in season.

1. Heat the olive oil in large heavy skillet over medium-high heat. Add the onions and garlic; sauté until the onions are soft, about 6 minutes. Add half of the kale and toss, cooking until it's just wilted, 2 to 3 minutes. Add the remaining kale and half of the pine nuts. Toss until the kale is just wilted but still bright green, about 3 minutes. Add the salt and pepper, then season to taste with more if needed.

2. Transfer to a large serving bowl, sprinkle with the remaining toasted pine nuts, and serve.

MAKES ABOUT 2 CUPS;
SERVES 6 TO 8
Nutrition information per
serving (based on 8 servings):
Calories: 97, Total Fat: 5.5g,
Cholesterol: 0mg, Sodium:
20.9mg, Total Carbohydrates:
12.9g, Dietary Fiber: 3.6g,
Sugars: 0g, Protein: 1.1g

Roasted Butternut Squash

1 large butternut squash,
    peeled and cut into
    1-inch cubes
¼ cup olive oil
1 tablespoon kosher salt
Freshly ground black
    pepper

If you can't find whole butternut squash, use precut and packaged fresh or frozen squash. This recipe is also delicious with fresh pumpkin instead of the butternut squash.

If you buy the squash whole, reserve the seeds for making the sweet or salty toasted pepitas (see the tip below). They make a great snack, or try them in soups, salads, and even desserts.

1. Position a rack in the center of the oven and heat the oven to 200°F.

2. In a large bowl, toss together the cubed butternut squash, olive oil, salt, and a few grinds of pepper. Spread onto a rimmed baking sheet in a single layer and roast for 25 to 30 minutes, until golden brown and caramelized. Serve as roasted chunks or allow to cool, then transfer to a blender and process to a purée.

COOK'S TIP

Use the seeds from the butternut squash to make sweet or spicy pepitas. Use the sweet toasted pepitas to top cakes, muffins, and breads, and try the spicy ones in soups and salads.

To make sweet toasted seeds, combine 1 teaspoon olive oil, 1½ teaspoons sugar, ½ teaspoon ground cinnamon, and a pinch of sea salt. For the spicy mixture, combine 1 teaspoon olive oil, ½ teaspoon cayenne, ½ teaspoon cumin, a pinch of sea salt, and a few grinds of black pepper.

When ready to toast, follow these instructions for either mixture. Heat the oven to 350°F. Combine the sweet or spicy mix with the seeds, spread on a rimmed baking sheet, and toast for 5 to 10 minutes, until golden brown and crisped. Let cool completely, then store in an airtight container.

Roasted Lime Carrots

1 pound heirloom baby carrots, with tops

1 tablespoon olive oil

1 lime, zested and juiced

1 tablespoon honey

1½ teaspoons kosher salt

½ teaspoon ground cumin

½ teaspoon paprika

2 scallions (white and light green parts), thinly sliced

½ cup finely chopped fresh mint

½ cup finely chopped fresh cilantro

This recipe showcases the beauty—and sweetness—of heirloom baby carrots. They're cooked with the tops left on, so they make a fancy presentation when entertaining.

1. Position a rack in the center of the oven and heat the oven to 400°F. Line a rimmed baking sheet with foil or parchment.

2. Spread the carrots on the prepared baking sheet. Drizzle with the olive oil, lime juice, and honey, then sprinkle with the lime zest, salt, cumin, and paprika. Roast the carrots for 20 to 25 minutes, until tender and golden brown. If the carrots are tender but not yet golden brown, leave in the oven for another 5 minutes.

3. Let the carrots cool slightly, then transfer to a flat serving dish and sprinkle with the scallions, mint, and cilantro (you don't have to use all of the herbs). Drizzle with more lime juice if you like, then serve.

VARIATION

 Replace the honey with 1 teaspoon agave nectar.

SERVES 4 TO 6
Nutrition information per serving (based on 6 servings): Calories: 102.3, Total Fat: 4.5g, Cholesterol: 0mg, Sodium: 45.5mg, Total Carbohydrates: 14.3g, Dietary Fiber: 0.9g, Sugars: 0g, Protein: 0g

Oven-Roasted Fingerling Potatoes

1 pound fingerling potatoes

1 bunch fresh rosemary, tied in a bundle with kitchen twine

2 teaspoons kosher salt, plus more as needed

1 teaspoon freshly ground black pepper, plus more as needed

2 tablespoons olive oil

COOK'S TIP

You'll find many recipes that call for tying sprigs of fresh herbs with kitchen twine before using them. The traditional tied herb bundle is referred to as a *bouquet garni* and includes thyme, parsley, and bay leaf. But you can tie any herbs into a bundle before using it to flavor soups, stews, stock, and more. The twine makes it easy to remove the herbs when called for in the recipe.

Kids and adults will love this simple dish, and it's gorgeous when you use multicolored fingerlings, which have purple and pink tones. You're most likely to find colored fingerlings at a farmers' market, but many supermarkets carry them as well. If you can't find fingerlings, use new potatoes, with their thin skin and sweet flavor.

1. Position a rack in the center of the oven and heat the oven to 425°F.

2. Put the potatoes, rosemary, salt, and pepper in a large stockpot. Cover with cold water and bring to a boil. Cook the potatoes until fork-tender, 15 to 20 minutes, then drain in a large colander. Let the potatoes cool slightly. Remove and discard the rosemary.

3. Once the potatoes have cooled, cut them in half lengthwise and arrange them on a large baking sheet in a single layer. Drizzle with the olive oil, sprinkle generously with more salt and pepper, and toss to coat.

4. Transfer the baking sheet to the oven and roast the potatoes until golden brown, 20 to 25 minutes.

SERVES 4 TO 6
Nutrition information per serving (based on 6 servings): Calories: 108.7, Total Fat: 9.3g, Cholesterol: 0mg, Sodium: 3.6mg, Total Carbohydrates: 6.1g, Dietary Fiber: 1.8g, Sugars: 3.6g, Protein: 2.1g

Mashed Summer Squash

5 medium yellow summer squash, unpeeled and cut into 2-inch chunks

1 tablespoon kosher salt, plus more as needed

1 teaspoon freshly ground black pepper, plus more as needed

¼ cup olive oil

4 large cloves garlic, finely minced

My Auntie Paula is the inspiration behind this recipe. One of my last memories of her was when she arrived for Thanksgiving sporting her usual hippie attire and a mesh sack of garden-fresh summer squash. She proceeded to tell us how her mother (my grandmother) would make this recipe for her and her siblings (including my father) when they were kids and how the most important ingredient in this recipe is and always will be butter—lots and lots of butter!

I've lightened up the original recipe, but if you dare, replace the olive oil with 1 stick of unsalted butter in honor of Auntie Paulie. Replacing the olive oil with butter makes this recipe no longer milk-free and vegan.

1. Put the squash in a large stockpot, cover with cold water, and add the salt and pepper. Bring to a simmer over medium heat and cook until a knife inserted in a couple of chunks of squash comes out easily. Drain the squash, then return to the pot.

2. Using a potato masher, mash the squash until smooth. Stir in the olive oil and garlic (or use 1 stick of unsalted butter in place of the olive oil). Season to taste with more salt and pepper. Serve warm.

SERVES 4 TO 6

Nutrition information per serving
(based on 6 servings): Calories: 233.8,
Total Fat: 17.5g, Cholesterol: 0mg,
Sodium: 683.2mg, Total Carbohydrates:
19.2g, Dietary Fiber: 5.1g, Sugars: 7g,
Protein: 4.9g

Green Beans with Toasted Walnuts and Dried Cherry Vinaigrette

⅓ cup extra-virgin
   olive oil

¼ cup minced shallots

¼ cup sherry vinegar

2 teaspoons kosher salt

½ teaspoon black pepper

2 teaspoons sugar

⅓ cup dried tart cherries,
   halved

1½ pounds green beans,
   trimmed

½ cup walnuts, chopped
   and toasted

4 tablespoons chopped
   fresh mint

This green bean dish makes a great addition to a holiday table. Can't find cherries? Substitute dried cranberries or chopped dried apricots instead.

1. Make the vinaigrette by whisking together the olive oil, shallots, sherry vinegar, salt, pepper, and sugar. Mix in the dried cherries and toss to coat. Set aside.

2. Cook the green beans in a large pot of boiling salted water for 3 to 4 minutes. Drain and transfer immediately to a bowl of ice water to cool and stop the cooking. Drain after 2 minutes.

3. To serve, toss the green beans with the walnuts and vinaigrette, sprinkle with the mint, and serve.

VARIATION

 Leave out the walnuts.

COOK'S TIP

Having an ice bath at the ready is important when cooking vegetables. The cold water will shock the vegetables, allowing them to maintain their color and stop the cooking. Be sure you have a large bowl filled with ice and water close by your colander so that you can quickly drain veggies, then plunge them into the icy water.

SERVES 4 TO 6
Nutrition information per serving
(based on 6 servings): Calories: 184.8,
Total Fat: 15.2g, Cholesterol: 0mg,
Sodium: 79.9mg, Total Carbohydrates:
11.5g, Dietary Fiber: 4.5g, Sugars: 0.5g,
Protein: 5g

Balsamic Roasted Cauliflower with Pine Nut–Tahini Dressing

FOR THE CAULIFLOWER

1 head cauliflower

3 tablespoons olive oil

2 tablespoons balsamic vinegar

1 teaspoon kosher salt

1 teaspoon freshly ground black pepper

FOR THE DRESSING

2 cloves garlic, minced

3 tablespoons tahini paste (read ingredient statement)

1 lemon, juiced

¼ cup pine nuts, toasted

Kosher salt and freshly ground black pepper

¼ cup chopped fresh flat-leaf parsley, plus more for garnish

After living in the Mediterranean, tahini paste became a staple in my pantry. The rich nuttiness of this dressing enhances the flavor of roasted vegetables like cauliflower and eggplant—two of my favorites—but feel free to experiment with other vegetables and tahini dressing variations (see p. 244 for an option). Omit the tahini if you have a sensitivity or allergy to sesame seeds.

1. Position a rack in the center of the oven and heat the oven to 400°F.

2. Trim the florets from the head of cauliflower, then thinly slice them and transfer to a large bowl. Add the olive oil, vinegar, salt, and pepper and toss to coat. Arrange the seasoned cauliflower in a single layer on a rimmed baking sheet and cook, uncovered, for 25 to 30 minutes, until the cauliflower is golden brown and caramelized.

3. While the cauliflower is roasting, make the dressing by combining all of the ingredients in a small bowl.

4. Return the roasted cauliflower to the original large bowl, then add the dressing. Season with salt and pepper and toss to coat. Transfer the cauliflower to a serving platter and garnish with more parsley.

VARIATION

 Leave out the pine nuts or substitute with ¼ cup golden raisins. Adjust the salt and pepper.

SERVES 4 TO 6
Nutrition information per serving (based on 6 servings): Calories: 91.3, Total Fat: 3.8g, Cholesterol: 0mg, Sodium: 16mg, Total Carbohydrates: 12.7g, Dietary Fiber: 1.0g, Sugars: 1.7g, Protein: 1.5g

Thai Coconut Rice

1 tablespoon olive oil

1 clove garlic, minced

4 scallions (white and light green parts), thinly sliced

1 teaspoon kosher salt, plus more as needed

1 lime, zested and juiced

1½ cups basmati rice

One 14-ounce can coconut milk

¼ cup finely chopped fresh cilantro

After traveling through Thailand for 2 months, cooking with the locals and eating the local cuisine, I discovered some delicious dishes that have become favorites, like this side dish. I eat this subtly sweet coconut rice for breakfast, lunch, or dinner (you might too if there are leftovers), but it pairs perfectly with any Asian-inspired meal you serve. Try it topped with fresh sliced mango or pineapple.

1. Warm the oil over medium-high heat in a medium saucepan. Add the garlic, scallions, salt, and lime zest. Stir constantly as you add in the rice. Cook for 3 to 4 minutes, continuing to stir, until the rice begins to turn opaque.

2. While the rice is cooking, combine the coconut milk and 2½ cups water in a medium saucepan and bring to a boil over high heat.

3. Pour the boiling coconut milk over the rice and stir to combine. Bring to a boil, reduce the heat to low, and cover the pan. Cook the rice for 15 minutes, remove the pan from the heat, and let the rice sit, covered, for another 5 minutes.

4. Fluff the rice with a fork and transfer to a serving dish. Squeeze the lime juice over the top, season with salt to taste, and sprinkle with the cilantro.

MAKES ABOUT 2½ CUPS POLENTA;
SERVES 4 TO 6

Nutrition information per serving (based on 6 servings): Calories: 175.1, Total Fat: 12g, Cholesterol: 0.1mg, Sodium: 13.6mg, Total Carbohydrates: 15.9g, Dietary Fiber: 1.5g, Sugars: 0.4g, Protein: 1.9g

Creamy Polenta

5 tablespoons olive oil

1 tablespoon kosher salt, plus more as needed

1 cup uncooked polenta

3 tablespoons milk

Freshly ground black pepper

The longer you cook the polenta, the more likely the seasoning will cook out and the thicker it will become, so wait until serving to season with salt and pepper. If the polenta becomes hard or dry, add a bit more water and oil (a teaspoon of each at a time) until you have reached the consistency you like.

Bring 5 cups water, 2 tablespoons of the olive oil, and the salt to a boil in a large saucepan. Add the polenta in a slow stream, stirring constantly with a wooden spoon. Reduce the heat to medium high and cook the polenta, stirring constantly, for 4 to 6 minutes until thickened to a sauce-like consistency. Remove the pan from the heat and stir in the milk and the remaining 3 tablespoons olive oil. Season to taste with more salt and pepper.

VARIATION

Replace the cow's milk with the same amount of soy or almond milk. Using soy milk means this recipe is no longer soy-free. Using almond milk means the recipe is no longer nut-free.

**MAKES ABOUT 6 CUPS;
SERVES 6 TO 8**
Nutrition information per ³/₄ cup:
Calories 204.1, Total Fat: 8.2g, Cho-
lesterol: 0mg, Sodium: 408.4mg, Total
Carbohydrates: 28.5g, Dietary Fiber:
7.1g, Sugars: 0.9g, Protein: 7.2g

Jalapeño, Black Bean, and Roasted Corn Salad

Two 15-ounce cans black
beans, rinsed and
drained

4 ears sweet corn, boiled
or grilled and kernels
removed

¹/₂ cup finely diced
red onions

¹/₂ cup finely diced
red bell peppers

2 jalapeños, minced

¹/₄ cup olive oil

¹/₄ cup balsamic vinegar

¹/₄ teaspoon cayenne

¹/₂ teaspoon ground
cumin

¹/₂ teaspoon dried
oregano

1 clove garlic, minced

Kosher salt and freshly
ground black pepper

2 tablespoons chopped
fresh cilantro

A cross between a salad and a salsa, this is best made with fresh corn kernels cut from the cob, and it's even better if you have time to grill the corn,
which adds a smoky flavor to the salsa. I love to serve this with Blackened
Fish Tacos (p. 155) or any other Mexican-style meal. Use as a chunky salsa
when entertaining, too.

In a large bowl, toss together the beans, corn kernels, onions, red bell peppers,
and jalapeño. Add the olive oil, balsamic vinegar, cayenne, cumin, oregano, and
garlic; toss to coat. Season to taste with salt and pepper. Cover and refrigerate
overnight to let the flavors meld. Before serving, toss again and sprinkle with the
chopped cilantro.

COOK'S TIP
If you're short on time, use
2 cans whole-kernel corn,
drained, in place of the
fresh corn.

SERVES 6 TO 8
Nutrition information per serving (based on 8 servings): Calories: 68.9, Total Fat: 5.3g, Cholesterol: 0mg, Sodium: 11.3mg, Total Carbohydrates: 5.2g, Dietary Fiber: 1.8g, Sugars: 1.7g, Protein: 1.6g

Brussels Sprouts with Lemon and Sage

2 pounds (4 cups) Brussels sprouts, stems trimmed, halved lengthwise

3 tablespoons olive oil

1 clove garlic, finely minced

2 teaspoons chopped fresh sage

1 lemon, juiced

1 teaspoon sugar

Coarse salt and freshly ground black pepper

Even if you don't like Brussels sprouts, you'll love this recipe. Cutting the veggies in half allows more surface to brown and caramelize, lending sweetness to the sometimes bitter taste. Add a sprinkling of fresh sage before serving if you like.

1. Bring a large pot of water to a boil. Add the Brussels sprouts and boil until just tender, 4 to 6 minutes. Transfer to a bowl.

2. Heat the olive oil in a large skillet over medium heat. Add the garlic and sage and cook for about 2 minutes. Add the Brussels sprouts and continue to cook for about 4 minutes, turning the vegetables a couple of times during cooking, until the Brussels sprouts are browned and just tender when poked with the tip of a knife. Season with the lemon juice, sugar, salt, and pepper and serve.

Chapter 6

Desserts

MAKES 36 TO 48 MINI TARTLETS
Nutrition information per tartlet (based on 48 tartlets): Calories: 147.7, Total Fat: 9.7g, Cholesterol: 23.9mg, Sodium: 13.6mg, Total Carbohydrates: 15.6g, Dietary Fiber: 0.9g, Sugars: 9.5g, Protein: 1.5g

Mini Chocolate Pecan Pie Tartlets

FOR THE CRUST

2½ cups unbleached all-purpose flour (read ingredient statement)

2 tablespoons sugar

2 teaspoons kosher salt

1 cup (2 sticks) very cold Earth Balance or butter substitute (read ingredient statement), cut into small pieces, plus more for the pan (optional)

½ cup ice water

Nonstick cooking spray (read ingredient statement); optional

FOR THE FILLING

2 cups pecans, toasted and finely chopped

3 large eggs

¾ cup light corn syrup

3 tablespoons granulated sugar

¼ packed cup dark brown sugar

3 tablespoons Earth Balance or butter substitute (read ingredient statement), melted

½ teaspoon kosher salt

2 teaspoons pure vanilla extract

1 cup semisweet dairy-free chocolate chips (read ingredient statement)

These mini tarts will be a huge hit on any dessert table and they couldn't be easier to make. I bake these in mini muffin tins, but you could also make them in 4-inch tart pans, as shown, which will yield 20 to 24 tartlets.

1. Make the crust by mixing together the flour, sugar, salt, and butter substitute in the bowl of a stand mixer. Mix until combined. Add in the water slowly and mix until a dough forms. Turn the dough out onto a clean surface and knead until it holds together. Divide the dough in half and flatten into two 6-inch disks. Wrap each disk in plastic and refrigerate for at least 20 minutes.

2. Position a rack in the center of the oven and heat the oven to 350°F. Lightly grease (with butter substitute or nonstick spray) two mini muffin pans.

3. Working with one disk of dough at a time, roll out the dough to a ⅛-inch thickness. Using a 2-inch round cookie cutter, cut out circles from the dough and fit them into the prepared pans, using your fingers to press the dough in the cups; set aside.

4. In a large bowl, whisk together all the filling ingredients except the chocolate chips. Sprinkle 2 to 3 chocolate chips in each dough cup, then pour 1 to 2 tablespoons of the filling over the top of the chocolate chips. Be sure the filling doesn't overflow. As you work, be sure to give the filling mixture a good stir because it settles at it sits.

5. Bake the tartlets for 15 to 20 minutes, until the tops are golden brown and the filling has set. Serve warm, alone or topped with a dollop of whipped cream or vanilla ice cream.

VARIATIONS

Instead of the all-purpose flour, use a gluten-free flour mix, like Bob's Red Mill. Because the consistency of this dessert doesn't rely on gluten to hold it together, the change in flour won't alter the taste much either.

Replace the corn syrup with ¾ cup honey or agave nectar. Check the ingredient statement of the butter substitute—many contain corn oil.

MAKES 48 BROWNIE BITES
Nutrition information per brownie bite: Calories: 85.4, Total Fat: 5.9g, Cholesterol: 34.6mg, Sodium: 59.5mg, Total Carbohydrates: 7.7g, Dietary Fiber: 0.5g, Sugars: 6.6g, Protein: 1.2g

Mini Fudge Brownie Bites

1 cup bittersweet chocolate chips (read ingredient statement)

1 cup (2 sticks) unsalted butter, cut into 1-inch chunks, plus more as needed

1¼ cups sugar

6 large eggs

1 cup unsweetened cocoa powder (read ingredient statement)

1 teaspoon kosher salt

1 teaspoon pure vanilla extract

These fudgy and delicious brownies happen to be naturally gluten-free since they contain no flour. I have served these a number of ways: à la mode, as brownie bite snacks in a lunchbox, and topped with frosting as mini cupcakes at a birthday party. Whichever way you choose, they are sure to be a huge hit!

1. Position racks in the upper and lower thirds of the oven and heat the oven to 350°F. Butter four mini muffin pans or line the cups with mini muffin paper liners.

2. In a double boiler or metal bowl set over a saucepan of barely simmering water, melt the chocolate and butter, stirring constantly until smooth. Remove the double boiler from the heat and whisk in the sugar, eggs, cocoa powder, salt, and vanilla until just combined.

3. Using a mini ice cream scoop, portion the batter into the prepared pans, filling each cup to the top. Bake for 8 to 12 minutes, or until the tops have formed a thin crust and they bounce back when poked (rotate the position of the pans halfway through baking). Cool the brownie bites in the pan on a rack for 10 minutes. Invert and let cool completely.

VARIATION

Use 1 cup (2 sticks) dairy-free butter substitute or margarine, like Earth Balance, instead of the butter. Use dairy-free chocolate chips. Be sure to read the ingredients, as they contain other potential allergens. Butter substitutes often use corn and soy and chocolate chips can contain soy or be at risk for nut contamination.

MAKES 12 COOKIES
Nutrition information per cookie: Calories: 161, Total Fat: 10.1g, Cholesterol: 7.8mg, Sodium: 159.4mg, Total Carbohydrates: 17.7g, Dietary Fiber: 1.5g, Sugars: 14.7g, Protein: 3g

Peanut Butter Huhus

1 cup sugar

1 large egg

1 cup peanut butter (read ingredient statement)

1 teaspoon kosher salt

½ teaspoon baking powder

1 teaspoon pure vanilla extract

One 12-ounce bag semisweet dairy-free chocolate chips (read ingredient statement)

Until writing this book, I never shared the recipe for these cookies, which gave me my "big break" into *Bon Appétit* magazine in 2009. They are surprisingly simple and extremely addictive. I always make a double batch and freeze some—my husband and I like to eat them right out of the freezer or crush them up onto ice cream.

The cookies happen to be gluten-free, but you would never know it. This is the perfect cookie to make for a large group of kids with varied allergies.

1. Position a rack in the center of the oven and heat the oven to 350°F. Line a rimmed baking sheet with parchment.

2. In the bowl of a stand mixer fitted with the paddle attachment (or in a large bowl and using a hand-held electric mixer), beat the sugar and egg for 2 to 3 minutes, until pale and fluffy. Reduce the speed to low; add the peanut butter, salt, baking powder, and vanilla. Beat until well mixed, about 1 minute. Stir in the chocolate chips.

3. Using a tablespoon-sized ice cream scoop, drop heaping balls of dough about 1 inch apart on the prepared baking sheet.

4. Bake the cookies until golden around the edges, 12 to 15 minutes. Let the cookies cool on the baking sheet for 1 to 2 minutes, then transfer to a wire rack and let cool completely. Store the cookies in an airtight container at room temperature for up to 1 week or freeze for up to 1 month.

COOK'S TIP
You can also make these cookies with the same amount of almond butter instead of peanut butter.

MAKES 24 BISCOTTI
Nutrition information per biscotti: Calories: 101.1, Total Fat: 5.9g, Cholesterol: 15.5mg, Sodium: 73.8mg, Total Carbohydrates: 10.7g, Dietary Fiber: 0.9g, Sugars: 8.5g, Protein: 2g

Lemon, Cranberry, and Pistachio Biscotti

¼ cup olive oil

¾ cup sugar

2 teaspoons pure vanilla extract

1 teaspoon lemon juice

1 tablespoon lemon zest

2 large eggs

2¼ cups unbleached all-purpose flour (read ingredient statement)

½ teaspoon kosher salt

1 teaspoon baking powder

½ cup dried cranberries

1½ cups pistachios

Biscotti in Italian means "twice baked," which is exactly how you make biscotti—and also what gives them their unique dry, crunchy quality.

1. Position a rack in the center of the oven and heat the oven to 350°F. Line a rimmed baking sheet with parchment.

2. In a large bowl, mix together the oil and sugar until well blended. Mix in the vanilla extract, lemon juice, zest, and eggs. Combine the flour, salt, and baking powder in a separate large bowl and stir to blend; gradually stir the flour mixture into the egg mixture. Mix in the cranberries and nuts.

3. Turn out the dough; you might need to lightly flour your work surface so the dough is easier to handle. Divide the dough in half and shape both halves into two logs about 2 x 8 inches and place on the prepared baking sheet.

4. Bake the logs for 15 to 25 minutes, or until golden brown and firm. Remove from the oven, cover with a clean kitchen towel and set aside to cool for 5 minutes. Cut the logs on the diagonal into ½-inch-thick slices. Lay the cookies on their sides on the baking sheet and bake for an additional 8 to 10 minutes, or until the biscotti are golden and have dried out. Transfer to a rack to cool. The biscotti will keep in an airtight container at room temperature for 5 to 7 days or in the refrigerator for up to 3 weeks.

VARIATIONS

 Leave out the pistachios or replace them with chocolate chips or another ingredient. This recipe is very adaptable, so just follow the basic technique and feel free to mix up the add-ins every time. Be sure to read the ingredient statements of substitute ingredients.

 Leave out the eggs and add the flour mixture into the sugar mixture slowly until you have reached a dough-like consistency. If the batter is too liquidy, add more flour ¼ cup at a time.

MAKES 12 CUPCAKES AND ABOUT 4 CUPS FROSTING

Nutrition information per cupcake: Calories: 541, Total Fat: 20.6g, Cholesterol: 21.1mg, Sodium: 570.4.mg, Total Carbohydrates: 85.2g, Dietary Fiber: 2.3g, Sugars: 64.9g, Protein: 3.9g

Apple Spiced Cupcakes with Cream Cheese Frosting

FOR THE CUPCAKES

1 cup sugar

2 cups unbleached all-purpose flour (read ingredient statement)

2 teaspoons baking soda

1 teaspoon kosher salt

1 teaspoon ground cinnamon

2 medium Gala apples, peeled, cored, and finely diced

2 large eggs

1 cup milk

½ cup (1 stick) unsalted butter, melted

FOR THE FROSTING

One 8-ounce package cream cheese, at room temperature

½ cup (1 stick) unsalted butter, at room temperature

1 tablespoon pure vanilla extract

½ teaspoon kosher salt

4 cups confectioners' sugar, plus more as needed

If you would like to try a healthy version of this recipe, replace the butter in the cake recipe with ½ cup applesauce. Although there isn't a healthy substitute for the butter in the frosting, you can use whipped mascarpone or plain yogurt as a cupcake topping instead.

MAKE THE CUPCAKES

1. Position a rack in the center of the oven and heat the oven to 400°F. Line a standard cupcake tin with paper liners and set aside.

2. Whisk together the sugar, flour, baking soda, salt, and cinnamon in a large bowl. Add the diced apples and toss to coat.

3. In a medium bowl, whisk together the eggs, milk, and butter. Gently fold the egg mixture into the flour mixture until just combined. Using a large ice cream scoop, portion the batter among the cups, filling them about three-quarters full. Bake for 15 to 18 minutes, or until golden brown and the center bounces back when poked. Let the cupcakes cool in the pan for a few minutes, then transfer to a wire rack to cool completely, about 15 minutes.

MAKE THE FROSTING

While the cupcakes are cooling, make the frosting. In a large bowl and using a hand-held electric mixer, beat the cream cheese and butter until smooth. Beat in the vanilla extract and salt. Gradually add the confectioners' sugar, beating until the frosting is smooth and creamy, about 2 minutes.

FINISH THE CUPCAKES

Frost the cooled cupcakes (you will probably have a bit of frosting left over) and serve.

SERVING SUGGESTION

After frosting the cupcakes, top each with a candied or toasted pecan and some maple sanding sugar for added presentation points. Doing so will make the recipe no longer nut-free.

COOK'S TIP

The consistency of your frosting can change with the weather, so always have extra confectioners' sugar on hand just in case your frosting is too runny.

The frosting and cupcakes can be made 1 day ahead and stored separately in the refrigerator. Bring to room temperature 2 hours before frosting.

VARIATIONS

 Replace the cow's milk with 1 cup soy or almond milk, and use ½ cup butter substitute for the unsalted butter. Using soy milk makes the recipe no longer soy-free. Using almond milk makes the recipe no longer nut-free. Be sure to read the ingredient statement for the butter substitute.

 Substitute the all-purpose flour with 2½ cups of your favorite gluten-free flour blend.

 To make this recipe vegan, replace the eggs, milk, and butter in the cupcakes recipe with 1 cup soy milk, ½ cup butter substitute, and 1 tablespoon apple cider vinegar. Allow to rest for 5 minutes, then continue with the recipe. Use the vegan frosting on p. 198. Doing so makes this recipe no longer soy-free. Be sure to read the ingredient statement for the butter substitute.

MAKES 36 BARS
Nutrition information per bar: Calories: 173.1,
Total Fat: 6.7g, Cholesterol: 1.7mg, Sodium: 2mg,
Total Carbohydrates: 28.1g, Dietary Fiber: 2.8g,
Sugars: 14.7g, Protein: 3.8g

Granola Bars

8 cups certified gluten-
free oats

2 cups nuts, roughly
chopped (a mix of
your choice)

¼ cup sesame seeds

1 cup dried fruit (a mix of
your choice), roughly
chopped

1 cup agave nectar

½ cup brown sugar

2 tablespoons vegan
butter substitute, such
as Earth Balance (read
ingredient statement)

1 teaspoon pure vanilla
extract

1 teaspoon sea salt

COOK'S TIP
Water stops the conduct-
ing of heat, so keep your
hands wet while pushing
the hot mixture into the
pan so you don't burn
yourself.

The best thing about this recipe is its flexibility—one day I make it with cherries, hazelnuts, and chocolate, and the next with almonds and apricots. Don't be afraid to try new flavor combinations every time. If you are anything like me, you will use whatever you have left over in your cabinets.

If you don't eat vegan, use honey instead of the agave nectar—it's less sweet.

1. Position two racks in the upper and lower thirds of the oven and heat the oven to 350°F.

2. In a large bowl, mix together the oats, nuts, and sesame seeds; spread out in a single layer on two baking sheets and toast for 10 to 15 minutes, or until golden brown and nutty smelling. Pour the hot oat mixture back into the bowl, add the dried fruit, and stir to combine. Let cool.

3. Meanwhile, combine the agave nectar, brown sugar, butter substitute, vanilla, and sea salt in a small saucepan. Bring the mixture to a boil over medium heat, then pour the syrup over the oat mixture and use a heatproof spatula to stir everything together, making sure the oat-nut mixture is evenly coated.

4. Scrape the mixture into a parchment-lined 13 x 9-inch baking dish. Wet your hands and immediately pat the mixture down firmly—it will be hot so be careful and keep your hands wet. Smooth the top with wet hands or a rubber spatula. Allow to cool at room temperature for up to 1 hour, then cut into bars approximately 2½ x 2¾ inches or another desired shape. Store the granola bars in an airtight container for up to 1 month at room temperature or up to 3 months in the fridge.

VARIATION

 Leave out the nuts and use extra dried fruit or chocolate chips instead. Be sure to read the ingredient statements of any substitute ingredients.

MAKES 24 COOKIES
Nutrition information per cookie: Calories: 125.1,
Total Fat: 5.8g, Cholesterol: 15.5mg, Sodium: 49.4mg,
Total Carbohydrates: 12.8g, Dietary Fiber: 0.2g,
Sugars: 7.5g, Protein: 0.8g

Mexican Wedding Cookies

1⅓ cups unbleached all-purpose flour (read ingredient statement)

½ teaspoon kosher salt

¾ cup (1½ sticks) unsalted butter, softened

¾ cup granulated sugar

¾ cup ground almonds

½ teaspoon pure vanilla extract

1 cup confectioners' sugar

I grew up calling these Mexican wedding cookies, but every culture has its own name—crescent cookies, Moroccan nut cookies, and several others. No matter what you call them, they're buttery and delicious!

1. Position racks in the upper and lower thirds of the oven and heat the oven to 325°F. Line two baking sheets with parchment.

2. Whisk together the flour and salt in a medium bowl; set aside. Put the butter, granulated sugar, and ground almonds in the bowl of a stand mixer fitted with the paddle attachment (or in a large bowl and using a hand-held electric mixer); beat on medium-high speed until pale and fluffy, about 2 minutes, scraping down the sides of the bowl as needed. Add the vanilla and beat to combine. Gradually add the flour mixture and beat until just combined.

3. Scoop tablespoon-size balls of dough onto the baking sheets and flatten them slightly with the back of a large spoon. Bake the cookies until golden brown but still soft, 15 to 20 minutes, rotating the sheets halfway through cooking. Transfer the baking sheets to a wire rack and let the cookies cool completely. Toss the cooled cookies in confectioners' sugar to coat. Store the cookies in an airtight container; they will keep for 5 to 7 days at room temperature or up to 3 weeks in the refrigerator.

VARIATIONS

  Use ¼ cup dairy-free butter substitute or margarine in place of the unsalted butter. Read the ingredient statement for potential other allergens.

  Replace the all-purpose flour with the same amount of your favorite gluten-free flour blend.

 Eliminate the nuts altogether. Instead make a dimple in each cookie prior to baking, and fill with raspberry jam.

MAKES 36 COOKIES
Nutrition information per cookie: Calories: 155.5,
Total Fat: 8.8g, Cholesterol: 24.1mg, Sodium: 87.6mg,
Total Carbohydrates: 21.7g, Dietary Fiber: 0.9g,
Sugars: 15.g, Protein: 1g

Salted Chocolate Chip Cookies

2 cups unbleached all-purpose flour (read ingredient statement)

½ teaspoon baking soda

1 teaspoon kosher salt

1 cup (2 sticks) unsalted butter, at room temperature

½ cup granulated sugar

1 cup packed light brown sugar

2 teaspoons pure vanilla extract

1 large whole egg

1 large egg yolk

One 12-ounce bag semisweet chocolate chips (read ingredient statement)

Sea salt

Everyone needs a go-to chocolate chip cookie recipe and this is it! The salty-sweet mix will send you to heaven and back. I always double the recipe because these cookies tend to disappear quickly.

1. Position racks in the upper and lower thirds of the oven and heat the oven to 350°F. Line two baking sheets with parchment.

2. In a small bowl, whisk together the flour, baking soda, and salt; set aside.

3. In the bowl of a stand mixer fitted with the paddle attachment (or in a large bowl and using a hand-held electric mixer), combine the butter and both sugars and beat on medium speed until light and fluffy. Reduce the speed to low and add the vanilla, egg, and egg yolk. Beat until well mixed, about 1 minute. Add the flour mixture and mix until just combined. Stir in the chocolate chips until just incorporated.

4. Using a tablespoon-size ice cream scoop, drop heaping balls of dough about 2 inches apart onto the prepared baking sheets. (You will have dough remaining for a third sheet; reuse one of the baking sheets once the first batch of cookies are baked.) Sprinkle with sea salt.

5. Bake the cookies until they are golden around the edges but still soft in the center, 8 to 10 minutes. Let the cookies cool on the baking sheets for 1 to 2 minutes, then transfer to a wire rack and let cool completely. Bake the remaining dough on one of the baking sheets. Store the cookies in an airtight container at room temperature for up to 1 week.

VARIATION

Substitute 1 cup dairy-free butter substitute or margarine, such as Earth Balance, for the butter. Use dairy-free chocolate chips. Be sure to read the ingredient statements for substitute ingredients. Butter substitutes often contain corn and soy and chocolate chips often contain soy.

MAKES 12 WHOOPIE PIES (24 INDIVIDUAL COOKIES)
Nutrition information per sandwich cookie: Calories: 693.7, Total Fat: 43.2g, Cholesterol: 129.9mg, Sodium: 641.9mg, Total Carbohydrates: 66.8g, Dietary Fiber: 2.5g, Sugars: 28.6g, Protein: 13g

Vanilla Whoopie Pies with Peanut Butter Filling

FOR THE WHOOPIE PIES

1 cup (2 sticks) unsalted butter

2 teaspoons kosher salt

2 teaspoons pure vanilla extract

1 tablespoon baking powder

1½ cups sugar

3 large eggs

4½ cups unbleached all-purpose flour (read ingredient statement)

1 cup milk

FOR THE PEANUT BUTTER FILLING

1 cup (2 sticks) unsalted butter, softened

1 cup creamy peanut butter (read ingredient statement)

5 cups confectioners' sugar, plus more as needed

¼ cup milk

1 teaspoon pure vanilla extract

I like to mix up the flavors of this recipe. For a strawberry cheesecake whoopie pie, replace the 1 teaspoon vanilla extract with 1 teaspoon strawberry extract. Fill the pies with the cream cheese frosting on p. 198 and roll the completed whoopie pie in graham cracker crumbs to serve. To make a Boston cream whoopie pie, make the whoopie pie as directed and fill with a whipped cream filling. Top with a drizzle of warm chocolate ganache (recipe on p. 207).

MAKE THE WHOOPIE PIES

1. Position racks in the upper and lower thirds of the oven and heat the oven to 400°F. Line two baking sheets with parchment.

2. In a large bowl, beat together the butter, salt, vanilla, baking powder, and sugar. Add the eggs one at a time, beating well after each addition. Add the flour and milk to the wet ingredients alternating each, beginning and ending with the flour.

3. Using a 1½-tablespoons-size ice cream scoop (about 1 ounce), drop mounds of dough 2 inches apart onto the prepared baking sheets.

4. Bake the cookies for 11 to 15 minutes, or until they are barely set on top but do not jiggle; they won't have colored at all or only very slightly. Allow to cool on the sheet for a few minutes, then transfer to a wire rack and let cool completely before filling.

MAKE THE FILLING

In a medium bowl and using a hand-held electric mixer, beat the butter on medium until pale and fluffy. Beat in the peanut butter, ½ cup of the confectioners' sugar, the milk, and vanilla. Gradually beat in the remaining confectioners' sugar, beating until smooth. Add more confectioners' sugar ½ cup at a time if the filling is too thin.

ASSEMBLE THE WHOOPIE PIES

1. Turn over half of the cooled cookies so the flat side is facing up. Transfer the filling to a piping bag fitted with a large flower tip and pipe about 2 tablespoons filling onto the flat cookies. If you don't have a pastry bag, use a tablespoon-size ice cream scoop to dollop filling onto the cookies, then spread with a butter knife.

2. Top the filled cookie halves with the remaining cookies (flat side down), then sandwich the cookies together.

VARIATION

 To make this dessert nut-free, replace the peanut butter filling with the vegan cream cheese frosting on p. 198. This frosting contains soy.

MAKES 18 CUPCAKES AND 3 TO 4 CUPS
FROSTING
Nutrition information per cupcake: Calories: 329.7,
Total Fat: 14.8g, Cholesterol: 0mg, Sodium: 438.7mg,
Total Carbohydrates: 46.4g, Dietary Fiber: 0.3g,
Sugars: 37.5g, Protein: 1.9g

Vanilla Cupcakes with Cream Cheese Frosting

FOR THE CUPCAKES

1½ cups unbleached
  all-purpose flour (read
  ingredient statement)

1 cup sugar

1 teaspoon baking soda

½ teaspoon kosher salt

½ cup vegetable oil (read
  ingredient statement)

1 cup soy milk (read
  ingredient statement)

1 tablespoon vanilla
  extract

1 tablespoon apple cider
  vinegar

FOR THE FROSTING

One 8-ounce package
  tofu cream cheese, at
  room temperature (read
  ingredient statement)

½ cup (1 stick) Earth
  Balance or butter
  substitute, at room
  temperature (read
  ingredient statement)

2 teaspoons pure vanilla
  extract

½ teaspoon kosher salt

4 cups confectioners'
  sugar, plus more as
  needed

Everyone deserves delicious desserts! As someone who is allergic to dairy, I cannot tell you how happy one of these cupcakes makes me when I eat it. It's all about the simple pleasures in life!

MAKE THE CUPCAKES

1. Position a rack in the center of the oven and heat the oven to 350°F. Line two standard cupcake tins with paper liners and set aside.

2. In a large bowl, whisk together the flour, sugar, baking soda, and salt. Add the vegetable oil, soy milk, and vanilla; whisk until the batter is smooth. Add the vinegar and stir for about 10 seconds.

3. Immediately spoon the batter into the cups, filling them about three-quarters full. Bake for 15 to 20 minutes, until the cupcakes turn golden brown on the edges and the center bounces back when poked. Let cool in the pan for a few minutes, then transfer to a wire rack and let cool completely for about 15 minutes.

MAKE THE FROSTING

Beat the cream cheese and butter substitute in a stand mixer on high until light and fluffy, about 1 minute. Add the vanilla and salt and beat to combine. Reduce the speed to low and add the confectioners' sugar, ½ cup at a time, mixing until the sugar is combined. Increase the speed to high and beat until you reach the desired consistency. Add more confectioners' sugar, a few tablespoons at a time, if the frosting is too thin.

FINISH THE CUPCAKES

Frost the cooled cupcakes (you will probably have a bit of frosting left over) and serve.

COOK'S TIP

To make these cupcakes lighter, substitute ½ cup applesauce for the ½ cup vegetable oil. It will slightly affect how much the cupcakes rise, but if you top them with frosting, you won't be able to tell the difference.

VARIATIONS

  Replace the all-purpose flour with a gluten-free flour mix. I like Bob's Red Mill.

 For the cupcakes, use 1 cup almond milk in place of the soy milk. Do not use rice milk, as it will effect the consistency of the cupcakes. For the frosting, replace the tofu cream cheese with a soy-free butter substitute. Using almond milk means this recipe is no longer nut-free. Read the ingredient statement of the butter substitute for other potential allergens.

MAKES 2 DOZEN COOKIES
Nutrition information per cookie: Calories: 212.2,
Total Fat: 9g, Cholesterol: 36.2mg, Sodium: 161.1mg,
Total Carbohydrates: 34.8g, Dietary Fiber: 1.6g,
Sugars: 16.7g, Protein: 2.9g

Oatmeal, Ginger, and Golden Raisin Cookies

1 cup (2 sticks) unsalted butter

1 cup packed dark brown sugar

½ cup granulated sugar

2 large eggs

1 teaspoon pure vanilla extract

1½ cups unbleached all-purpose flour (read ingredient statement)

1 teaspoon baking soda

1 teaspoon ground cinnamon

½ teaspoon ground allspice (read ingredient statement)

½ teaspoon ground ginger

½ teaspoon nutmeg

1 teaspoon kosher salt

3 cups old-fashioned oats

1 cup golden raisins

The flavor combination of all the spices makes these oatmeal-raisin cookies different from others. Golden raisins instead of dark ones add a touch of sweetness.

1. Position racks in the upper and lower thirds of the oven and heat the oven to 350°F.

2. In the bowl of a stand mixer fitted with the paddle attachment (or in a large bowl and using a hand-held electric mixer), cream the butter, brown sugar, granulated sugar, eggs, and vanilla until smooth.

3. In a large bowl, combine the flour, baking soda, cinnamon, allspice, ginger, nutmeg, and salt; stir into the sugar mixture. Once combined, stir in the oats and raisins. Using a tablespoon-size ice cream scoop, drop rounded balls of dough 1 inch apart onto ungreased cookie sheets (you'll need two).

4. Bake the cookies for 10 to 12 minutes, until light and golden. Do not overbake or they won't be chewy. Let the cookies cool for 2 minutes on the pans, then transfer to a wire rack to cool completely. Store in an airtight container for up to 1 week.

VARIATIONS

 Substitute ¾ cup dairy-free butter substitute or margarine for the unsalted butter. Read the ingredient statement for other potential allergens.

 Replace the 1½ cups all-purpose flour with 2 cups of your favorite gluten-free flour mix. Replace the oats with certified gluten-free oats.

MAKES 16 WEDGES
Nutrition information per wedge: Calories: 325.1, Total Fat: 12.1g, Cholesterol: 0mg, Sodium: 188.6mg, Total Carbohydrates: 59.5g, Dietary Fiber: 4.4g, Sugars: 39.3g, Protein: 3.5g

Oatmeal and Fig Crumble Wedges

FOR THE FILLING

2 cups dried figs, stemmed and finely chopped

1/3 cup sugar

1/2 teaspoon kosher salt

1 lemon, zested and juiced

1 teaspoon pure vanilla extract

FOR THE CRUST

1 3/4 cups old-fashioned oats

1 cup unbleached all-purpose flour (read ingredient statement)

3/4 cup whole wheat flour (read ingredient statement)

1 1/4 packed cups dark brown sugar

2 teaspoons ground cinnamon

1/4 teaspoon nutmeg

1 teaspoon baking soda

1/2 teaspoon kosher salt

1 cup (2 sticks) vegan butter substitute, chilled (read ingredient statement)

Nonstick cooking spray (read ingredient statement)

This is a great basic crumble bar recipe; experiment with different fillings or dried fruits in place of the figs. Leftover wedges will keep, covered with foil or in an airtight container, at room temperature for up to 5 days.

1. Make the filling by combining the chopped figs, 1 cup water, the sugar, and salt in a medium saucepan over medium heat. Bring the mixture to a simmer until the sugar dissolves, stirring constantly. Cover and simmer over low heat for 5 minutes. Uncover and continue cooking for about 10 minutes, or until the mixture has thickened. Stir in the lemon zest, juice, and vanilla. Set aside and let cool completely.

2. Position a rack in the center of the oven and heat the oven to 350°F. Spray an 8-inch springform pan with nonstick spray.

3. To make the crust, combine the oats, flours, brown sugar, cinnamon, nutmeg, baking soda, and salt in large bowl, whisking to blend. Using your fingers, blend in the butter substitute until small pea-size clumps form.

4. Transfer half of the crust mixture to the prepared pan and use your fingers to pack it into the bottom. Spread the filling evenly over the crust, then sprinkle the remaining crust mixture over the filling.

5. Bake the crumble until golden brown, about 35 minutes. Transfer the pan to a wire rack to cool, then cut into 16 wedges and serve.

VARIATION

  Use 1¾ cups of a gluten-free flour mix and 1¾ cups of certified gluten-free oats to make these wedges gluten-free.

MAKES 12 BARS

Nutrition information per bar: Calories: 243.6, Total Fat: 16.1g, Cholesterol: 15.5mg, Sodium: 409.6mg, Total Carbohydrates: 22g, Dietary Fiber: 2.4g, Sugars: 17.2g, Protein: 6.5g

Nutella–Peanut Butter Blondies

Nonstick cooking spray (read ingredient statement)

1 cup peanut butter (read ingredient statement)

1 large egg, beaten

¼ cup honey

1 teaspoon baking soda

1 large ripe banana, mashed

1 teaspoon pure vanilla extract

½ teaspoon kosher salt

½ cup semisweet chocolate chips (read ingredient statement)

⅓ cup Nutella® (or other chocolate hazelnut spread; read ingredient)

Sea salt, for sprinkling

When lining the pan with foil or parchment, leave a couple of inches overhanging on two opposite sides. These "handles" make removing the block of blondies from the pan easy.

1. Position a rack in the center of the oven and heat the oven to 350°F. Grease a square 9x9-inch pan with nonstick cooking spray and line it with foil or parchment for easy lifting.

2. In a large bowl, combine the peanut butter, egg, honey, baking soda, banana, vanilla, and salt; using a hand-held electric mixer, beat the ingredients on medium speed until well combined and the batter is smooth. Fold in the chocolate chips.

3. Scrape the batter into the prepared pan and smooth the top. Warm the Nutella to loosen it up, then dollop it 1 teaspoon at a time all over the top of the batter. Gently swirl the Nutella into the peanut butter mixture with a skewer or knife; don't swirl so much that the two completely blend together—you should still see streaks of Nutella on top of the peanut butter. Sprinkle with sea salt.

4. Bake for 20 to 30 minutes, or until the edges become golden brown and the center doesn't jiggle. Allow the blondies to cool for about 20 minutes, then use the foil or parchment handles to transfer the blondies to a rack to cool completely. Once cool, cut into 12 bars about 2¼x3 inches. The blondies will keep in an airtight container for up to 7 days.

VARIATIONS

 Replace the Nutella with dairy-free chocolate spread or eliminate it altogether and use additional peanut butter or any other nut butter. Read the ingredient statement of any substitute ingredient.

 Make these vegan by leaving out the egg, replacing the honey with ¼ cup agave nectar, using dairy-free chocolate chips, and replacing the Nutella with the same amount of peanut butter or any other nut butter. Read the ingredient statement of any substitute ingredient.

MAKES ONE 9-INCH CAKE (SERVES 8 TO 12)
AND ABOUT 4 CUPS FROSTING
Cake nutrition information per serving (based on 12 servings): Calories:
415.8, Total Fat: 20.3g, Cholesterol: 62mg, Sodium: 348.3mg, Total
Carbohydrates: 54.5g, Dietary Fiber: 0.8g, Sugars: 34g, Protein: 5.3g

Four-Layer Lemon Coconut Cake with Buttercream Frosting and Lemon Curd

FOR THE CAKE

1 cup vegetable oil, plus more for the pans (read ingredient statement)

2½ cups unbleached all-purpose flour (read ingredient statement)

1 teaspoon kosher salt

1 tablespoon baking powder

1 cup soy milk (read ingredient statement)

1 teaspoon pure vanilla extract

1 tablespoon lemon zest

2 cups sugar

4 large eggs

FOR THE LEMON CURD

1 cup fresh lemon juice

2 tablespoons lemon zest

1⅓ cups sugar

4 large eggs

1 teaspoon kosher salt

1¾ sticks Earth Balance or dairy-free butter substitute, cut into tablespoons (read ingredient statement)

I made this cake for my family in the winter of 2012, when we had 6 feet of snow in Boston and were snowed in. Needless to say, we finished the cake by the time we were able to get out of the house. This recipe is very easily adaptable to satisfy gluten-free eaters without anyone being the wiser.

MAKE THE CAKE

1. Position a rack in the center of the oven and heat the oven to 350°F. Brush two 9-inch round cake pans with oil and line the bottom of each with a round of parchment.

2. In a medium bowl, whisk together the flour, salt, and baking powder until well combined. In another medium bowl, stir together the soy milk, 1 cup vegetable oil, vanilla extract, and lemon zest.

3. In a stand mixer fitted with the paddle attachment, beat together the sugar and eggs at medium speed just until combined. Reduce the speed to low and add the flour and milk mixtures, alternating one at a time and mixing until just combined.

4. Divide the batter evenly between the cake pans and bake for 35 to 40 minutes, until the cakes are golden brown and the center bounces back when poked.

5. Cool the cake in the pans for at least 10 minutes, then invert onto a wire rack to cool completely before frosting (leave the parchment on the cake for now).

MAKE THE LEMON CURD

Whisk together the lemon juice, zest, sugar, eggs, and salt in a medium saucepan. Add the butter substitute and cook over medium-low heat, whisking constantly, until the curd thickens, about 10 minutes. Immediately pour the lemon curd through a fine-mesh sieve into a medium bowl, cover with plastic wrap (press the wrap directly on top of the curd), then chill. The curd will keep, refrigerated, for up to 1 week.

Lemon curd nutrition information per serving (based on 12 servings): Calories: 232.6, Total Fat: 15g, Cholesterol: 98.2mg, Sodium: 219.6mg, Total Carbohydrates: 24.2g, Dietary Fiber: 0.2g, Sugars: 22.8g, Protein: 2.3g

Buttercream frosting nutrition information per serving (based on 12 servings): Calories : 338.6, Total Fat: 15.3g, Cholesterol: 41.5mg, Sodium: 3.4mg, Total Carbohydrates: 50.3g, Dietary Fiber: 0g, Sugars: 48.6g, Protein: 0.3g

---

FOR THE BUTTERCREAM FROSTING

1 cup (2 sticks) Earth Balance or dairy-free butter substitute (read ingredient statement)

3 tablespoons soy milk (read ingredient statement)

2 teaspoons pure vanilla extract

5 cups confectioners' sugar, plus more as needed

2 to 3 cups shredded sweetened coconut, toasted, for serving

SERVING SUGGESTIONS

To amp up the coconut flavor, make coconut frosting. Replace 1 teaspoon of the vanilla extract with ½ teaspoon coconut extract.

This recipe can be adapted to make 24 cupcakes. Follow steps 1 through 3 for making the cake and divide the batter evenly among 2 standard cupcake tins, filling the cups three-quarters full. Bake the cupcakes for 15 to 20 minutes, or until golden brown and the tops bounce back when poked. Let cool completely then use a paring knife to cut a cone shape in the center of each cupcake. Fill with curd and then frost.

MAKE THE FROSTING

In a stand mixer or in a large bowl and using a hand-held electric mixer, beat the butter substitute on high until light and fluffy, about 1 minute. Add the soy milk and vanilla and beat to combine. Add the confectioners' sugar, ½ cup at a time, and mix on low until combined, then increase the speed to high and beat until you reach the desired consistency. Add more confectioners' sugar, ½ cup at a time, if the frosting is too thin.

ASSEMBLE AND FROST THE CAKE

1. Peel off the parchment from the cakes.

2. With a serrated knife, cut each cake layer in half horizontally. Spread the cut side of each cake layer with half of the lemon curd, then top with the remaining cake layers (cut side down) to form two sandwiched cakes.

3. Put 1 sandwiched cake on a cake stand or platter and spread ½ cup frosting over the top, then cover with the remaining sandwiched cake. Frost the top and sides of the 4-layer cake with the remaining frosting.

4. Pat the sides of the cake with toasted coconut and serve.

VARIATION

 Replace the soy milk with 1 cup almond milk to keep this recipe milk-free or use regular cow's milk, if you don't have a milk allergy or intolerance.

MAKES ONE 8-INCH ROUND CAKE (SERVES 12 TO 14) OR 24 CUPCAKES

Nutrition information per serving (based on 14 servings): Calories: 344.2, Total Fat: 10.9g, Cholesterol: 26.6mg, Sodium: 341mg, Total Carbohydrates: 58.7g, Dietary Fiber: 1.5g, Sugars: 41.5g, Protein: 4.3g

Dark Chocolate Cake with Chocolate Ganache

FOR THE CAKE

Butter substitute, for the pans

1 cup unbleached all-purpose flour (read ingredient statement), plus more for the pans

2 cups sugar

1 cup whole wheat flour (read ingredient statement)

3/4 cup unsweetened cocoa powder (read ingredient statement)

2 teaspoons baking soda

1 teaspoon baking powder

1 teaspoon kosher salt

2 large eggs

1 cup soy milk (read ingredient statement)

1 cup strong black brewed coffee (read ingredient statement)

1/2 cup applesauce (read ingredient statement)

1 teaspoon pure vanilla extract

This will become your go-to cake recipe because it easily adapts from a layer cake, to a bundt cake or cupcakes. Plus it's just really good! While the cake can be made with regular milk and butter, I find that the dairy-free version is much richer and produces better results.

This recipe uses 1 cup of coffee, which acts as an active rising agent in the cake. Regular coffee will not flavor the cake. I like to use espresso, for a richer flavor, but any kind of coffee works.

If you're making cupcakes, bake them for 18 to 20 minutes. When poked, they should bounce back fast and the center should not jiggle.

MAKE THE CAKE

1. Position a rack in the center of the oven and heat the oven to 350°F. Grease and flour two 9-inch round baking or springform pans and set aside.

2. Stir together the sugar, white and wheat flours, cocoa powder, baking soda, baking powder, and salt in large bowl. Add the eggs, soy milk, coffee, apple-sauce, and vanilla. Beat by hand or using a hand-held electric mixer on medium speed for 2 minutes (the batter will be thin). Divide the batter between the prepared pans.

3. Bake the cakes for 30 to 35 minutes, until the edges are beginning to brown and the center bounces back when poked. Cool for 10 minutes in the pan, then invert onto a wire rack and cool completely.

FOR THE GANACHE

One 12-ounce bag dairy-
free semisweet chocolate
chips, chopped (read
ingredient statement)

½ cup soy milk (read
ingredient statement)

¼ cup butter substitute
(read ingredient
statement)

MAKE THE GANACHE

1. Put the chocolate chips in a medium bowl.

2. In a small saucepan, bring the soy milk and butter substitute to a boil, then immediately remove the pan from the heat and pour it over the chocolate. Let the mixture rest for a minute, then using a rubber spatula, stir the ingredients together gently in a circular motion, working from the center out as an emulsion is formed.

FINISH THE CAKE

Pour a third of the warm ganache over one cake layer and spread it out to the edges. Top with the second cake layer, then pour the remaining ganache over the top, allowing it to drizzle down the sides.

VARIATION

Replace the soy milk with almond milk to keep the recipe dairy-free or feel free to use regular cow's milk if you don't have a milk allergy or intolerance. Using almond milk means this recipe is no longer nut-free.

MAKES ONE 9-INCH CHEESECAKE AND 3 CUPS
GLAZE; SERVES 12 TO 14

Nutrition information per serving (based on 14 serv-
ings): Calories: 181.7, Total Fat: 13g, Cholesterol: 26.6mg,
Sodium: 335.7mg, Total Carbohydrates 30g, Dietary
Fiber: 0.2g, Sugars: 18.2g, Protein: 3.2g

Classic Cheesecake Topped with Cranberry Glaze

FOR THE CRUST

1½ cups graham cracker crumbs (read ingredient statement)

3 tablespoons sugar

⅓ cup Earth Balance or butter substitute (read ingredient statement)

FOR THE CHEESECAKE

Two 8-ounce packages soy cream cheese (read ingredient statement)

One 12-ounce package soy sour cream (read ingredient statement)

¾ cup sugar

1 tablespoon lemon juice

1 teaspoon pure vanilla extract

2 large eggs, beaten

FOR THE CRANBERRY GLAZE

4 cups cranberries

2 cups sugar, plus more as needed

½ teaspoon ground cinnamon

1 lemon, juiced

½ teaspoon kosher salt, plus more as needed

¼ cup bourbon

Everyone has their kryptonite and cheesecake is mine. Because of my dairy allergy I can't eat regular cheesecake. This milk-free version will knock your socks off.

MAKE THE CRUST

1. Position a rack in the center of the oven and heat the oven to 325°F.

2. In a medium bowl, mix together the graham cracker crumbs, sugar, and melted butter substitute; press into the bottom of a 9-inch springform pan. Bake for 10 to 15 minutes, or until slightly golden.

MAKE THE CHEESECAKE

1. In a large bowl and using a hand-held electric mixer, beat together the cream cheese, sour cream, sugar, lemon juice, and vanilla until well blended. Add the eggs, one at a time, mixing on low after each addition until blended. Pour the mixture over the crust.

2. Bake the cheesecake for 50 to 60 minutes, or until the center doesn't move when you jiggle the pan and the edges are golden brown. Cool completely in the refrigerator (at least 2 hours), then loosen the cake from the pan. Refrigerate for 4 hours before serving.

MAKE THE GLAZE

Combine the cranberries, sugar, and cinnamon in a medium saucepan over medium-low heat. Cook until the cranberries have popped and the sugar has dissolved, stirring often, about 10 minutes. Once the mixture is reduced, remove the pan from the heat and stir in the lemon juice, salt, and bourbon. Season to taste with additional sugar and salt. Refrigerate the cranberry sauce until well chilled.

TO SERVE

Top the chilled whole cheesecake with the cranberry glaze, then slice and serve, or cut the cheesecake into individual slices and serve the cranberry glaze along side.

VARIATION

  Use gluten-free graham crackers and process into crumbs to make this cake gluten-free.

MAKES ONE 9-INCH TART; SERVES 12 TO 14
Nutrition information per serving (based on 12 servings): Calories: 284.5, Total Fat: 22.7g, Cholesterol: 190mg, Sodium: 19.5mg, Total Carbohydrates: 16.7g, Dietary Fiber: 0.4g, Sugars: 5.3g, Protein: 4.2g

Lemon Shortbread Tart

Nonstick cooking spray (read ingredient statement)

FOR THE CRUST
1¼ cups unbleached all-purpose flour (read ingredient statement)
½ cup confectioners' sugar
½ teaspoon kosher salt
1 cup (2 sticks) unsalted butter, at room temperature

FOR THE LEMON FILLING
7 large egg yolks
2 large eggs
1 cup plus 2 tablespoons granulated sugar
¼ cup lemon zest (from 3 to 4 lemons)
⅔ cup lemon juice (from about 5 lemons)
Pinch of kosher salt
¼ cup unsalted butter, cut into small pieces

If you make nothing else in this book, make this tart. This is always first on the menu for every dinner party and dessert buffet I cater or host, and now I'm happy to share this joy with you.

1. Spray a 9-inch fluted tart pan with a removable bottom with nonstick cooking spray. Position a rack in the center of the oven and heat the oven to 350°F.

2. Make the crust by mixing together the flour, confectioners' sugar, and salt in a large bowl. Using an electric hand-held mixer, mix in the butter until combined. Scrape the dough into the prepared pan and press firmly with your fingers into an even layer over the entire pan, including the sides. Refrigerate for 30 minutes, then bake the crust until golden brown, 15 to 20 minutes.

3. In a medium bowl, whisk together the yolks and whole eggs. Add the granulated sugar and whisk until just combined, then add the lemon zest, lemon juice, and salt. Transfer the egg–sugar mixture to a medium saucepan, heat on medium, and add the butter pieces. Cook, stirring constantly, until the mixture thickens to a pudding consistency, 6 to 8 minutes.

4. Immediately pour the filling through a single-mesh stainless-steel strainer set over a clean bowl. Once strained, pour the filling into the crust.

5. Bake the tart until the filling is shiny and doesn't jiggle when shaken, 15 to 20 minutes. Cool on a wire rack for about 45 minutes before serving. Don't cut before then or the filling will not have set.

VARIATIONS

 Replace the butter in the recipe with the same amount of Earth Balance or other butter substitute. Read the ingredient statement.

  Replace the all-purpose flour with a gluten-free flour mix, like Bob's Red Mill. Because the consistency of this dessert doesn't rely on gluten to hold it together, the change in flour won't alter the taste much either.

MAKES ONE 9-INCH PIE; SERVES 12 TO 14

Nutrition information per serving (based on 14 servings): Calories: 477.9, Total Fat: 20.5g, Cholesterol: 53.3mg, Sodium: 13.6mg, Total Carbohydrates: 76.6g, Dietary Fiber: 4.6g, Sugars: 42.2g, Protein: 5g

Blueberry Lemon Crumble Pie

FOR THE CRUST

2½ cups unbleached all-purpose flour (read ingredient statement), plus more as needed

2 tablespoons granulated sugar

2 teaspoons kosher salt

1 cup (2 sticks) very cold unsalted butter, cut into small pieces

½ cup ice water

FOR THE CRUMBLE TOPPING

1 cup old-fashioned oats

1 cup unbleached all-purpose flour (read ingredient statement)

1 packed cup brown sugar

1 teaspoon ground cinnamon

1 teaspoon kosher salt

½ cup (1 stick) unsalted butter, melted

FOR THE FILLING

8 cups (about 4 pints) blueberries, picked over for stems

½ cup granulated sugar

¼ cup cornstarch

1 teaspoon kosher salt

2 lemons, juiced and zested

The lemon juice and zest in the filling are what make this pie so special, adding brightness and tang. You won't need all the crumble topping, so freeze the extra and use it to top a pie or to add streusel to a muffin recipe, like the one for blueberry muffins on p. 225.

MAKE THE CRUST

1. In the bowl of a stand mixer fitted with the paddle attachment, mix the flour, sugar, salt, and butter until combined. Add the water slowly and mix until a dough forms. Turn the dough out onto a clean surface and knead until it holds together. Divide the dough in half and flatten each half into a 6-inch disk. Wrap each disk in plastic and refrigerate for at least 20 minutes.

2. On a lightly floured piece of parchment, roll out one disk of dough to a 12-inch round (save the other disk to make a second pie at a later date). With a dry pastry brush, sweep off excess flour; fit the dough into a 9-inch glass pie plate, pressing it into the edges. Trim the dough to a ½-inch overhang all around. Fold the edge of the dough over or under, and crimp as desired. Chill the prepared pie shell until firm, about 30 minutes.

MAKE THE TOPPING

In a medium bowl, mix together all the crumble topping ingredients and set aside.

MAKE THE FILLING AND FINISH THE PIE

1. Position a rack in the center of the oven and heat the oven to 400°F.

2. Put the blueberries in a large bowl. Add the sugar, cornstarch, salt, lemon juice, and zest. Toss to combine. Spoon the mixture into the chilled pie shell, mounding the berries in the center. Top with the crumble topping.

(continued)

3. Put the pie on a baking sheet and bake for 20 minutes, or until the crust begins to turn golden. Reduce the oven temperature to 350°F and continue baking, rotating the baking sheet halfway through, for 40 to 50 minutes, or until the juices are bubbling. (If the juices aren't bubbling after 50 minutes you can leave the pie in for another 5 to 10 minutes; just be careful the crust doesn't burn.) Transfer the pie to a wire rack to cool completely.

VARIATIONS

  Turn this into a lighter, gluten-free blueberry crumble. Skip making the crust and instead transfer the blueberry filling into a lightly greased 9-inch pie plate. Top with the crumble topping and bake for 40 minutes. For the crumble topping, be sure to use a gluten-free flour mix in lieu of the all-purpose flour, and use certified gluten-free oats.

 Replace the butter in the recipe with the same amount of Earth Balance or other butter substitute. Read the ingredient statement for other potential allergens.

 Replace the cornstarch with 3 tablespoons flour to thicken the juices when baking.

Chapter 7

Breads & Breakfast

MAKES 3 BAGUETTES
Nutrition information per serving (based on 8 servings): Calories: 187.5, Total Fat: 0.9g, Cholesterol: 0mg, Sodium: 292.6mg, Total Carbohydrates: 37.8g, Dietary Fiber: 1.2g, Sugars: 0.5g, Protein: 6.2g

Basic Baguette

3 cups bread flour (read ingredient statement), plus more for rolling the dough

1 teaspoon kosher salt

1 teaspoon sugar

1 teaspoon instant yeast (read ingredient statement)

1½ cups warm water

Olive oil, for drizzling

Sea salt, for sprinkling

SERVING SUGGESTION

Serve these baguettes with the Eggplant Caponata on p. 45 for a delicious appetizer or snack.

COOK'S TIP

This recipe is very flexible, so feel free to add flavorful ingredients during the first step of mixing. I've had great success with olives, sun-dried tomatoes, herbs, and pine nuts. Or try walnuts, cranberries, and 2 tablespoons honey—delicious! If you'd rather, shape the baguettes, top with the ingredients, and then bake to get baguettes that look like those shown in the photo.

If you're afraid of baking yeast breads, try this recipe. It's super simple and will build the confidence you need to expand your baking repertoire!

1. In a large bowl, mix the flour, salt, sugar, and yeast. Stir in the water, cover the bowl with plastic wrap and a clean kitchen towel, and let rest at room temperature for 2 to 3 hours, until the dough has doubled in size.

2. Position a rack in the center of the oven and heat the oven to 475°F. Line a baking sheet with parchment.

3. Scrape the dough onto a lightly floured work surface. Roll out the dough and shape into a ball, adding more flour to the surface and your hands as needed to prevent sticking. Cut the ball into thirds.

4. Roll out each ball into a long baguette (about 1½ inches wide by 7 or 8 inches long) and arrange on the prepared baking sheet. Drizzle with olive oil and sprinkle with sea salt. Bake for 15 to 20 minutes, until the baguettes are golden brown.

Pizza Dough

1¹/₂ cups unbleached all-purpose flour (read ingredient statement), plus more for rolling the dough

1¹/₂ cups bread flour (read ingredient statement)

2 teaspoons kosher salt

2 teaspoons sugar

1 teaspoon instant yeast (read ingredient statement)

1¹/₂ cups warm water

Topping of your choice

SERVING SUGGESTION

For a fun afternoon or evening, host a BYOT (bring your own toppings) party. You supply the dough for the crust and guests bring and share toppings. This makes for a great time with kids and adults. Just be mindful of allergens and be sure to read the ingredient statements.

You can go with traditional toppings for your pizza (be sure they are appropriate for any allergens you're dealing with), but why not get creative? Try one of these: tomato sauce, garlic, and basil; thinly sliced potatoes, yellow onions, and rosemary; arugula, sliced fresh tomatoes, and grated Parmesan; for dessert: Nutella, olive oil, sea salt, bananas, and confectioners' sugar.

1. In a large bowl, mix the flours, salt, sugar, and yeast. Stir in the water, cover the bowl with plastic wrap and a clean kitchen towel, and let rest at room temperature for 2 to 3 hours, until the dough has doubled in size.

2. Position racks in the upper and lower thirds of the oven and heat the oven to 475°F. Line 2 rimmed baking sheets with parchment.

3. Scrape the dough onto a lightly floured work surface. Roll the dough in the flour then shape into a ball, adding more flour to your hands and to the surface as needed to prevent sticking. Cut the dough in half, then roll out each half to your preferred shape and thickness. Transfer the dough to the prepared baking sheets, then top with your desired toppings.

4. Bake the pizzas for 15 to 20 minutes, until they're golden brown and the cheese has melted (if using).

MAKES ONE LOAF, ABOUT 7 INCHES IN DIAMETER

Nutrition information per serving (based on 12 servings): Calories: 169.2, Total Fat: 5.6g, Cholesterol: 0mg, Sodium: 631.7mg, Total Carbohydrates: 26.1g, Dietary Fiber: 2.2g, Sugars: 0g, Protein: 4.1g

Whole Wheat Olive Bread

1½ cups bread flour (read ingredient statement)

1½ cups whole wheat flour (read ingredient statement)

1 teaspoon instant yeast (read ingredient statement)

1½ teaspoons kosher salt

1 cup chopped Kalamata olives

1½ cups warm water

Cornmeal, for dusting the surface

The term whole wheat refers to the whole-grain version of wheat (as all parts of the grain, including the germ, bran, and endosperm, are used). When working with whole wheat flour, you'll need to include a portion of regular bread flour because that's what makes the bread airy and springy.

If you don't like olives, you can leave them out or replace them with walnuts, raisins, or even a mixture of herbs of your choice. If you don't use olives, add 1½ teaspoons more kosher salt (for a total of 1 tablespoon) to make up for the salt in the olives.

1. In a large bowl, stir together the flours, yeast, salt, and olives until just combined. Stir in the water, cover the bowl with plastic wrap and a clean kitchen towel, and let rest at room temperature for 12 to 18 hours, until the dough has doubled in size.

2. Once the dough has risen, position a rack in the center of the oven and heat the oven to 475°F.

3. Dust your work surface with cornmeal, then shape the dough into a ball (or your preferred shape) for baking. Transfer to a baking sheet and bake the bread for 15 to 20 minutes, until golden brown. Transfer the loaf to a wire rack and let cool for at least 10 minutes before cutting to prevent an early release of steam (which would dry out the bread).

VARIATION

 If you are allergic to corn, use bread flour or whole wheat flour for rolling out the dough instead of the cornmeal.

MAKES 8 TO 10 SCONES
Nutrition information per serving (based on 10 servings): Calories: 165.6, Total Fat: 7.8g, Cholesterol: 37.3mg, Sodium: 157.6mg, Total Carbohydrates: 20.6g, Dietary Fiber: 1.3g, Sugars: 0.5g, Protein 3.5g

Iced Pumpkin Scones

FOR THE SCONES

2 cups unbleached all-purpose flour (read ingredient statement)

1/3 cup firmly packed brown sugar

1 tablespoon baking powder

1 teaspoon kosher salt

1/2 teaspoon ground cinnamon

1/2 teaspoon ground nutmeg

1/2 teaspoon ground ginger

6 tablespoons (3/4 stick) cold butter, cut into pieces

1/2 cup canned pure pumpkin purée

3 tablespoons soy milk (read ingredient statement)

1 large egg

FOR THE SPICED ICING

1 cup confectioners' sugar

2 tablespoons soy milk (read ingredient statement), plus more as needed

1/4 teaspoon ground cinnamon

Pinch of ground nutmeg

Pinch of ground ginger

Toasted pepitas (optional; see "Cook's Tip" on p. 169)

These scones are delicious with or without the pepitas. If you use them, try the sweet variation.

MAKE THE SCONES

1. Position a rack in the center of the oven and heat the oven to 425°F. Line a baking sheet with parchment; set aside.

2. In the bowl of a stand mixer fitted with a paddle attachment, mix the flour, sugar, baking powder, salt, cinnamon, nutmeg, and ginger. With the mixer on medium, add the butter to the dry ingredients and mix until the mixture is crumbly.

3. In a separate bowl, whisk the pumpkin purée, soy milk, and egg. Pour the wet ingredients into the dry and mix until combined. Scrape the dough onto a lightly floured surface and shape it into a rectangle about 1 inch wide and 8 inches long. Using a sharp knife, cut the dough into 8 to 10 triangles. Arrange the scones on the prepared baking sheet, leaving space between them, and bake for 13 to 15 minutes, until golden brown. Let cool completely before icing the scones.

MAKE THE ICING

Whisk all the ingredients in a small bowl until creamy. Add more soy milk if the icing is too thick. Drizzle over each scone and top with the pepitas, if using.

VARIATIONS

 Replace the butter with Earth Balance or another butter substitute. Read the ingredient statement.

 Substitute the all-purpose flour with a gluten-free flour.

 Substitute the soy milk with almond milk. Doing so will make this recipe no longer nut-free.

 Replace the egg with an additional 1 tablespoon soy milk and 1 teaspoon apple cider vinegar.

MAKES ABOUT 14 SCONES
Nutrition information per serving: Calories: 149.6,
Total Fat: 7g, Cholesterol: 17.8mg, Sodium: 241.2mg,
Total Carbohydrates: 21.7g, Dietary Fiber: 1.1g,
Sugars: 7.5g, Protein: 2g

Lemon-Ginger-Corn Scones

1 cup unbleached
all-purpose flour (read
ingredient statement),
plus more as needed

1/2 cup whole wheat
flour (read ingredient
statement)

1/2 cup cornmeal

2 teaspoons baking
powder

1 teaspoon kosher salt

1/2 cup (1 stick) butter
substitute (read
ingredient statement)

3 tablespoons granulated
sugar, plus more for
sprinkling

3 tablespoons brown
sugar

1 to 2 lemons, zested
and juiced

1/4 cup candied ginger,
chopped (read
ingredient statement)

1/3 cup soy milk (read
ingredient statement),
plus more for brushing

Sanding sugar

COOK'S TIP

When baking with a milk-
free substitute, don't use
rice milk, as it will affect
the consistency of your
baked goods.

When I feel a cold coming on, I make these for the perfect pick-me-up treat. Infused with ginger, they make me feel better in no time!

1. Position a rack in the center of the oven and heat the oven to 400°F. Line a baking sheet with parchment.

2. In a large bowl, mix the flours, cornmeal, baking powder, and salt. Using a fork or your fingers, add the butter substitute and mix until crumbs form. Mix in the sugars, lemon zest, and candied ginger, then stir in the soy milk and the juice of 1 lemon. If the mixture is too sticky, add more all-purpose flour, ¼ cup at a time; if it's too crumbly, add more lemon juice, 1 teaspoon at a time. You are looking for a workable dough-like consistency.

3. Turn out the dough onto a lightly floured surface and knead it for 2 minutes, until it's smooth and has come together. Stretch and shape the dough into a long rectangle about 3 inches wide by 12 inches long; using a sharp knife, cut the dough into 14 triangles. Arrange the triangles on the baking sheet, leaving space between, and brush the tops with more soy milk and sprinkle with the sanding sugar.

4. Bake for 15 to 20 minutes, until the tops just start to turn golden brown. The scones can be stored, covered, at room temperature for up to 5 days.

VARIATION

 Use almond milk instead of soy milk. Doing so will make the recipe no longer nut-free.

MAKES ABOUT 1 DOZEN MUFFINS
Nutrition information per muffin: Calories: 224.2, Total Fat: 9.9g, Cholesterol: 41.4mg, Sodium: 387.4mg, Total Carbohydrates: 30.8g, Dietary Fiber: 1.2g, Sugars: 11.5g, Protein: 3.7g

Lemon and Olive Oil Corn Muffins

1 cup yellow cornmeal

1 cup unbleached all-purpose flour (read ingredient statement)

2/3 cup sugar, plus more for sprinkling

1 tablespoon baking powder

1 teaspoon baking soda

1 teaspoon kosher salt

1/4 cup olive oil

1/4 cup (1/2 stick) unsalted butter, melted

2 large eggs, lightly beaten

1/3 cup cream cheese (read ingredient statement)

1 lemon, zested

1/2 teaspoon pure lemon extract

1/2 teaspoon pure vanilla extract

2/3 cup soy milk (read ingredient statement) or water

Olive oil adds a rich complexity to these muffins while maintaining healthy fats and delicious texture and taste.

1. Position a rack in the center of the oven and heat the oven to 350°F. Line one standard 12-cup muffin tin with paper liners.

2. In a medium bowl, combine the cornmeal, flour, sugar, baking powder, baking soda, and salt; set aside.

3. In the bowl of a stand mixer fitted with the paddle attachment, combine the olive oil, butter, eggs, cream cheese, lemon zest, lemon extract, vanilla extract, and soy milk (or water). With the mixer on low, slowly add the dry ingredients and process until just combined.

4. Portion the batter evenly into the muffin cups and sprinkle with more sugar. Bake the muffins until they're golden around the edges and bounce back when poked, 18 to 20 minutes. Let the muffins cool before removing them from the tin.

VARIATIONS

 Replace the butter with a butter substitute, and replace the cream cheese with tofu cream cheese or 1/4 cup soy yogurt. Read all the ingredient statements.

 Use almond milk instead of soy milk. Doing so will make the recipe no longer nut-free.

MAKES ONE 9 X 5-INCH LOAF
Nutrition information per serving (based on 12 servings): Calories: 201.5, Total Fat: 4.3g, Cholesterol: 0mg, Sodium: 487.5mg, Total Carbohydrates: 42.1g, Dietary Fiber: 3.5g, Sugars: 26g, Protein: 2.5g

Chocolate Chip–Banana Bread

Nonstick cooking spray (read ingredient statement)

1½ cups whole wheat flour (read ingredient statement)

2 teaspoons baking soda

2 teaspoons baking powder

1 teaspoon kosher salt

1 cup semisweet chocolate chips (read ingredient statement)

1 cup sugar

½ cup unsweetened applesauce (read ingredient statement)

3 mashed ripe bananas

¼ cup soy milk (read ingredient statement)

1 teaspoon pure vanilla extract

This recipe can be made as a loaf, regular-size muffins, or mini muffins. If making standard-size muffins, bake for 15 to 20 minutes, until the tops are golden brown and bounce back when poked; for mini muffins, bake for 10 to 15 minutes.

1. Position a rack in the center of the oven and heat the oven to 350°F. Spray a 9 x 5-inch loaf pan with nonstick cooking spray or line it with parchment.

2. In a medium bowl, whisk the flour, baking soda, baking powder, salt, and chocolate chips; set aside.

3. In another medium bowl, beat the sugar, applesauce, mashed bananas, soy milk, and vanilla until well combined. Stir in the flour mixture until just incorporated.

4. Pour the batter into the prepared pan. Bake the bread for 45 to 55 minutes, until a tester inserted into the center comes out clean. Turn out onto a rack and let cool completely.

VARIATIONS

  Use a gluten-free flour mix, like Bob's Red Mill, in place of the whole wheat flour.

 Substitute almond milk for the soy milk. Doing so will make this recipe no longer nut-free. In addition, many chocolate chips contain soy lecithin, so if you are allergic to soy be sure to read the ingredient statements.

MAKES 1¹/₂ DOZEN MUFFINS
Nutrition information per muffin: Calories: 180.1,
Total Fat: 4.8g, Cholesterol: 41.4mg, Sodium:
223.4mg, Total Carbohydrates: 31.2g, Dietary
Fiber: 1.5g, Sugars: 14.4g, Protein: 3.6g

Crumb-Topped Blueberry Muffins

**FOR THE CRUMB
TOPPING**

1¹/₄ cups unbleached
all-purpose flour (read
ingredient statement)

¹/₂ cup firmly packed
brown sugar or
granulated sugar

¹/₂ teaspoon kosher salt

³/₄ teaspoon ground
cinnamon

¹/₂ cup (1 stick) unsalted
butter, melted

FOR THE MUFFINS

2¹/₂ cups unbleached
all-purpose flour (read
ingredient statement)

¹/₂ cup whole wheat
flour (read ingredient
statement)

1 tablespoon baking
powder

1 teaspoon kosher salt

6 tablespoons (³/₄ stick)
unsalted butter,
softened

1 cup granulated sugar

1 large whole egg

2 large egg yolks

2 teaspoons pure vanilla
extract

1 lemon, zested

1¹/₄ cups milk

3 cups fresh blueberries

If fresh blueberries aren't in season, simply use frozen blueberries, but be sure to add them to the batter directly from the freezer or they will become too mushy and turn your batter blue.

If you'd rather not use the crumble topping, sprinkle some extra granulated sugar on top of the muffins before baking to give them the crunchy bakery-like top (but I highly recommend the crumble!).

MAKE THE CRUMB TOPPING

In a bowl, whisk together the flour, brown sugar, salt, and cinnamon. Pour in the melted butter and toss until large crumbs form. Set aside.

MAKE THE MUFFINS

1. Position a rack in the center of the oven and heat the oven to 375°F. Line two standard 12-cup muffin tins with paper liners.

2. Sift together both flours, baking powder, and salt into a large bowl.

3. In the bowl of a stand mixer fitted with the paddle attachment, cream the butter with the sugar until the mixture becomes pale and fluffy. Add the egg and yolks, vanilla, and lemon zest and continue to mix until well combined. Reduce the speed to low and add the flour and milk, alternating between additions. Gently fold in the blueberries by hand.

4. Portion the batter evenly among the prepared cups, filling them three-quarters of the way full. Sprinkle the crumb topping evenly over the batter in each cup.

5. Bake the muffins for 20 to 30 minutes, until they're golden brown and spring back when poked. Let cool on a wire rack for 15 minutes before removing from the tin.

(continued)

Crumb-Topped Blueberry Muffins *(continued)*

COOK'S TIP

If you want to make these muffins or other baked goods with whole wheat flour, use three-quarters wheat flour and one-quarter all-purpose flour or the baked goods will be too dense. For example, if the recipe calls for 1 cup of all-purpose flour, use ¾ cup whole wheat flour and ¼ cup all-purpose flour.

VARIATION

Replace the butter with Earth Balance or another butter substitute. Replace the milk with 1 cup soy milk or 1 cup tofu sour cream for an even richer flavor. Using soy milk and/or tofu sour cream means the recipe is no longer soy-free. Be sure to read the ingredient statements of alternate ingredients.

MAKES 12 TO 14 BUNS
Nutrition information per bun (based on 14):
Calories: 300.5, Total Fat: 7.9g, Cholesterol: 47.5mg,
Sodium: 439.5mg, Total Carbohydrates: 49.4g,
Dietary Fiber: 1.4g, Sugars: 8.7g, Protein: 7.5g

Brioche Buns

3 cups unbleached all-purpose flour (read ingredient statement), plus more for the work surface

3 cups bread flour (read ingredient statement)

1 teaspoon active dry yeast

2½ teaspoons kosher salt

¾ cup sugar

1¾ cups milk, heated until warm

½ cup (1 stick) unsalted butter, melted, plus more for the bowl and the pan

3 large eggs, divided

SERVING SUGGESTIONS
Serve these buns with the Sloppy Joes recipe on p. 120 or make French toast from them.

COOK'S TIP
In the winter when it's cold outside, it will take longer for dough to rise than in the warmer months. Heat, like salt and sugar, is essential "food" for the yeast and makes the yeast react and activate.

You can sprinkle sea salt, sesame seeds, poppy seeds, or any number of other toppings on top of the egg wash just before baking the buns. Or sprinkle with cinnamon-sugar for a sweet variation.

This recipe makes 2-inch buns; you can adjust the size up or down, but adjust the cooking time, too.

1. In the bowl of a stand mixer fitted with the paddle attachment, mix both flours, the yeast, salt, and sugar. In a medium bowl, stir together the milk, melted butter, and 2 eggs. With the mixer on low, slowly pour in the milk mixture and beat until a soft dough has formed. Beat on high for another 5 minutes, until shiny.

2. Butter the inside of a large bowl and put the dough ball in the bowl, turning to coat with the butter. Cover the bowl with plastic wrap and let stand in a warm spot for 1 to 2 hours, until the dough has doubled in size.

3. Position a rack in the center of the oven and heat the oven to 375°F. Butter a 9-inch round pan and set aside. Lightly flour your work surface.

4. Scrape the dough onto the prepared work surface and roll it in the flour. Cut the dough into 2-inch pieces, then shape into balls. Arrange the dough balls in a circle in the prepared pan; the dough balls should be touching. Cover the pan loosely with a clean kitchen towel and let stand on top of the oven while it's heating until the rolls have risen slightly, about 30 minutes.

5. In a small bowl, whisk the remaining egg, then generously brush it onto the rolls. Sprinkle with your desired toppings (if any; see the headnote).

6. Bake the buns until golden brown, 20 to 25 minutes, rotating the pan halfway through cooking. Let the rolls cool for at least 10 minutes before serving.

VARIATION

Replace the butter with Earth Balance or another butter substitute. Replace the milk with 1½ cups soy milk, almond milk, or warm water. Using soy milk makes this recipe no longer soy-free. Using almond milk makes this recipe no longer nut-free. Read the ingredient statements of all alternate ingredients for potential allergens.

MAKES THREE 9X5-INCH LOAVES
Nutrition information (based on 12 servings from 1 loaf): Calories: 279.1, Total Fat: 14.7g, Cholesterol: 41.4mg, Sodium: 106.8mg, Total Carbohydrates: 36.1g, Dietary Fiber: 1.6g, Sugars: 19.9g, Protein: 3.3g

Chocolate Babka

FOR THE STREUSEL TOPPING (MAKES ABOUT 4 CUPS)

1²/₃ cups confectioners' sugar

1¹/₃ cups unbleached all-purpose flour (read ingredient statement)

³/₄ cup (1¹/₂ sticks) unsalted butter, at room temperature

FOR THE DOUGH

1¹/₂ cups milk, heated until warm

2 teaspoons instant yeast

³/₄ cup sugar, plus more for the yeast

2 large eggs

2 egg yolks

6 cups unbleached all-purpose flour (read ingredient statement), plus more for the work surface

2 teaspoons kosher salt, plus more as needed

1 cup (2 sticks) unsalted butter, cut into 1-inch chunks, at room temperature, plus more as needed

The babka can be stored at room temperature, covered, for up to 5 days or frozen for up to 1 month. If freezing, freeze the babka before baking (wrap well in plastic) and then thaw and bake just before serving. If you'd rather, use one of the dough balls to make the Cinnamon Sticky Buns (recipe on p. 232).

MAKE THE STREUSEL

In a large bowl, combine the confectioners' sugar, flour, and butter. Using a fork, stir and mash the mixture until the ingredients are fully combined with clumps ranging in size from crumbs to 1 inch. Set aside.

FOR THE DOUGH

1. Pour the milk into a small bowl. Sprinkle the yeast and a pinch of sugar over the milk and let it sit for about 5 minutes.

2. In a medium bowl, whisk the sugar, eggs, and yolks. Add the yeast mixture to the sugar–egg mixture and whisk to combine.

3. In the bowl of a stand mixer fitted with the paddle attachment, combine the flour and salt. With the mixer on low, add the sugar–yeast mixture and beat until the flour is well incorporated. Add the butter and beat until a soft, shiny dough forms, about 10 minutes.

4. Turn the dough out onto a lightly floured surface and knead until smooth. Grease a large bowl with butter, add the dough ball, and turn to coat evenly. Cover the bowl tightly with plastic wrap and set aside in a warm place to rise, about 1 hour.

MAKE THE FILLING

While the dough is rising, make the filling. Put the chocolate, sugar, and cinnamon in a large bowl and toss to combine. Using your fingers, mix in the butter until well combined; set the filling aside.

FOR THE FILLING

2¼ pounds semisweet chocolate (read ingredient statement), very finely chopped

1 cup sugar

2½ tablespoons ground cinnamon

¾ cup (1½ sticks) unsalted butter, at room temperature

FOR THE EGG WASH

1 large egg

1 tablespoon milk

PREPARE THE BABKA

1. Generously butter three 9x5-inch loaf pans and line them with parchment. Make the egg wash by beating the egg with the milk; set aside.

2. Punch down the dough, then transfer to a clean surface and cut it into three equal pieces. Keep two pieces covered with plastic wrap while working with the remaining piece. On a floured surface, roll out the dough into a ⅛-inch-thick square.

3. Brush the edges of the dough square with some of the egg wash. Crumble a third of the chocolate filling evenly over dough, leaving a ¼-inch border. Roll up the dough tightly, jelly-roll style, then pinch the ends together to seal. Twist the whole roll five or six times and set it in one of the prepared pans. Repeat with the remaining two pieces of dough and filling.

4. Position racks in the upper and lower thirds of the oven and heat the oven to 350°F.

5. Brush the top of each loaf with egg wash, then crumble a third of the streusel topping over each loaf. Loosely cover each pan with plastic wrap and let stand in a warm place for 20 to 30 minutes.

6. Bake the loaves until golden brown, about 55 minutes. Lower the oven temperature to 325°F and bake for another 15 to 20 minutes. Remove the pans from the oven and transfer to wire racks until completely cooled. Cut the loaf right from the pan—it will last longer than if you remove it from the pan.

VARIATION

 Replace the butter with Earth Balance or another butter substitute. Replace the cow's milk with soy milk or almond milk. Don't use rice milk, as it will affect the consistency of the final product. Using soy milk makes this recipe no longer soy-free. Using almond milk makes this recipe no longer nut-free. Be sure to read the ingredient statements of all substitute ingredients.

MAKES 12 CINNAMON BUNS
Babka dough nutrition information (based on 1 ball): Calories: 110.7, Total Fat: 4.4g, Cholesterol: 25.9mg, Sodium: 104.3mg, Total Carbohydrates: 15.5g, Dietary Fiber: 0.4g, Sugars: 3.6g, Protein: 2.3g

Sticky bun filling nutrition information (based on 1 roll): Calories: 137.2, Total Fat: 4.8g, Cholesterol: 0mg, Sodium: 27.7mg, Total Carbohydrates: 28.5g, Dietary Fiber: 0.7g, Sugars: 27.7g, Protein: 0.6g

Cinnamon Sticky Buns

Nonstick cooking spray (read ingredient statement)

2¼ cups light corn syrup

1½ cups firmly packed dark brown sugar

2½ cups chopped pecans

1 dough ball from the Chocolate Babka recipe (see pp. 230–231)

½ cup sour cream (read ingredient statement)

1 tablespoon ground cinnamon

COOK'S TIP

It's important that you turn out the buns from the muffin pan immediately after removing the pan from the oven. Otherwise, the buns will stick to the pan and will be impossible to get out. Once you've removed the sticky buns, put the pan in the sink and soak in hot water for easier cleanup later.

This recipe uses one of the dough balls from the babka as the base, so if you have an extra in your freezer, these cinnamon buns will come together quickly. Be sure to thaw the dough in the refrigerator the night before you want to make these buns. (Note: This recipe calls for only a third of the dough recipe on pp. 230–231. You can use more of the dough if you like and make double or triple the amount of cinnamon buns; just adjust the amount of topping and filling accordingly.)

1. Position a rack in the center of the oven and heat the oven to 350°F. Spray a regular muffin tin with nonstick cooking spray.

2. Into each individual muffin cup, pour 3 tablespoons corn syrup, 1 tablespoon brown sugar, and 2 tablespoons pecans; set the filled muffin pan aside.

3. Roll out the dough to a 15 x 20-inch rectangle that's ¼ inch thick. Using a spatula, spread the sour cream over the surface of the dough, leaving a ½-inch border. Dust the sour cream with the cinnamon, sprinkle with the brown sugar, then sprinkle with the remaining chopped pecans. Starting on one short side, roll up the dough jelly-roll style to form a roll that's about 18 inches long by 3 inches in diameter (trim the ends or tuck them in so that you end up with a roll about 18 inches).

4. Using a sharp knife, cut the dough into twelve 1½-inch-thick slices; set one slice in each muffin cup. Cover the muffin pan with a clean, dry kitchen towel and let the dough rise in a warm place for 20 to 30 minutes.

5. Once the dough has risen, bake the buns until dark golden brown, about 40 minutes.

6. Remove the pan from the oven and immediately invert the buns onto a parchment-lined cookie sheet. Let them cool completely before serving.

VARIATION

 Replace the sour cream with tofu sour cream and follow the milk-free variation for the Chocolate Babka dough.

MAKES 15 TO 20 MINI BUNS
Nutrition information per bun (based on 20):
Calories: 79.8, Total Fat: 4.7g, Cholesterol: 12mg,
Sodium: 143.3 mg, Total Carbohydrates: 8.2g,
Dietary Fiber: 0g, Sugars: 0.4g, Protein: 1.6 g

Mini Goat Cheese Brioche Buns

½ cup milk

⅓ cup canola oil

1½ cups tapioca flour
(read ingredient
statement)

½ cup soft goat cheese

1 teaspoon kosher salt

1 large egg

Nonstick cooking spray
(read ingredient
statement)

The goat cheese makes this recipe special. It creates a taste and texture that will sway your pickiest gluten-free eater.

You can use any kind of milk in this recipe. Try sheep's or goat's milk if you have an allergy to cow's milk.

1. Position a rack in the center of the oven and heat the oven to 375°F.

2. Mix all the ingredients together in the order listed in a stand mixer fitted with the paddle attachment. Beat for 3 minutes until the dough is shiny, then let the dough rest for 15 minutes before continuing.

3. Grease a mini muffin pan with nonstick cooking spray or use mini muffin paper liners.

4. Using a mini ice cream scoop, scoop out tablespoon-size balls of dough and set them in the muffin cups so they are three-quarters full. Bake for 30 to 35 minutes until golden brown.

5. Let the buns cool slightly in the pan, then remove from the pan and serve immediately. Store leftovers in an airtight container for up to 3 days.

Chapter 8

Dressings, Sauces & Dips

MAKES 8 CUPS
Nutrition information per serving (based on ¾ cup): Calories: 69.1, Total Fat:4.4g, Cholesterol: 0mg, Sodium: 149.7mg, Total Carbohydrates: 6g, Dietary Fiber: 1.3g, Sugars: 2.8g, Protein: 1.2g

Spicy Tomato Sauce

3 tablespoons olive oil

1 medium onion, finely chopped

2 medium carrots, finely chopped

6 cloves garlic, minced

1 teaspoon oregano (fresh or dried)

1 tablespoon basil (fresh or dried)

1 teaspoon crushed red pepper flakes

Two 28-ounce cans diced San Marzano tomatoes, with their juices (read ingredient statement)

3 tablespoons tomato paste (read ingredient statement)

1 lemon, juiced

½ cup dry red wine

Kosher salt and freshly ground black pepper

1. Heat the oil in large heavy saucepan over medium heat. Add the onions, carrots, garlic, oregano, basil, and red pepper flakes. Cover and cook until the onions are golden and translucent, stirring occasionally, about 10 minutes. Add the tomatoes, tomato paste, lemon juice, and wine and bring to a gentle simmer. Cook uncovered, stirring occasionally and breaking apart the tomatoes, until the sauce thickens, about 1 hour.

2. Season the sauce to taste with salt and pepper. Let cool slightly, cover, and refrigerate. Use within 1 week.

COOK'S TIP

It's best to use San Marzano tomatoes, a variety of plum tomato, from Italy. They are very sweet and will add a fresh taste to this sauce.

MAKES ABOUT ³/₄ CUP
Nutrition information per serving (based on 2 table-spoons): Calories: 27, Total Fat: 0.5g, Cholesterol: 0mg, Sodium: 209.7mg, Total Carbohydrates: 5.7g, Dietary Fiber: 0.2g, Sugars: 2.9g, Protein: 0.4g

Ginger–Miso Dressing

2 tablespoons mirin (Japanese rice wine; read ingredient statement)

2 teaspoons white miso (read ingredient statement)

2 teaspoons grated fresh ginger

¹/₃ cup carrot juice

2 tablespoons fresh orange juice

2 teaspoons gluten-free soy sauce (read ingredient statement)

2 tablespoons distilled white vinegar (read ingredient statement)

¹/₂ teaspoon crushed red pepper flakes

¹/₂ teaspoon Asian sesame oil

Combine all of the ingredients in a small bowl, whisking until the miso dissolves. Transfer to an airtight container, cover, and refrigerate. Use within 5 days.

COOK'S TIP
Use this dressing on a simple green salad to serve as an appetizer to the Yakitori Beef Skewers on p. 126.

MAKES ABOUT ¾ CUP
Nutrition information per serving
(based on 2 tablespoons): Calories:
124.9, Total Fat: 12.6g, Cholesterol: 0mg,
Sodium: 43.3mg, Total Carbohydrate:
3.3g, Dietary Fiber: 1g, Sugars: 0.7g,
Protein: 1.8g

Pistachio Pesto

½ cup chopped fresh flat-
   leaf parsley

2 tablespoons chopped
   fresh tarragon

3 tablespoons unsalted
   natural pistachios

1 lemon, juiced

1 medium clove garlic,
   peeled

¼ cup olive oil

Kosher salt and freshly
   ground black pepper

Purée the herbs, nuts, lemon juice, and garlic in a blender or food processor. With the machine running, drizzle in the oil in a thin stream and blend until a coarse paste forms, then blend in 3 tablespoons water. Stir in salt and pepper to taste. Transfer to an airtight container, cover, and refrigerate. Use within 5 days.

COOK'S TIP

I love to use this pesto to top a simple seared fish or even as a dip for a festive crudité platter. It is a great naturally vegan substitute for pesto.

MAKES 1¼ CUPS
Nutrition information per serving (based on 2 tablespoons): Calories: 78.4, Total Fat: 7.9g, Cholesterol: 0mg, Sodium: 2.3mg, Total Carbohydrates: 1.6g, Dietary Fiber: 0.6g, Sugars: 0.4g, Protein: 1.1g

Arugula–Almond Pesto

1 clove garlic, peeled

⅓ cup almonds

5 cups arugula

2 teaspoons finely grated lemon zest

1 lemon, juiced, plus more as needed

⅓ cup olive oil

Kosher salt and freshly ground black pepper

Combine the garlic, almonds, arugula, lemon zest, and lemon juice in a blender or food processor. Process until the nuts are finely chopped and a coarse paste forms. With the machine running, drizzle in the oil in a thin stream and blend until smooth. Season the pesto with salt and pepper and more lemon juice if you like. Transfer to an airtight container, cover, and refrigerate. Use within 5 days.

MAKES 1 CUP
Nutrition information per serving (based on 2 tablespoons):
Calories: 21.5, Total Fat: 2g,
Cholesterol: 0mg, Sodium:
30.3mg, Total Carbohydrates:
0.9g, Dietary Fiber: 0.2g,
Sugars: 0.1g, Protein: 0.1g

Sweet Red Pepper Jam

3 tablespoons olive oil

1 red bell pepper, thinly sliced

1 medium red onion, thinly sliced

1 lemon, juiced

2 teaspoons sugar

2 sprigs fresh marjoram, chopped

1 spring fresh thyme, chopped

2 teaspoons kosher salt

Freshly ground black pepper

1. In a medium pan, heat the oil over medium heat; add the peppers and onions and cook, stirring occasionally, until the onions are translucent, about 10 minutes. Add the lemon juice, sugar, and herbs and continue cooking, stirring regularly, until the onions are caramelized, about another 15 minutes. Stir in the salt and season to taste with pepper.

2. Let the mixture cool completely, then transfer to an airtight jar, cover, and refrigerate. Use within 2 weeks.

COOK'S TIP

Dried herbs are fine for some recipes, but not this one. It's important that you use fresh herbs to bring out the most flavor.

MAKES 1½ CUPS
Nutrition information per serving (based on 2 tablespoons):
Calories: 92, Total Fat: 7.9g,
Cholesterol: 0.3mg, Sodium:
14mg, Total Carbohydrates:
5.1g, Dietary Fiber: 0.8g,
Sugars: 0.7g, Protein: 0.8g

Caramelized Onion Jam

½ cup olive oil

2 pounds onions, thinly
   sliced

½ cup vegetable stock
   (read ingredient
   statement) or water

1 tablespoon balsamic
   vinegar

2 teaspoons sugar

Sea salt and freshly
   ground black pepper

In a medium pot, heat the oil over medium-low heat, then add the onions;
cover and cook, stirring occasionally, until the onions are translucent, about 10
minutes. Add the stock, vinegar, and sugar. Cook, uncovered, stirring, until the
onions are caramelized, about 30 minutes more. Season to taste with salt and
pepper. Let cool completely. The jam can be stored for up to 1 week in the refrigerator in an airtight container.

COOK'S TIP

Be sure you cook the
onions over a low flame
so they don't burn before
they caramelize.

MAKES 1¹/₂ CUPS
Nutrition information per serving (based on 2 tablespoons): Calories: 160.8, Total Fat: 17.8g, Cholesterol: 5.1mg, Sodium: 93.4mg, Total Carbohydrate: 0.4g, Dietary Fiber: 0.0 g, Sugars: 0.1g, Protein: 0.2g

Cilantro–Lime Aïoli

1 large clove garlic, peeled

1 cup mayonnaise (read ingredient statement)

4 teaspoons fresh lime juice

2 tablespoons roughly chopped fresh cilantro

1 teaspoon kosher salt

¹/₄ cup extra-virgin olive oil, plus more as needed

Combine the garlic, mayonnaise, lime juice, cilantro, and salt in a blender or food processor; process to blend. With the machine running, drizzle in the oil in a thin stream and blend until smooth. Add more olive oil to thin out the consistency if needed. Cover and refrigerate if not using right away. Use within 7 days.

VARIATION

Instead of mayonnaise, use tofu sour cream or a vegan mayonnaise substitute. Tofu sour cream means this recipe is no longer soy-free. Be sure to read the ingredient statements for all substitute ingredients for potential allergens.

COOK'S TIP

To lighten up this recipe, swap out full-fat mayonnaise for a reduced-fat version (read ingredient statement for potential allergens).

MAKES 1 CUP
Nutrition information per serving (based on 2 tablespoons): Calories: 46.8, Total Fat: 4g, Cholesterol: 3.9mg, Sodium: 10.2mg, Total Carbohydrates: 2.3g, Dietary Fiber: 0.7g, Sugars: 0.2g, Protein: 1.2g

Spiced Mediterranean Dip

¼ cup fresh lemon juice

2 teaspoons dried oregano

½ teaspoon ground cinnamon

½ teaspoon ground coriander

½ teaspoon ground cumin

½ teaspoon freshly grated nutmeg

2 teaspoons kosher salt, plus more as needed

1 large clove garlic, pressed

½ cup sour cream (read ingredient statement)

¼ cup tahini paste (read ingredient statement)

A few grinds black pepper

Combine all of the ingredients in a blender until well blended. Season to taste with more salt and freshly ground black pepper. This dip can be stored for up to 1 week in the refrigerator in an airtight container.

VARIATION

Make this dip milk-free and vegan by substituting tofu sour cream for the regular sour cream. Doing so makes this recipe no longer soy-free.

COOK'S TIP
Because sesame seeds and tree nuts have proteins in common, eliminate the sesame seeds if you have a tree nut allergy.

MAKES 1 CUP
Nutrition information per serving (based on 2 tablespoons):
Calories: 46.4, Total Fat: 4.1g,
Cholesterol: 0mg, Sodium:
9.6mg, Potassium: 41.5mg, Total
Carbohydrates: 2g, Dietary Fiber:
0.8g, Sugars: 0.1g, Protein: 1.3g

Simple Tahini Dip

½ cup tahini paste (read
  ingredient statement)

1 lemon, zested and
  juiced

2 cloves garlic, mashed

¼ cup finely chopped
  fresh flat-leaf parsley

Kosher salt and freshly
  ground black pepper

Put the tahini paste, lemon zest and juice, and garlic in a medium bowl and mix to combine. Slowly stir in about 1 cup water a few tablespoons at a time until you reach the dressing consistency you like (you might not use all the water). Add the parsley and season with salt and pepper. This dip can be stored for up to 1 week in the refrigerator in an airtight container.

COOK'S TIP

The mixture will be clumpy when you first add water, but the mixture will start to thin out the more water you add and the more it gets incorporated into the tahini paste.

MAKES ABOUT 3 CUPS
Nutrition information per serving
(based on 2 tablespoons): Calories:
88.6, Total Fat: 9g, Cholesterol: 0mg,
Sodium: 304.3mg, Total Carbohydrates:
2.1g, Dietary Fiber: 0.3g, Sugars: 0.8g,
Protein: 0.5g

Asian Ginger Vinaigrette

1 onion, roughly chopped

1 carrot, roughly chopped

1 celery stalk, roughly
  chopped

1 cup rice wine vinegar

1 teaspoon finely grated
  fresh ginger

1 cup olive oil

1/2 cup gluten-free soy
  sauce (read ingredient
  statement)

1 large tomato, diced

Kosher salt and freshly
  ground black pepper

Combine all of the ingredients, except the salt and pepper, in a food processor and blend until smooth. Season to taste with salt and pepper. Store in an airtight container in the refrigerator and use within 1 week.

COOK'S TIP

Try this recipe with different kinds of vinegar, keeping in mind that each will alter the flavor of the dressing a bit.

MAKES ABOUT 4 CUPS
Nutrition information per
serving (based on 1/4 cup):
Calories: 26.7, Total Fat: 0.3g,
Cholesterol: 0mg, Sodium:
295.3mg, Total Carbohydrates:
6.2g, Dietary Fiber: 1.6g,
Sugars: 2.3g, Protein: 1.1g

Homemade Salsa

3 cups chopped tomatoes

1 green bell pepper, finely
  diced

1 cup finely diced onions

1/4 cup fresh cilantro,
  minced

3 tablespoons fresh lime
  juice, plus more as
  needed

4 teaspoons finely
  chopped jalapeño

1 teaspoon ground cumin,
  plus more as needed

1 teaspoon kosher salt,
  plus more as needed

1 teaspoon ground black
  pepper, plus more as
  needed

Stir together all ingredients and season with any additional spices to taste. Refrigerate and marinate overnight. Serve chilled. Refrigerate and use within 1 week.

SERVES 8 TO 10
Nutrition information per serving (based on 2 figs): Calories: 184.6, Total Fat: 0.3g, Cholesterol: 0mg, Sodium: 6.8mg, Total Carbohydrates: 48g, Dietary Fiber: 2.5g, Sugars: 42.3g, Protein: 0.9g

Balsamic Figs

1½ cups sugar

½ cup balsamic vinegar

2 tablespoons orange juice

1 sprig fresh thyme

1 cinnamon stick

½ teaspoon ground allspice (read ingredient statement)

4 black peppercorns

8 ounces dried figs, halved lengthwise

In a small saucepan set over medium-high heat, combine the sugar and ½ cup water, stirring until the sugar dissolves. Add the vinegar, orange juice, thyme, and spices; bring to a boil. Add the figs, turn the heat down to medium low, and cook until the mixture has reduced slightly and thickened, 5 to 10 minutes. Remove the pan from the heat and let the figs cool completely; remove the cinnamon stick. Transfer to an airtight container, refrigerate, and use within 2 weeks.

COOK'S TIP

Serve drizzled over the Perfect Roast Chicken on p. 99 and the Creamy Polenta on p. 179.

MAKES 2 CUPS
Nutrition information per serving (based on 2 tablespoons): Calories: 25.7, Total Fat: 0.1g, Cholesterol: 0mg, Sodium: 7.8mg, Total Carbohydrates: 6.6g, Dietary Fiber: 0.8g, Sugars: 5.1g, Protein: 0.1g

Strawberry Jam

1 pound strawberries, hulled and halved

1 lemon, zested and juiced, plus more juice as needed

½ cup sugar, plus more as needed

1 teaspoon kosher salt, plus more as needed

In a medium saucepan over medium heat, combine the strawberries, lemon zest and juice, and sugar. Bring to a boil over medium-high heat, stirring occasionally, then lower the heat to a simmer and cook, uncovered, until the jam thickens, 20 to 25 minutes. Add the salt, taste, and adjust with more sugar, salt, or lemon juice if needed. Let cool at room temperature for 1 hour, then transfer to an airtight container and refrigerate. Use within 1 week.

COOK'S TIP

Follow this same technique to make jam with whatever fruit is in season.

MAKES 2 CUPS
Nutrition information per serving (based on 2 tablespoons): Calories: 25.7, Total Fat: 0.1g, Cholesterol: 0mg, Sodium: 7.8mg, Total Carbohydrates: 6.6g, Dietary Fiber: 0.8g, Sugars: 5.1g, Protein: 0.1g

Raspberry Basil Jam

1 pound raspberries, fresh or frozen

1 lemon, zested and juiced, plus more juice as needed

½ cup sugar

2 tablespoons fresh basil, chopped

1 teaspoon kosher salt, plus more as needed

In a medium saucepan over medium heat, combine the raspberries, lemon zest and juice, and sugar. Bring to a boil over medium-high heat, stirring occasionally, then lower the heat to a simmer and cook, uncovered, until the jam thickens, 20 to 25 minutes. Stir in the basil and salt, and adjust to taste with additional salt or lemon juice.

Cool at room temperature for 1 hour, then transfer to an airtight container and refrigerate. Use within 1 week.

MAKES 2 CUPS
Nutrition information per serving (based on 2 tablespoons): Calories: 100.8, Total Fat: 10.8g, Cholesterol: 0mg, Sodium: 32.5mg, Total Carbohydrates: 1.3g, Dietary Fiber: 0g, Sugars: 0.2g, Protein: 0g

Mustard Vinaigrette

1 cup olive oil

½ cup balsamic vinegar

3 tablespoons whole-grain mustard (read ingredient statement)

1 shallot

1 clove garlic

1 teaspoon fresh thyme

1 teaspoon sugar

2 teaspoons kosher salt, plus more as needed

A few grinds of black pepper, plus more as needed

Combine all of the ingredients in a blender and process until smooth. Season to taste with more salt and pepper. Store the vinaigrette in the refrigerator but allow it to come to room temperature before serving. If the olive oil and vinegar separate, shake well before serving to bring back the emulsification.

Menu Options

When I was first starting out, the hardest thing for me wasn't making one dish but knowing what to serve together to make a meal so that the flavors of all dishes complemented each other. Here I've provided a list of menus based on recipes in the book. Some of these menus are designed with a particular allergy sensitivity in mind (you'll find menus that are all gluten-free, dairy-free, and nut-free), but others aren't, so be sure to check the allergen appropriateness for each recipe to be sure they are suitable for you and your guests.

MOROCCAN DINNER

Starter: Moroccan Stuffed Tomatoes (p. 52)
Salad: Moroccan Carrot Slaw (p. 75)
Main Course: Moroccan Tagine with Apricots and Almonds (p. 100)
Side Dish: Simple couscous
Dessert: Mexican Wedding Cookies (p. 194)

RUSTIC ITALIAN FEAST

Starter: Basic Baguette (p. 216)
Starter: Mushroom and Onion Flatbread (p. 48)
Soup: Turkey, Spinach, and White Bean Soup (p. 58)
Main Course: Slow-Cooker Provençal Lemon and Olive Chicken (p. 113)
Dessert: Lemon Shortbread Tart (p. 210)

ASIAN FEAST

Starter: Thai Chicken Lettuce Cups (p. 40)
Main Course: Yakitori Beef Skewers (p. 126)
Side Dish: Thai Coconut Rice (p. 178)
Dessert: Coconut and Mango Sorbets

MEDITERRANEAN TAPAS (MANY SMALL PLATES TO SHARE)

Tomato and Watermelon Salad (p. 74)

Moroccan Carrot Slaw (p. 75)

Pine Nut and Olive Orzo Salad (p. 80)

Fire-Roasted Eggplant (p. 165)

Deconstructed Sabich (p. 50)

Israeli Meatballs with Tahini Glaze (p. 49)

Balsamic Roasted Cauliflower with Pine Nut–Tahini Dressing (p. 176)

BRAZILIAN NIGHT

Starter: Tomato and Almond Gazpacho (p. 64)

Main Course: Roasted Sea Bass and Potatoes with Olive Dressing (p. 152)

Dessert: Four-Layer Lemon Coconut Cake with Buttercream Frosting and Lemon Curd (p. 204)

DAIRY-FREE MENU

Starter: Kale and Barley Soup (p. 68)

Salad: Quinoa and Baby Spinach Salad with Cranberries and Pecans (p. 87)

Main Course: Spicy Italian Poached Sea Bass (p. 140)

Dessert: Lemon, Cranberry, and Pistachio Biscotti (p. 188)

GLUTEN-FREE MENU

Starter: Herb Pesto–Stuffed Mushrooms (p. 39)

Soup: One-Pot Veggie Soup (p. 67)

Main Course: Rosemary Skillet Chicken with Mushrooms and Potatoes (p. 110)

Dessert: Nutella–Peanut Butter Blondies (p. 202)

NUT-FREE MENU

Salad: Barley, Fig, and Mixed Greens Salad (p. 81)

Soup: Broccoli–Cauliflower Soup (p. 69)

Main Course: Strip Steak with Red Wine–Mushroom Pan Sauce (p. 121)

Dessert: Dark Chocolate Cake with Chocolate Ganache (p. 206)

VEGETARIAN MENU

Salad: Spiced Butternut Squash and Lentil Salad (p. 78)

Soup: Caramelized Cauliflower Soup (p. 61)

Dessert: Oatmeal, Ginger, and Golden Raisin Cookies (p. 200)

VEGAN MENU

Starter: Tahini Tartlets with Spinach and Mushrooms (p. 46)

Main Course: Polenta "Steaks" with Spicy Tomato Sauce (p. 162)

Dessert: Oatmeal and Fig Crumble Wedges (p. 201)

NEW ENGLAND THANKSGIVING HARVEST

Starter: Basic Baguette (p. 216)

Starter: Lemon and Olive Oil Corn Muffins (p. 223)

Starter: Eggplant Caponata (p. 45)

Main Course: Oven-Roasted Herb and Ginger Turkey (p. 103)

Side Dish: Garlic Mashed Potatoes (p. 164)

Side Dish: Brussels Sprouts with Lemon and Sage (p. 181)

Side Dish: Green Beans with Toasted Walnuts and Dried Cherry Vinaigrette (p. 175)

Dessert: Mini Chocolate Pecan Pie Tartlets (p. 185)

Dessert: Apple Spiced Cupcakes with Cream Cheese Frosting (p. 190)

COCKTAIL PARTY FOR 20+

Mustard Raisin Marmalade on Toasted Crostini (p. 38)

Asparagus Beef Rolls with Horseradish Cream (p. 42)

Eggplant Caponata (p. 45)

Herb Pesto–Stuffed Mushrooms (p. 39)

Thai Peanut and Lime Chicken Skewers (p. 51)

Greek Salad Cucumber Cups (p. 37)

Blinis Topped with Lemon Whip and Smoked Salmon (p. 54)

NEW YEAR'S BRUNCH

Blinis Topped with Lemon Whip and Smoked Salmon (p. 54)

Mushroom and Onion Flatbread (p. 48)

Bloody Mary Salad (p. 77)

Spiced Butternut Squash and Lentil Salad (p. 78)

Chocolate Babka (p. 230)

Cinnamon Sticky Buns (p. 232)

GAME DAY OPEN HOUSE

Starter: Edamame Sliders with Sweet Red Pepper Jam (p. 44)

Salad: Jalapeño, Black Bean, and Roasted Corn Salad (p. 180)

Main Course: Blackened Fish Tacos with Guacamole and Cilantro–Lime Slaw (p. 155)

Dessert: Granola Bars (p. 193)

Dessert: Mini Fudge Brownie Bites (p. 186)

MOTHER'S DAY/FATHER'S DAY LUNCHEON

Starter: Thai Peanut and Lime Chicken Skewers (p. 51)

Starter: Basic Baguette (p. 216); Eggplant Caponata (p. 45)

Main Course: Balsamic Herb Skirt Steak (p. 117)

Salad: Barley, Asparagus, and Mushroom Salad Topped with Ginger Tofu (p. 88)

Salad: Garlic Arugula Crostini Salad (p. 82)

Dessert: Dark Chocolate Cake with Chocolate Ganache (p. 206)

BABY/BRIDAL SHOWER

Starters:

Tahini Tartlets with Spinach and Mushrooms (p. 46)

Herb Pesto–Stuffed Mushrooms (p. 39)

Greek Salad Cucumber Cups (p. 37)

Tomato and Watermelon Salad (p. 74)

Quinoa and Herbed Fennel Salad (p. 83)

Desserts:

Four-Layer Lemon Coconut Cake with Buttercream Frosting and Lemon Curd (p. 204)

Lemon, Cranberry, and Pistachio Biscotti (p. 188)

Mexican Wedding Cookies (p. 194)

Crumb-Topped Blueberry Muffins (p. 225)

Lemon–Ginger–Corn Scones (p. 222)

DESSERT BUFFET

Arrange on a mix of different platters and trays on a variety of heights on your table. Mix in some jars and bowls of candies and colorful objects for a themed display.

Lemon Shortbread Tart (p. 210)

Mini Chocolate Pecan Pie Tartlets (p. 185)

Apple Spiced Cupcakes with Cream Cheese Frosting (p. 190)

Dark Chocolate Cake with Chocolate Ganache (p. 206)

Salted Chocolate Chip Cookies (p. 195)

Oatmeal, Ginger, and Golden Raisin Cookies (p. 200)

Mini Fudge Brownie Bites (p. 186)

Peanut Butter Huhus (p. 187)

Metric Equivalents

liquid/dry measures		oven temperatures		
U.S.	METRIC	°F	GAS MARK	°C
¼ teaspoon	1.25 milliliters	250	½	120
½ teaspoon	2.5 milliliters	275	1	140
1 teaspoon	5 milliliters	300	2	150
1 tablespoon (3 teaspoons)	15 milliliters	325	3	165
1 fluid ounce (2 Tablespoons)	30 milliliters	350	4	180
¼ cup	60 milliliters	375	5	190
⅓ cup	80 milliliters	400	6	200
½ cup	120 milliliters	425	7	220
1 cup	240 milliliters	450	8	230
1 pint (2 cups)	480 milliliters	475	9	240
1 quart (4 cups; 32 ounces)	960 milliliters	500	10	260
1 gallon (4 quarts)	3.84 liters	550	Broil	290
1 ounce (by weight)	28 gram			
1 pound	454 grams			
2.2 pounds	1 kilogram			

Recipes by Allergen

WHEAT-FREE

MILK-FREE

NUT-FREE

EGG-FREE

SHELLFISH-FREE

All recipes in this book are Shellfish-Free

FISH-FREE

SOY-FREE

CORN-FREE

VEGETARIAN

VEGAN

GLUTEN-FREE

Index